Stock Market Events
That Mattered
(Or Did They?)
A Choose Your Own Experience
Stock Market Adventure Book
By Cody Willard
With Bryce

Published by Willard Media Ventures, LLC, New York, NY.

For general information on our other products and services or for technical support, please contact our Customer Care Department within the United States at (646) 397-7244.

Willard Media Ventures also publishes its books in a variety of electronic formats. For more information about Willard Media Ventures' publications, including Cody Willard's TradingWithCody.com products, visit our web site at www.TradingWithCody.com.

Willard Media Ventures
ISBN-13: 978-0615720586 (Custom)
ISBN-10: 0615720587

Note from the author

Long before I started a hedge fund or talked to Jay Leno on the Tonight Show about my favorite stocks, I spent years going back in history and looking at the headlines and how certain stocks or markets have performed in parallel scenarios from the past. And over the last year and a half of writing and building a very helpful community at TradingWithCody.com, I've realized just how underdeveloped most investors' and traders' sense of history really is. We all know that our brain distorts events when it pulls them up as memories. And so many times, we think we know how a stock should trade today based on a faulty memory of how it traded last time.

So with that in mind, I started building what I hope is the world's coolest, smartest and most-addictive Wall Street trading game ever – ***Stock Market Events** That Mattered (Or Did They?)*, a fantasy stock market world where the player would go back in time to some of the biggest events in markets history and choose how to play each set up. The players would be choose whether they want to be a short-term trader trying to turn $1 million into more than $150 million or if they want to see if they can invest $5 million with a buy-and-hold-forever approach to even greater fortunes. Just like in the real-world by using real-world events like the launching of the first iPhone or when Steve Jobs first came back to Apple in 1998.

- Did Apple go straight up after the first iPhone was announced and when Jobs came back on board for the first month?
- How about over the first year?
- Did RIMM crash or spike when they announced what eventually turned out to be the disastrous Playbook tablet?

But a great trader and investor need to go broader than anyone sector too of course, so we also added hundreds of setups and outcomes where the player has to choose such things as:

- Whether to trade (or invest in) GE as we invaded Iraq in March 2003
- How you should play biotech Gilead's potential blockbuster drug, Darusentan
- Or what's the best way to profit from Nike's rollout of the original Air Jordan.
- And many others.

The performance of these stocks and markets in the short-term, mid-term and long-term after each of these very significant junctures will absolutely blow your mind.

And what makes the book and game even cooler is that just like in the real-world, you get to compete against everybody else as you try to make the Top 10 Traders of All-Time list. Find out what kind of title you can attain (and keep) on Wall Street. Can you move up from Junior Trader to Managing Director and become a Wall Street Legend without first falling from grace and ending up an amateur daytrader?

Over the course of the next year, we'll be rolling out a steady stream of these books and games with various themes, including –

- ***Apple Events*** *That Mattered (Or Did They?)*
- ***Oil Events*** *That Mattered (Or Did They?)*
- ***War Events*** *That Mattered (Or Did They?)*
- ***Google Events*** *That Mattered (Or Did They?)*
- ***Tech Events*** *That Mattered (Or Did They?)*

On ThatMattered.com, we went and found historical footage of every event from the time it was happening with videos including:

- Bill Cosby announcing New Coke and a look back at New Coke and its impact on the cola industry from thirty years later
- Traders on the floor going crazy about one of oil's biggest spikes ever
- A profile on Enron's collapse as it was happening
- A profile on the promise of "The New Economy" from the peak of the bubble
- Or, yes, we found Steve Jobs' first presentation from when he returned to Apple in 1998.
- And many more historical videos.

The book and game are designed so that anybody, regardless of trading and investing experience can play it, learn from it, and have a blast doing it.

Sincerely,

Cody Willard

RANKINGS - WHERE DO YOU FIT IN ON WALL STREET?

If you start off trading $1 million, you need:

(Grab a pencil and keep your trading score history here)

Shoe Shiner	0	
Amateur Daytrader	$750000	
Wall Street Gopher	$850000	
Boutique Firm Sales Associate	$900000	
Junior Trader	$1000000	
VP of Sales	$1050000	
Branch Manager	$1100000	
Startup Fund Manager	$1200000	
Managing Director	$1300000	
Chief Investment Officer	$1400000	
Hedge Fund Rock Star	$1500000	
Warren Buffet-esque	$3000000	

If you start off investing $5 million, you need:

(Grab a pencil and keep your investment score history here)

Shoe Shiner	3500000	
Amateur Daytrader	4000000	
Wall Street Gopher	4500000	
Boutique Firm Sales Associate	4750000	
Junior Trader	5000000	
VP of Sales	6000000	
Branch Manager	7000000	
Startup Fund Manager	10000000	
Managing Director	20000000	
Chief Investment Officer	50000000	
Hedge Fund Rock Star	100000000	
Warren Buffet-esque	125000000	
Wall Street Legend	140000000	
Even Better Than Great Uncle Buster!	150000001	

Stock Market Events That Mattered (Or Did They?)

Stock Market Events That Mattered (Or Did They?)

The call

You're lost deep in thought as the flames crackle in the fireplace when your cell phone vibrates in your pocket, rousing you back to the real world. It's not a number you recognize, though you know that its 212 area code means it hails from NYC. You bring the phone to your ear to take the call, wondering who could be calling at this time on a Saturday morning of New Year's Eve and realizing your toes are so hot they itch inside your wool socks.

The caller on the line asks for you by name and introduces himself as "Thomas Topdollar, that is, Sir Topdollar." He begins explaining in a sophisticated British accent that he's got a client named Buster Smith who had passed away from natural causes at the age of 94 the night before, and that you have been included in the will for his "very sizable estate."

You step away from the warmth of the fireplace because your adrenalin is suddenly flowing. You ask this Sir Topdollar to repeat what he's just said. As he does, you can hardly believe your ears when he says "very sizable estate" for a second time.

"But," he continues in that suddenly harmonious-sounding British accent, "there's a catch." And those hot chills you just felt turn into butterflies in your stomach and you ask him to go on.

You step outside into the cold crisp air and you hear the crows overhead cawing. You don't notice the chill in the air, nor do you take note of the birds.

The esquire explains that your old Great Uncle Buster Smith (whom you didn't even know you had) was a former gas station attendent-turned banker-turned inventor whose lifetime of creations and wise investments in publicly-traded companies built an estate worth $150 million.

You shift your weight from one foot to the other and begin to pace around the the yard.

The attorney, Mr. Topdollar (or was it "Count Topdollar?" No, it was "Sir Topdollar" and you realize that means this guy is implying that he's literally been knighted by the Queen at some point) seems to be a straight shooter, as he goes on to explain that your old uncle was addicted to the stock market. Buster had died in front of his multiple Bloomberg and computer terminals in a tiny rent-controlled apartment in Brooklyn that he'd lived in with his grandmother since he was a little boy back in the Great Depression.

He goes on. "Your Great Uncle Buster also had a great sense of humor–or maybe just a desire to inspire you to love the stock markets, too. Because Great Uncle Buster left some very challenging stipulations in his will."

You wonder why the fine Sir on the line keeps calling this mystery man you're suddenly learning about "Your Great Uncle Buster," which sounds almost like "Yo-or graht Oon-kle Boo-stah" to your ears. And you wonder what the heck the old codger looked liked, too. You're picturing an old man in a wheel chair with oxygen tubes up his nostrils and wrapped around his ears.

No sooner have you had the thought when the man on the phone tells you that there's a video email starring your one and only "Graht Oon-kle Boo-stah" on its way to you with all the details. You're to call the attorney back at his 212 phone number as soon as you watch the video and make your decision.

An email awaits you in your inbox and there's a large attachment to it. After downloading the .mp4 attachment, the video starts and it's a clip of an old man, just almost exactly like you had pictured, and he's sitting in front of more computer terminals, both new flat ones and old tube ones that even look like they must have been useful back in the 1970s, but are still flashing with lights behind him as he speaks in a gravelly old voice into the camera.

Great Uncle Buster lays out the following stipulations for his will:

You can take $5 million, and cash out of the estate and walk away with no strings attached (including sending that money to your personal long-term investment account to invest in real historical companies at crucial events in their history with a buy-and-hold-forever approach).

OR

You can take a $1 million margin stock market trading account that he has set up in your name. If you can get a 50% return out of that money over the next year, you get the whole $150 million estate. Everything. You can buy and short stocks and options, and you can allocate the entire $1 million across as concentrated or as diverse as you want.

If you decide to go for the whole $150 million estate, turn to page 4.

If you decide to take the $5 million inheritance, turn to page 199.

Start trading January

You pick up your cell phone and call back the most recent number in its call history–the 212 number.

“I need to save that number with the rest of this guy’s contact info,” you think to yourself as the phone starts to ring in the earpiece.

The familiar British accent is on the other end and you realize you are smiling as he says, “I expected you to call back quickly, but not that quickly. I assume you have some questions.”

“No, not so much. I know what I want to do.”

And you tell him that you’re going for the full $150 million inheritance because you are confident that you can indeed turn that $1 million stock account that he left you into $1.5 million before this new year is over.

He gives you the online broker account information where your $1 million margin account is waiting for you. He tells you that he’ll be back in touch in a week to check up on you, and that you can call him at his 212 number at any time, as he has a 24-hour answering service and he or one of his partners is always available.

You get the idea that your Great Uncle Buster must have been a very important client to this guy’s firm.

It’s Sunday afternoon when you log back into the brokerage account, and you’ve got butterflies in your stomach as you realize you really do have to trade that money now. Where was that confidence you were feeling when you were picturing doing this earlier?

You pull up a chart of the DJIA, the S&P 500, and the Nasdaq. You remember on that video how your Great Uncle Buster had turned almost angry when he’d talked about how he had barely beaten the major indices last year.

You need to start trading if you're going to ever get that 50% profit you need to get your mitts on that whole $150 million nut. But should you buy stocks and call options to bet that they keep going higher or should you short some stocks and buy put options to bet that the big run is over and stocks are about to crack?

If you want to trade a hot new tech sector, turn to page 6.

If you want to trade a technology giant before they release their latest revolutionary product, turn to page 13.

If you want to trade financial and bank stocks, turn to page 19.

If you want to trade homebuilder stocks, turn to page 27.

If you'd rather move onto the next month's set of trading options, turn to page 33.

Internet Sector Setup

It's January 2000...There's a hot new tech sector called the "Internet" that enables people and companies to connect and do business easier than ever before through their computers. Most of the recent IPOs there are flying high, although you can also find some of the stocks in this sector have missed their earnings estimates and have been pummeled.

The NASDAQ, the exchange where all these high-flyers have been listing, was up 88% in 1999, almost 60% in the last 6 months alone. Last October a startup called Akamai that does something with the speed of the internet came public at $26 and closed that first day at $145.19 at a market capitalization of $15 billion.

Your friends who have never traded before in their life are opening accounts and all of them are making money buying and flipping internet stocks, doubling their Etrade accounts in a matter of months.

When you turn on the TV, analysts are saying that the right way to value companies without revenues and earnings is with "eyeball" and "click" multiples, not earnings. Absolutely everyone will be on the internet in the next five years; this is the most profound technology shift in 100 years.

Nasdaq Composite Index-1999

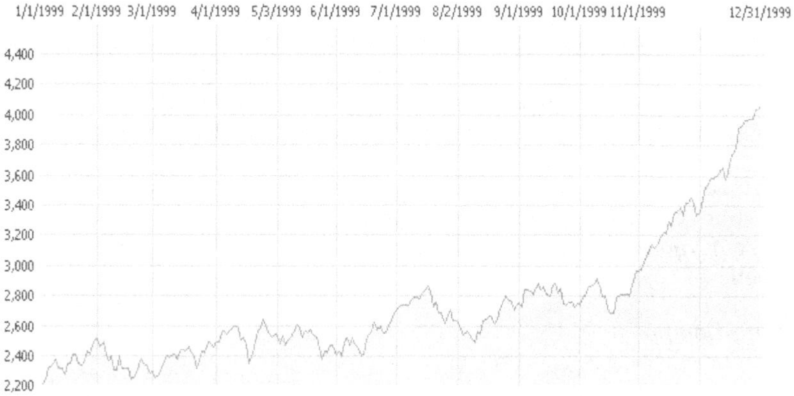

Source: MSN Money

If you are bullish and want to buy about $100,000 of common stock in this sector and hold them for the whole year, turn to page 8.

If you are bearish and want to short about $100,000 of common stock from this sector for the whole year, turn to page 9.

If you are bullish and want to buy about $50,000 of calls on this hot new sector for a short-term one month trade, turn to page 11.

If you are bearish and want to buy about $50,000 of puts on this hot new sector for a short-term one month trade, turn to page 12.

If you would rather find something else to trade this month, turn to page 4.

Internet Stock Bullish Outcome

Oops, you just lost 40% on your investment.

Sorry, you just literally top-ticked the Internet tech bubble. I mean, your timing couldn't be any worse. You bought Amazon at a split-adjusted $76 in January 2000, and by November of next year it was under $7 bucks. And that isn't even your worst trade. Lycos, HotBot, and a host of other internet portals are in Chapter 11 or have been sold for the office furniture. Globe.com was up 600% on its first day of trading in 1998; it was delisted in April 2001. You got in right at the end and only enjoyed about a 10% run-up before a 90% decline. Just to get to even you'll need a couple consecutive years of big performance.

You stare at the ceiling all night as your brain processes just how much money you've just lost on this dratted trade. Your portfolio needs a boost if you're going to get back out of the hole you've just dug for yourself.

Nasdaq Composite Index

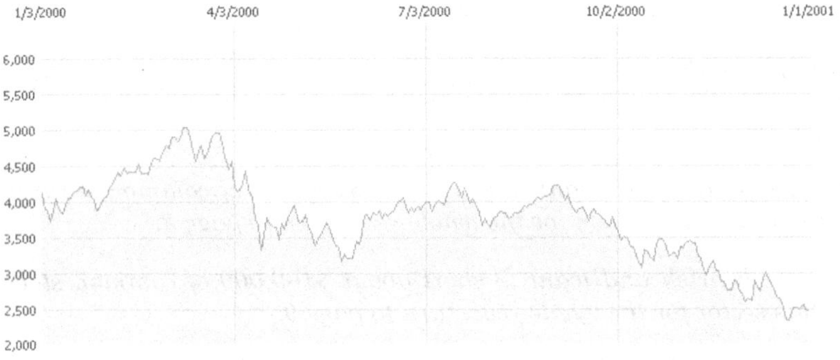

Source: MSN Money

If you'd like to do more trades before moving onto the next month, turn to page 7.

If you'd rather move onto the next month's trading options, turn to page 33.

Internet Stock Bearish Outcome

Congratulations, you just made a 40% return on your investment.

Congratulations, you just literally shorted the very tippy-top of one of the greatest stock market bubbles the world has ever seen: the Internet tech bubble. Few traders have ever done as well–and those who did typically go down in the history books when they're discovered.

Seriously, very few people saw this coming–basically just you and Warren Buffett. The NASDAQ peaked at 5048 in March of 2000. Then everything went very, very wrong and $5 trillion of wealth was obliterated from March 00' through October 2002. Infospace traded at $1305 in March 2000 and was trading at $22 in April next year. Companies that everyone wanted when they had zero revenue are penny stocks, trading below even liquidation values. You haven't heard from your friend with that six-figure Etrade account for a little bit now.

You find yourself dancing around the room in delight as your brain processes just how much money you've just made on this brilliant trade. Your portfolio is already a big part of the way towards getting you that $150 million jackpot.

Nasdaq Composite Index

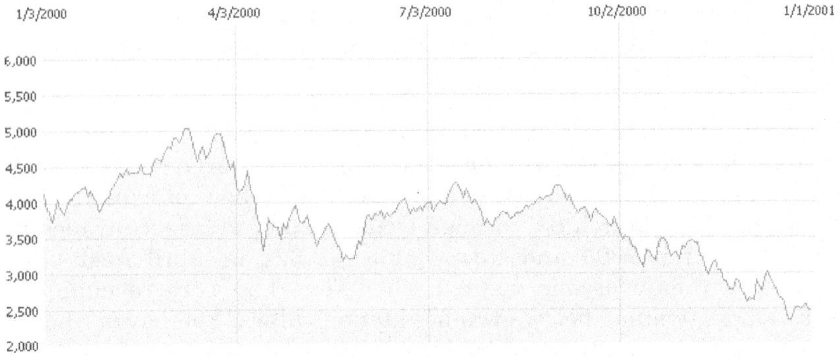

Source: MSN Money

If you'd like to do more trades before moving onto the next month, turn to page 4.

If you'd rather move onto the next month's set of trading options, turn to page 33.

Internet Option Bullish Outcome

Oops, you just lost 5% on your trade.

You have witnessed some of the biggest price moves in stock market history. The Nasdaq was down 10% the first week and back up 15% the next. These huge moves lead you to believe that a big move is just around the corner. As you look back at the fundamentals of these internet stocks, you are starting to think that you might be wrong on your bullish analysis. These companies have taken expensive to a new level–and many of them have never made a dime. Your call options are down slightly and things could definitely be worse right now. Your emotions led you to this trade–and luckily it didn't cost you that much.

Nasdaq Composite Index

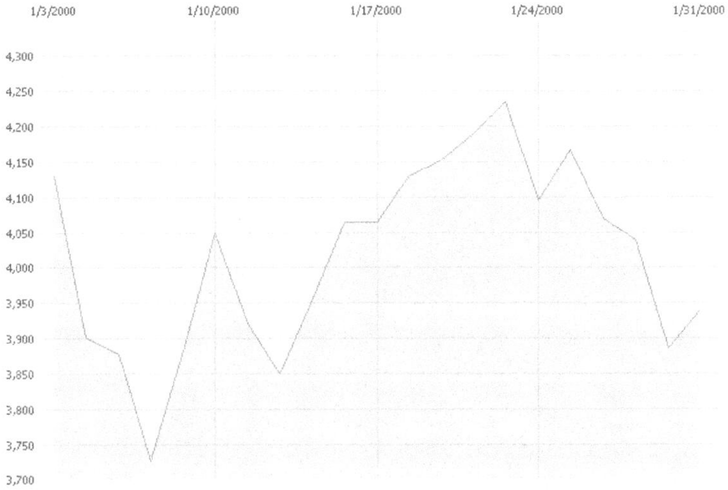

Source: MSN Money

If you would like to do more January trades, turn to page 4.

If you would rather skip to next month's set of trading options, turn to page 33.

Internet Option Bearish Outcome

Congratulations, you just made a 5% return on your trade.

Wow, these internet stocks look like they're on a roller coaster. The Nasdaq was down 10% this week, then up 15% the week after that! It is unknown which way this market will end up moving but into the end of the month, the markets fell significantly. This kind of choppy price action usually means that a big move is right around the corner. As you look back at the fundamentals, you remain confident in your decision to go bearish. Although your returns are not huge, your analysis is still right. From a value perspective, these prices are outlandish and you might have caught the top of giant bubble.

Nasdaq Composite Index

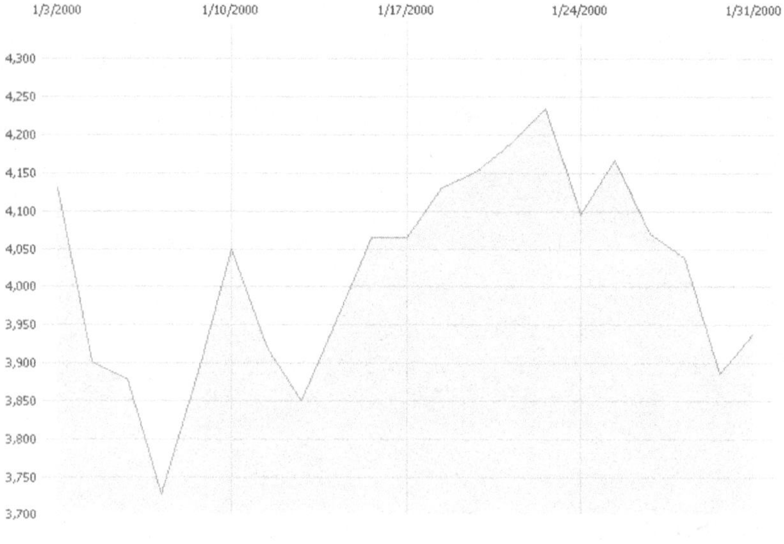

Source: MSN Money

If you would like to do more January trades, turn to page 4.

If you would rather skip to next month's set of trading options, turn to page 33.

First iPhone setup

It's January 2007...Apple's about to release their first-ever cell phone, rumored to be called the iPhone. There have been so many Apple whispers over the last couple years that it's hard to keep track.

Remember when everyone said Apple would buy a music label?

What isn't hard to keep track of is how Apple's stock has done since Steve Jobs returned in August of '97: it's up more than 1600%.

The market has bid up Apple almost 50% in the last six months and with good reason; the iPod is a monster hit and has obliterated every other mp3 player from the market.

But Apple isn't without missteps. You bought a Rokr in 2005, Apple's phone collaboration with Motorola, when renewing your Cingular contract. Blackberry and Nokia are already established giants in mobile devices, with enterprise and global consumer bases.

Apple has always been a niche player in computers–and smartphones are a totally new market for them and everyone else.

Apple Inc.

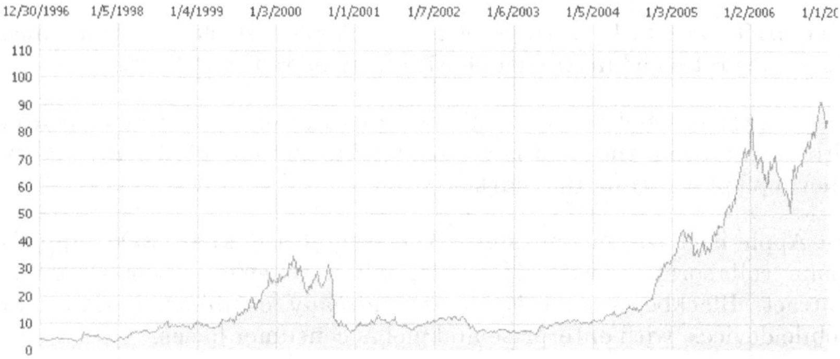

Source: MSN Money

If you are bullish and want to buy about $100,000 of Apple common stock and hold it for the whole year, turn to page 15.

If you are bearish and want to short about $100,000 of Apple common stock for the whole year, turn to page 16.

If you are bullish and want to buy about $50,000 of calls in Apple for a short-term one month trade, turn to page 17.

If you are bearish and want to buy about $50,000 of puts in Apple for a short-term one month trade, turn to page 18.

If you would rather find something else to trade this month, turn to page 4.

First iPhone Stock Bullish Outcome

Congratulations, you just made a 135% return on your trade.

Wow! This stock is on fire and on the rise. It has more than doubled in price since you bought it. The iPhone is being met with huge demand and service providers are struggling to provide all of the data that the phones are using. Apple has sold 1.65 million units in 6 months at a price of $599 a piece. The iPhone has even been called the “Jesus phone.”

The iPhone has further expounded on the already-successful Apple ecosystem. The company continues to lock users into its platform via devices, operating systems, software, and music. As Apple continues to innovate, they will continue to profit and grow. Apple is still a growth company at $200. You really did well on this trade.

Apple Corp.

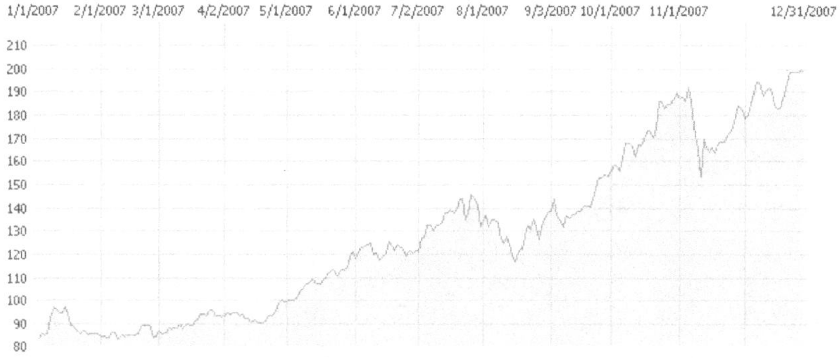

Source: MSN Money

If you would like to do more January trades, turn to page 4.

If you'd rather move onto the next month's set of trading options, turn to page 33.

First iPhone Stock Bearish Outcome

Oops, you just lost 58% on your investment.

Wow this stock is through the roof. Since you sold the stock, it has more than doubled in price. The iPhone is selling like hotcakes. People are lining up all around the world to get their hands on the new Apple phone–it has even been called the "Jesus phone." Apple has sold 1.46 million units this year, and they are selling for $599 a piece.

Service carriers are swamped and providing more data than they can handle. The iPhone clicks right in place with the Apple ecosystem. You can load your music on it through iTunes on your Mac. More people are integrating Apple into their lives. With the rise in social networks, the iPhone helps connect people like never before. You really messed up shorting this stock.

Apple Corp.

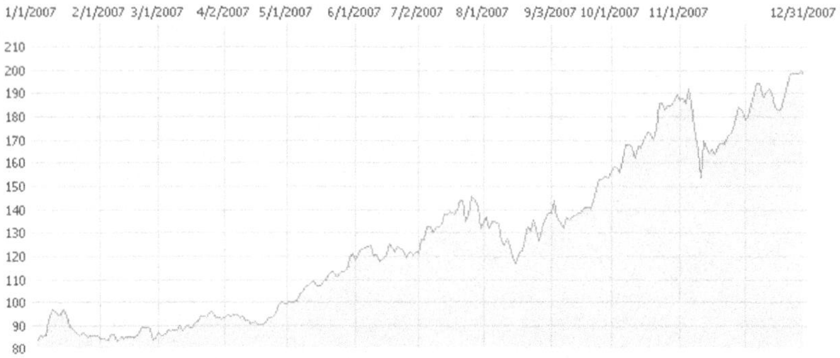

Source: MSN Money

If you would like to do more January trades, turn to page 4.

If you would rather skip to next month's set of trading options, turn to page 33.

First iPhone Option Bullish Outcome

You broke even on your trade. There is no change to your portfolio value.

The first iPhone is being met with a very warm welcome. The phone will go on sale later this year and people will surely be lining up at the door to get their hands on it. The new Apple phone has even be called the "Jesus phone."

The stock popped after the announcement and soon fell back to your purchase price. Your call options are up slightly. The emotions around the iPhone have seemed to fade off and the critics are quick to pick out all of the issues. This new phone will nicely integrate into the Apple ecosystem, but it will take some time before the real earnings start to roll in.

Apple Corp.

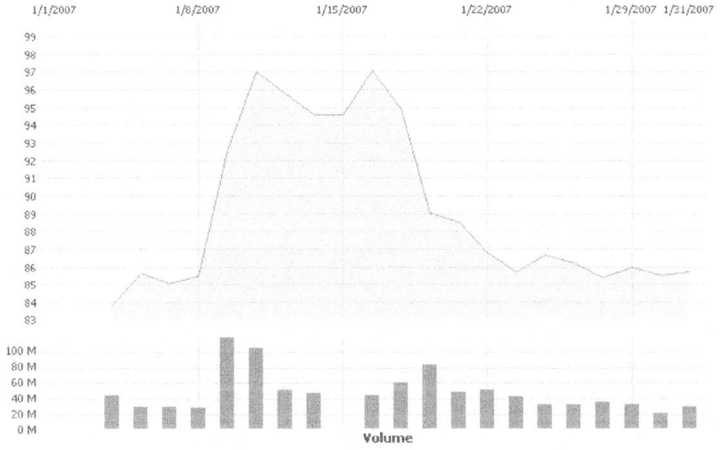

Source: MSN Money

If you would like to do more January trades, turn to page 4.

If you would like to skip to next month's set of trading options, turn to page 33.

First iPhone Option Bearish Outcome

You broke even on your trade. You have no change to your portfolio value.

This new iPhone looks really cool. It will go on sale later this year and it is being met with a positive response. It has even been called the "Jesus phone." People can't wait to get their hands on the new iPhone, and will most likely be lining up at the doors to get their own.

The stock popped in the days after the announcement; however, it has fallen back close to the price where you bought in. This iPhone looks like it will expound on the already great Apple platform (iTunes, iPod, Mac) and will probably lead to great profits. For now you break even on the trade.

Apple Corp.

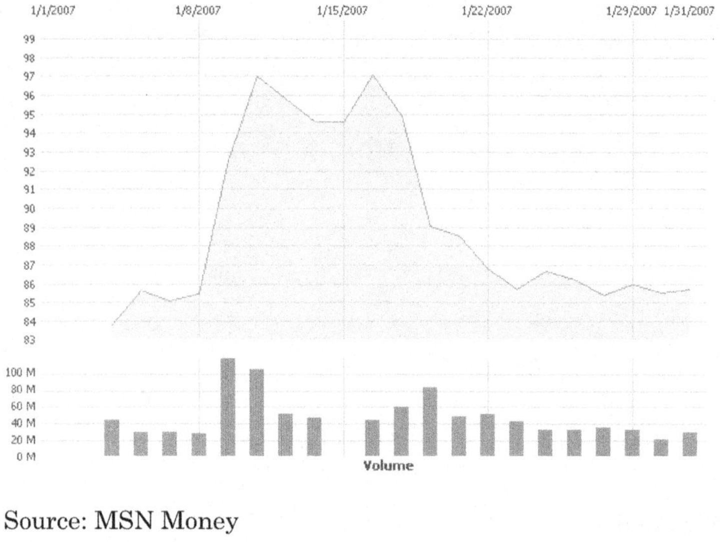

Source: MSN Money

If you would like to do more January trades, turn to page 4.

If you would like to skip to next month's set of trading options, turn to page 33.

Financials in Collapse Setup

It's January 2008 and financials have been taking it on the chin. The XLF is down 25% in the last six months. The housing bubble is in full scale collapse and the fallout is starting to hit Wall Street. Last July, Bear Stearns had to close two multi-billion dollar mortgage hedge funds when their holdings cratered in a matter of days. Even vaunted Goldman Sachs is down 15% since just October.

But the Fed and the Treasury insist that there is no issue with the financial system; Treasury Secretary Paulson is even saying that the fallout from the subprime mortgage crisis is "largely contained."

The Dow was just at an all-time high and money center banks are trading below their long-term earnings multiples. Citigroup, Bank of America and Lehman Brothers pay healthy dividends that provide a buffer against stock market volatility.

Financial Select Sector SPDR (AMEX: XLF)

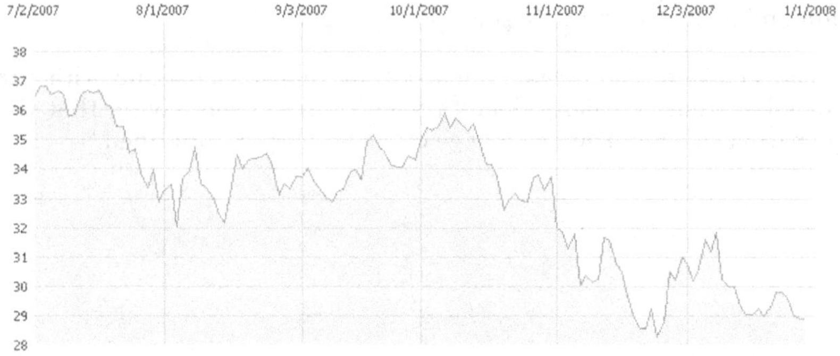

Source: MSN Money

If you are bullish and want to buy about $100,000 of common stock in this sector and hold it for the whole year, turn to page 21.

If you are bearish and want to short about $100,000 of financial sector common stock for the whole year, turn to page 23.

If you are bullish and want to buy about $50,000 of calls in the financial sector for a short-term one month trade, turn to page 25

If you are bearish and want to buy about $50,000 of puts in the financial sector for a short-term one month trade, turn to page 26.

If you would rather find something else to trade this month, turn to page 4.

Financials in Collapse Stock Bullish Outcome

Oops, you just lost 50% on your investment.

It was only a matter of time.

The entire banking system was fragile and literally every single giant bank was insolvent–despite what their balance sheets they were filing with the SEC indicated, and despite every CEO denial that the system was collapsing. Over the course of the year, there was a total run on the banking system and it took trillions of dollars of covert and overt bailouts and welfare distributions to the banks to keep them afloat.

And you blew it.

But the amount of pain from this disastrous trade depends upon the time frame you had for it. The short term returns on the options weren't nearly as painful as the returns for those who held on for the whole year and bet on the sector stocks going to all-time new highs. The system truly collapsed and the stocks did too, but it wasn't overnight. It took months.

Financial Select Sector SPDR (AMEX:XLF)

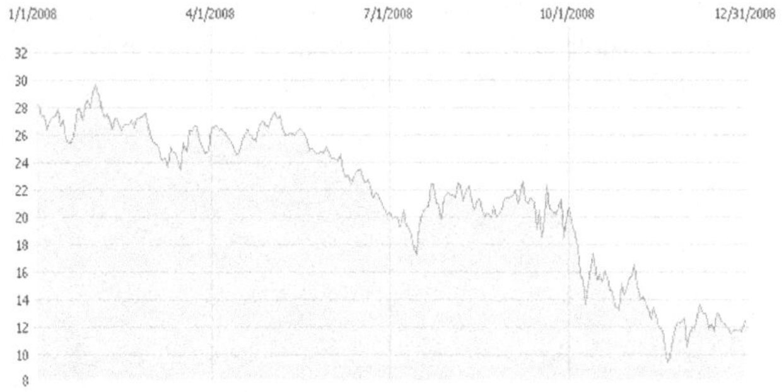

Source: MSN Money

On November 11, 2008, it was announced that the XLF would be moved from AMEX to the NYSE Arca.

If you'd like to do more trades before moving onto the next month, turn to page 4.

If you'd rather move onto the next month's set of trading options, turn to page 33.

Financials in Collapse Stock Bearish Outcome

Congratulations, you just made a 50% return on your investment.

It was only a matter of time.

The entire banking system was fragile and literally every single giant bank was insolvent–despite what their balance sheets they were filing with the SEC indicated, and despite every CEO denial that the system was collapsing. Over the course of the year, there was a total run on the banking system and it took trillions of dollars of covert and overt bailouts and welfare distributions to the banks to keep them afloat.

And you nailed it.

But the amount of pain from this disastrous trade depends upon the time frame you had for it. The short term returns on the options weren't nearly as painful as the returns for those who held on for the whole year and bet on the sector stocks going to all-time new highs. The system truly collapsed and the stocks did too, but it wasn't overnight. It took months.

Bank of America went from $40 to $21 in a few months (January to July). By December it was an $11 stock. Citigroup, Goldman Sachs, and Morgan Stanley were all down by April, but seven months later were worth a third of what they were at the beginning of the year. Betting against the short term prices of Lehman Brothers and Bear Stearns was a good trade; betting against their continued existence was a great one.

Financial Sector Select SPDR (AMEX:XLF)

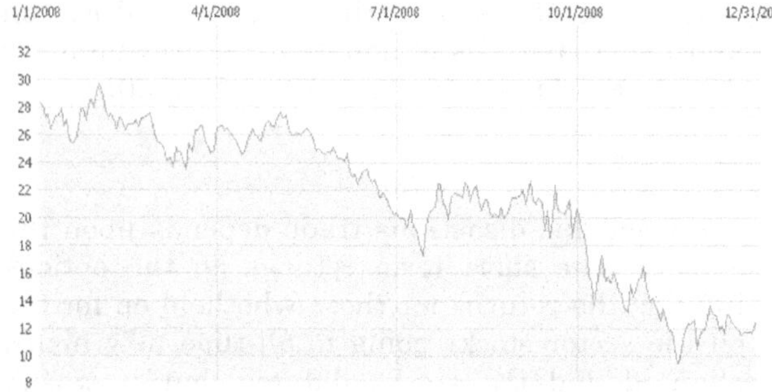

Source: MSN Money

On November 11, 2008, it was announced that the XLF would be moved from the AMEX to NYSE Arca.

If you'd like to do more trades before moving onto the next month, turn to page 4.

If you'd rather move onto the next month's set of trading options,turn to page 33.

Financials in Collapse Option Bullish Outcome

Congratulations, you made a 4% return on your trade.

Wow, the Financials keep climbing. Despite everything that appears to be going wrong with our financial system, people are still buying financial stocks. Your call options have posted some nice gains and you lock in some profits today. There appears to be a lot of faith in this system and virtually no one has anything bad to say about the stocks. It's another great lesson about how unpredictable this market can be. Nice gains for now.

Financial Select Sector (XLF)

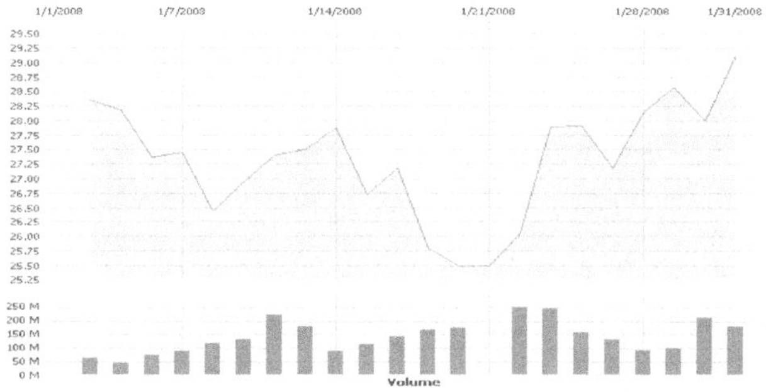

Source: MSN Money

On September 7, 2008, the XLF was delisted from the AMEX to the NYSE Arca.

If you would like to do more January trades, turn to page 4.

If you would rather skip to next month's set of trading options, turn to page 33.

Financials in Collapse Option Bearish Outcome

Oops, you just 4% on your trade.

Unbelievable! The Financial Sector is still climbing, climbing, climbing higher! The gears of the financial sector keep grinding and spinning for now. Over this past month, there have not been any big catalysts that would drive the stock either direction. The price action has been a little choppy but there is still a lot of support at these levels. The American/Investor/Government/Rating Agency faith in the financial system is really phenomenal.

Another loss goes on the books.

Financial Select Sector (XLF)

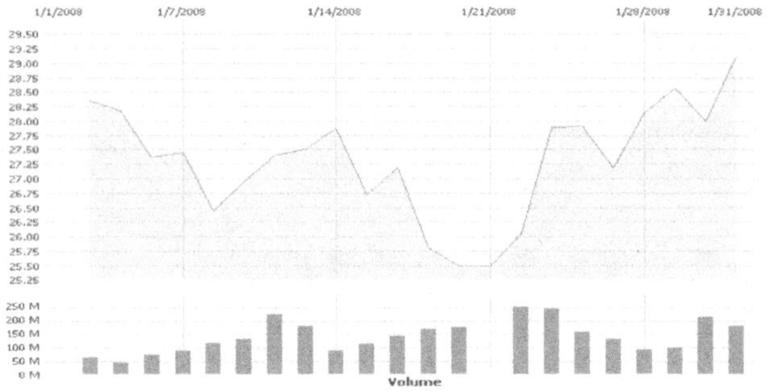

Source: MSN Money

On September 7, 2008, the XLF was delisted from the AMEX to the NYSE Arca.

If you would like to do more January trades, go to page 4.

If you would rather skip to next month's set of trading options, turn to page 33.

Housing Sector Setup

It's January 2005 and housing stocks have been on a multi-year run. Okay that's an understatement. Hovanian Enterprises is up almost 1400% in the last five years. Lennar is up 500% and KBH is up 300%. Every time you're up late (instead of sleeping and resting up for the trading day) you see a new infomercial about buying and flipping houses.

Your junk mail is full of mortgage offers. Some company called Ditech has been able to offer loans over the phone with increasingly weird terms: 10% down, nothing down, adjustable rates, and now something called a 1+3+6+20 year loan. And they promise that you can refinance later.

Something smells funny to you. You look at Department of Labor and Federal Reserve data. Your alarm bells go off.

The line of housing prices is starting to veer away from everything that could justify those prices (income, rents). Median housing prices have increased faster than median incomes! You don't see how people can keep buying houses on credit.

Lennar Corp.

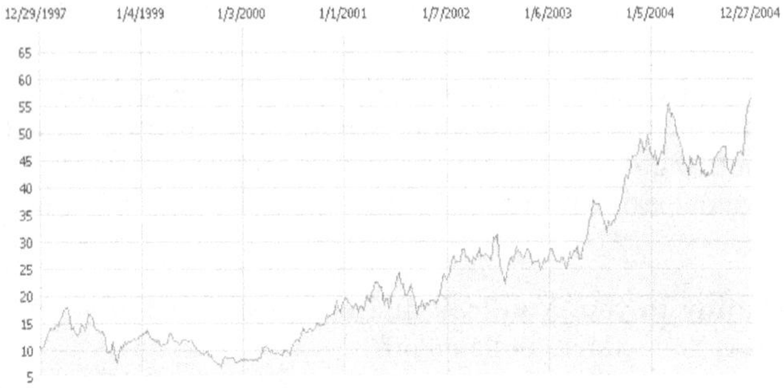

Source: MSN Money

If you are bullish and want to buy about $100,000 of common stock in this sector and hold it for the whole year, turn to page 29.

If you are bearish and want to short about $100,000 of common stock from this sector for the whole year, turn to page 30.

If you are bullish and want to buy about $50,000 of calls on this hot new sector for a short-term one month trade, turn to page 31.

If you are bearish and want to buy about $50,000 of puts on this hot new sector for a short-term one month trade, turn to page 32.

If you would rather find something else to trade this month, turn to page 4.

Housing Sector Stock Bullish Outcome

Congratulations, you just made a 10% return on your investment.

Who's better than you? Your foresight and/or luck of being able to look past all those reasons for housing and real estate to collapse have paid off in spades. You bought KBH in January and made 50% in just six months. Lennar was up about 10% in the same time frame. People are still snapping up homes, and prices for raw land are still going up. Also going up? Your bank account.

Lennar Corp.

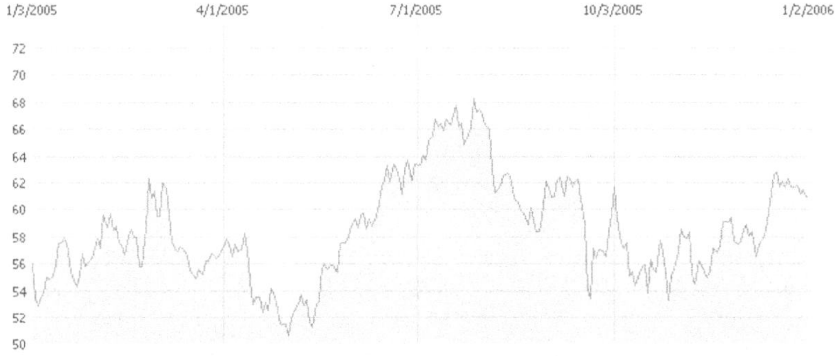

Source: MSN Money

If you would like to do more January trade, turn to page 4.

If you'd rather move onto the next month's set of trading options, turn to page 33.

Housing Sector Stock Bearish Outcome

Oops, you just lost 10% on your investment.

"Man oh man, that's brutal," you think to yourself as you see the homebuilder stocks climb through the roof, despite every reason for the real estate market to start collapsing. Toll Brothers, KBR and everyone else throwing up McMansions are totally killing it! Wachovia is buying GoldenWest for $25 billion to have access to California's housing market, especially the Inland Empire. Housing prices have increased sequentially every month for three years and almost anyone can get credit. The suppliers to housing builders, like drywall maker USG, have doubled. You got this one exactly backwards.

Lennar Corp

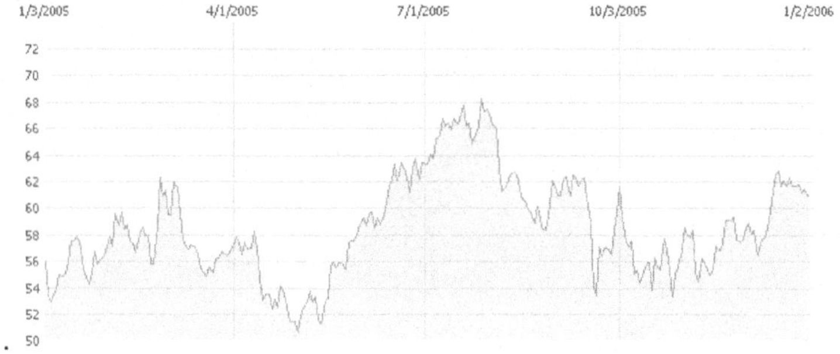

Source: MSN Money

If you'd like to do more trades before moving onto the next month, turn to page 4.

If you'd rather move onto the next month's set of trading options, turn to page 33.

Housing Sector Option Bullish Outcome

You broke even on your investment. There is no change to your portfolio value.

The housing stocks have had mixed price action over this past month. Lennar closed slightly above the price where you bought the call options, and there is no catalyst to move the stock in either direction. For now it looks like the housing market will continue on its current trend. This kind of displacement could also lead to larger price movements in the near future. As a stock becomes more volatile, it is a good indicator that it may pop or crash in the coming weeks, or even days. Your timeline has unfortunately run out and it looks like you won't get to play, whatever happens to this market.

Lennar Corp.

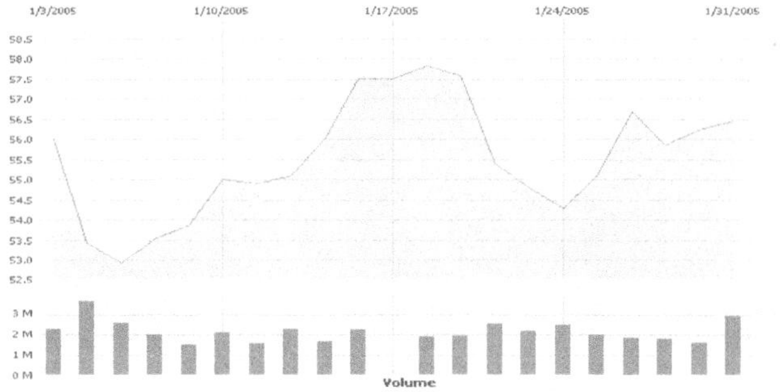

Source: MSN Money

If you would like to do more January trade, turn to page 4.

If you would rather skip to next month's set of trading options, turn to page 33.

Housing Sector Option Bearish Outcome

You broke even on your trade. There is no change to your portfolio value.

The housing stocks have had mixed price action over this past month. Lennar closed slightly above the price where you bought the put options, and there is no catalyst to move the stock in either direction. For now it looks like the housing market will continue on its current trend. This kind of displacement could also lead to larger price movements in the near future. As a stock becomes more volatile, it is a good indicator that it may pop or crash in the coming weeks or even days. Your timeline has unfortunately run out and it looks like you won't get to play, whatever happens to this market.

Lennar Corp.

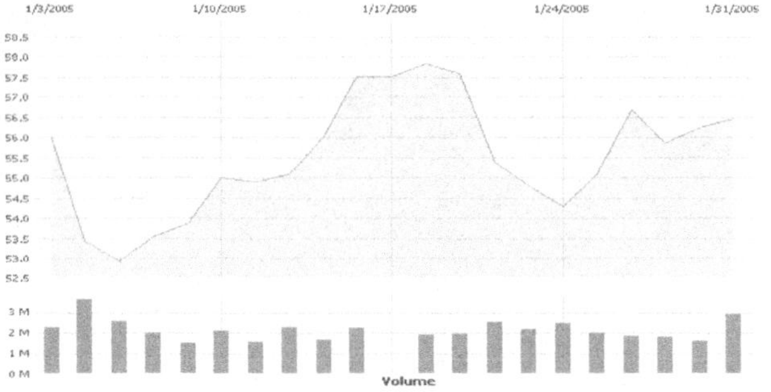

Source: MSN Money

If you would like to do more January trade, turn to page 4.

If you would rather skip to next month's set of trading options, turn to page 33.

Start trading February

You pull up a chart of the DJIA, the S&P 500, and the Nasdaq. You remember on that video how your Great Uncle Buster had turned almost angry when he'd talked about how he had barely beaten the major indices last year.

And here you are supposed to be getting 50% in a single year's timeframe.

If you want to trade the health care sector, turn to page 34.

If you want to trade a company that just released a new state-of-the-art smart phone, turn to page 39.

If you'd rather move onto the next month's set of trading options, turn to page 46.

Obamacare Setup

Today is February 24, 2009. In a joint session of Congress, newly-elected President Barack Obama said, "So let there be no doubt: Healthcare reform cannot wait, it must not wait, and it will not wait another year." This is a very powerful statement. Throughout his campaign, Barack Obama pledged that he would make healthcare affordable for all Americans. He has some big plans to change America's current health insurance industry. Most likely, health insurers will have to provide insurance regardless of preexisting conditions. They will also not be allowed to cap the amount of insurance you can receive. For example, if you get cancer and have millions of dollars worth of treatment, there is a good chance that your insurance has a cap around $1 million dollars. This could spell doom for the current insurance providers in America if they are forced to pay these extra costs.

UnitedHealth Group (UNH) is America's largest insurance provider. This bill could seriously cut into their profits. On the other hand, this company is known for spending big bucks on lobbyists. They may be able to sway politicians to make the bill where it could actually increase their profits. If they can get subsidized for providing this insurance, they will likely double or triple their revenue as people who were never allowed to get insurance before (preexisting condition, low income) are now being paid for by the government. One thing to consider is that 65% of healthcare providers had a disapproval rating on UnitedHealth Group, the lowest of all insurance providers.

UnitedHealth Group Inc.

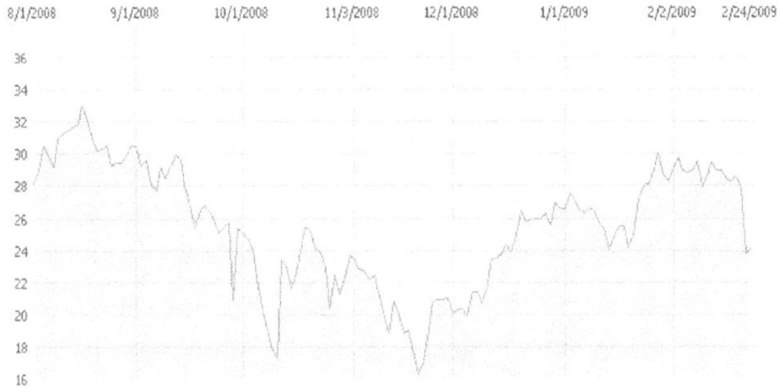

Source: MSN Money

If you are bullish and want to buy about $100,000 of UnitedHealth Group common stock and hold it for the whole year, turn to page 36.

If you are bearish and want to short about $100,000 of UnitedHealth Group common stock for the whole year, turn to page 37.

If you are bullish and want to buy about $50,000 of calls in UnitedHealth Group for a short-term one month trade, turn to page 38.

If you are bearish and want to buy about $50,000 of puts in UnitedHealth Group for a short-term one month trade, turn to page 39.

If you would rather find something else to trade this month, turn to page 33.

Obamacare Stock Bullish Outcome

Congratulations, you just made a 93% return on your investment!

Great Call. You caught the bottom of this healthcare stock. You have enjoyed a nearly straight-up ride as UNH is now up 93% from your purchase price. Since you bought the stock, the Affordable Healthcare Act went through committee and passed the Senate on December 24.

Investors have continued faith in management's ability to navigate through the government and still generate returns. Not long after you bought in the common stock jumped 33%. Healthcare in the United States is now going to be a different animal as this 2,074 page bill is picked through and administered by the Bureaucracy.

UnitedHealth Group Inc.

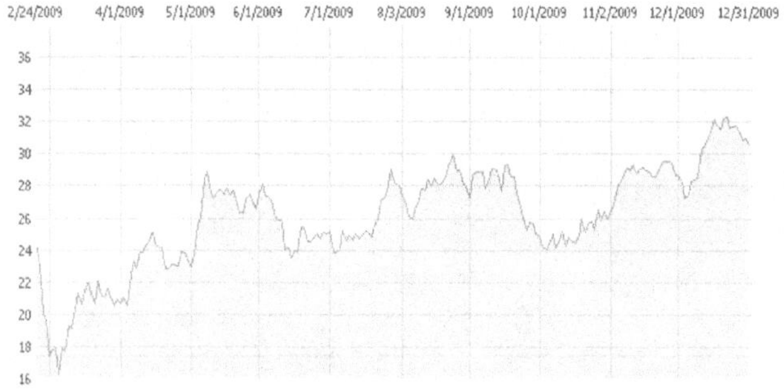

Source: MSN Money

If you want to do more February trades, turn to page 33.

If you'd rather move onto the next month's set of trading options, turn to page 46.

Obamacare Stock Bearish Results

Oops, you just lost 93% on your investment!

Look out! You shorted at the bottom of this healthcare stock. This has been an extremely ugly trade as the stock shot upward immediately after you bought it, and then closed up 94% into the end of the month. Since you shorted the stock, the Affordable Healthcare Act went through committee and passed the Senate on December 24.

Investors have continued faith in management's ability to navigate through the government and still generate returns. Not long after you shorted it, the common stock jumped 33%. Healthcare in the United States is now going to be a different animal as this 2,074 page bill is picked through and administered by the Bureaucracy.

UnitedHealth Group Inc.

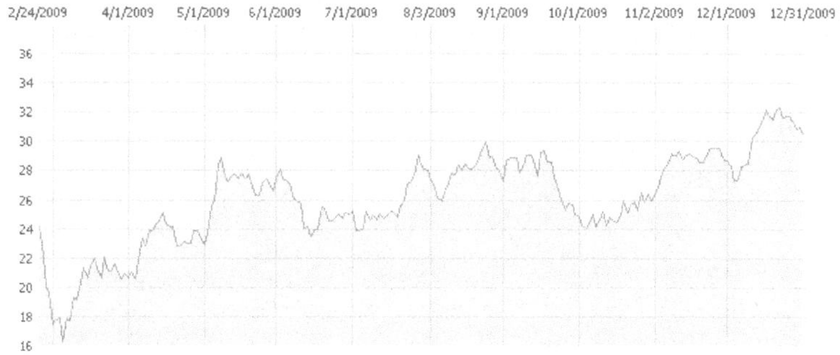

Source: MSN Money

If you want to do more February trades, turn to page 33.

If you'd rather move onto the next month's set of trading options, turn to page 46.

Obamacare Option Bullish Outcome

Oops, you just lost 13% on your trade!

It looks like a bit of uncertainty is driving UnitedHealth in the short-term. The Affordable Healthcare Act is 2,074 pages, and it is going to take some time to figure out what all it entails. Until we see a direct effect on insurance providers, UnitedHealth will most likely behave very cyclically.

The Affordable Healthcare Act is a revision of healthcare reform in the past. Many presidents have attempted to change the healthcare system but this is the first time any significant reform has taken place. There is a lot of criticism and praise surrounding the bill. Some are saying that it is a socialization of the American healthcare system, while others say that it is one of the greatest and most-needed pieces of legislation to ever come out of Washington. It will take some time to see how this one plays out, and today you take a loss on your call options.

UnitedHealth Group Inc.

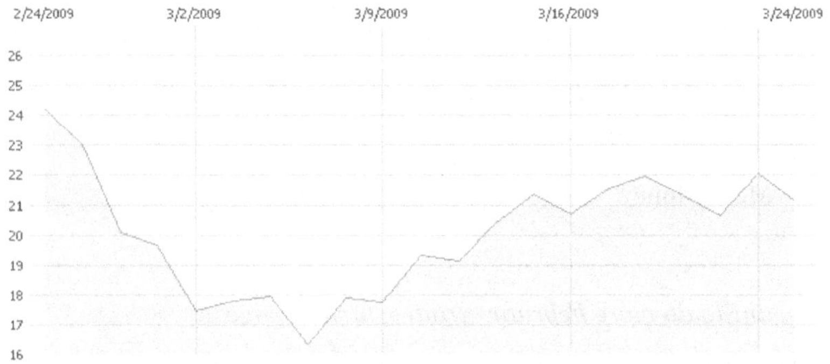

Source: MSN Money

If you would like to do more February trades, turn to page 33.

If you would like to skip to next month's set of trading options, turn to page 46.

RIM 8800 Setup

Today is February 12, 2007. The famous smartphone company Research in Motion just released their all-new lineup of Blackberrys known as the RIM 8800 series. These new phones are everything good about the previous models with new features and a sleek new look. These series of smartphones now come standard with the trackball and will now feature Wi-Fi capability. Research in Motion is one of the most innovative companies on the planet and continues to rock the world with their great lineup of unique smartphones. RIM has doubled in price over the last year, and is facing resistance around the $47 level. It has had some big displacement in the last few months and looks primed for a breakout or a crash. This new product launch is likely to be spectacular as this phone faces high demand from businesses as well as consumers. People love their PDAs and businesses have a lot of utility for them. RIM has been making phones for several years, and new competition is starting to come out. Apple just released their first version of a Phone called the iPhone in January. Samsung and Motorola also have similar smartphones. Unstrung describes the new RIM 8800 phones as "for the cognoscenti, almost as hotly anticipated as was the iPhone."

The Blackberry 8800 will be a wider version of the Blackberry 8100 Pearl, with a full ASCII keyboard. There will be two versions — with and without a camera.

Like the Pearl, the 8800 series will play heavily on multimedia functions (a camera and a music player) alongside the existing strong email functions. By comparison, the iPhone is taking multimedia, and adding phone and email — though without a Qwerty keyboard, it's never going to appeal to Blackberry users. Another Blackberry upgrade will come later in the year, when RIM is expected to launch a 9000 series, which will operate on 3G (and one might hope, Wi-Fi) and will "feature a completely redesigned Blackberry GUI." It is also expected to feature a full system back-up and restore to a micro-SD card.

Research in Motion

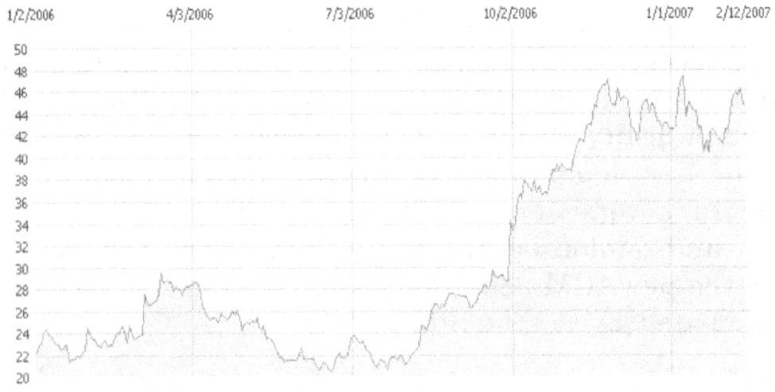

Source: MSN Money

If you are bullish and want to buy about $100,000 of RIMM common stock hold it for the whole year, *turn to page 41.*

If you are bearish and want to short about $100,000 of RIMM common stock for the whole year, *turn to page 43.*

If you are bullish and want to buy about $50,000 of calls in RIMM for a short-term one month trade, *turn to page 44.*

If you are bearish and want to buy about $50,000 of puts in RIMM for a short-term one month trade, *turn to page 45.*

If you would rather find something else to trade this month, *turn to page 33.*

RIM 8800 Stock Bullish Outcome

This stock has really rallied. You sit back in your Lazy Boy recliner and smoke your $50 cigar as you see your RIMM stock up massively. RIMM went on to release three other smartphones this year which all had great success. The company also increased their revenue by 47% year over year! This is phenomenal growth for a company that is now worth over $64 billion dollars.

Their product line is being snatched up by businesses around the world as RIM's software allows them to do business better. The RIM platform gives business everything they could possibly need in the palm of their hands. Although RIM still faces serious competition (especially from Apple) investors are confident in the company's innovative capability to stay on top of the market.

This was a great long opportunity and you have really made some money. The common stock is up 150% from where you bought in at. The stock was slow to react but it finally caught speed. Ahhh the sweet smell of money.

Research in Motion

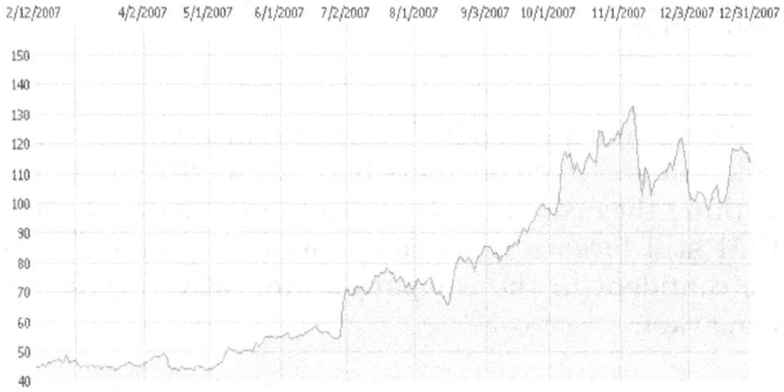

Source: MSN Money

If you would like to do more February trades, turn to page 33.

If you'd rather move onto the next month's set of trading options, turn to page 46.

RIM 8800 Stock Bearish Outcome

Man o' man, this is horrible. This common stock looks like it may leave Earth. RIMM stock is up 150% on the year and the fundamentals are great. The company grew its revenue a stunning 47% year-over-year, and their products continue to be eaten up by consumers and businesses alike. Competition still exists and the Apple iPhone is really taking off. Investors remain confident in the company's ability to remain on top.

The RIM software is really the most useful part of the phone. It brings together email, internet, IM, and usage in such a way that it will surely remain the envy of the smartphone world for many years to come. It took awhile for this stock to gain momentum, but once it got past that initial level of resistance, the stock was unstoppable.

Research in Motion

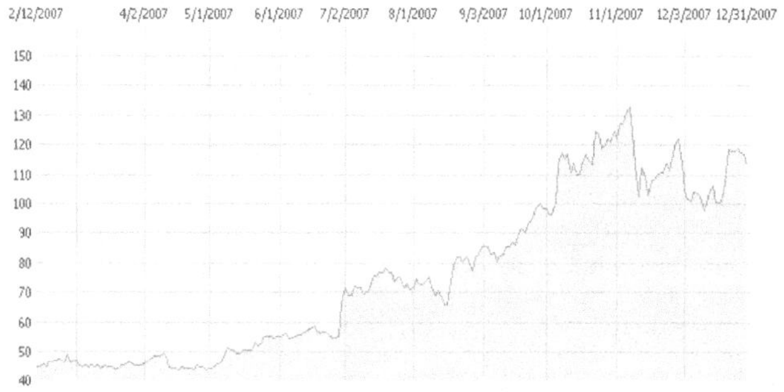

Source: MSN Money

If you would like to do more February trades, turn to page 33.

If you'd rather move onto the next month's set of trading options, turn to page 46.

RIM 8800 Option Bullish Outcome

You made a whopping 2% on your trade!

The stock bounced immediately following the announcement. Your options were up nicely but then into the end of the month, the stock fell back to just 2% above your purchase price. The RIM 8800 series of phones will most likely be a widely-sold and very successful phone. However, it seems that investors aren't willing to keep buying up the stock at higher prices. If the phones create real earnings for the company, we will then see a significant rise in the price of the stock. RIM continues to innovate and is already set to release two more phones throughout the year. For now the stock is still slightly in the money for you and you actually made money on the trade.

Research in Motion

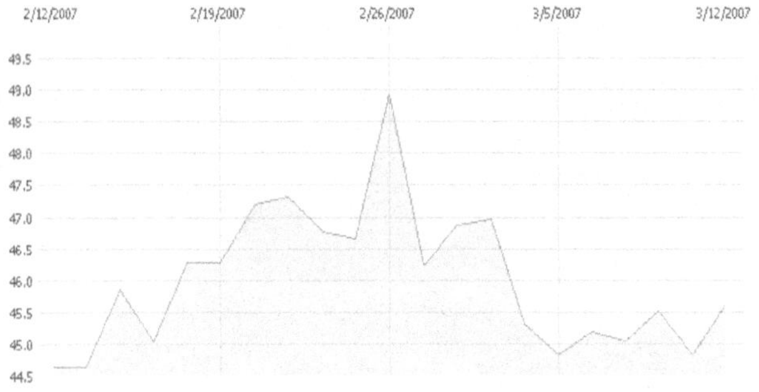

Source: MSN Money

If you would like to do more February trades, turn to page 33.

If you would rather skip to next month's set of trading options, turn to page 46.

RIM 8800 Option Bearish Outcome

You lost a whopping 2% on your trade!

The stock bounced immediately following the announcement. Your put options were down significantly, but then into the end of the month, the stock fell back to just 2% above your purchase price. The RIM 8800 series of phones will most likely be a widely-sold and very successful phone. However, it seems that investors aren't willing to keep buying up the stock at higher prices. If the phones create real earnings for the company, we will then see a significant rise in the price of the stock. RIM continues to innovate and is already set to release two more phones throughout the year. For now the stock is still slightly out of the money and you are going to take a small loss on this trade.

Research in Motion

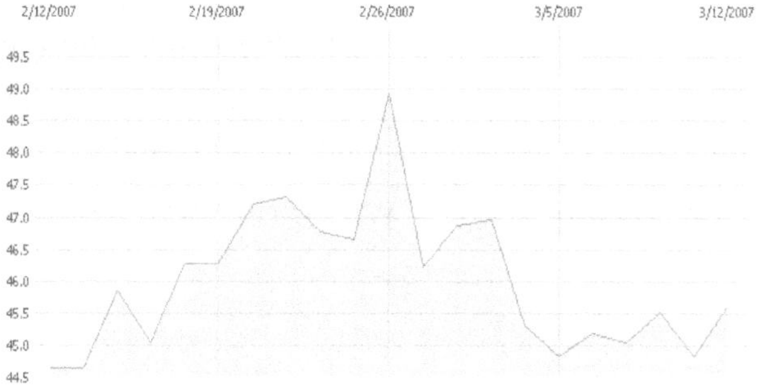

Source: MSN Money

If you would like to do more February trades, turn to page 33.

If you would rather skip to next month's set of trading options, turn to page 46.

Start trading March

You pull up a chart of the DJIA, the S&P 500, and the Nasdaq. You remember on that video how your Great Uncle Buster had turned almost angry when he'd talked about how he had barely beaten the major indices last year.

And here you are supposed to be getting 50% in a single year's timeframe.

If you want to trade stocks just before a new war is started, turn to page 47.

If you want to trade a technology stock just before they roll out a new service, turn to page 53.

If you'd rather move onto the next month's set of trading options, turn to page 59.

If you've hit $1.5 million and are ready to cash in, turn to page 308.*

*(*PLEASE DO NOT GO TO PAGE 308 IF YOU HAVE NOT HIT $1.5 MILLION).*

Operation Iraqi Freedom Setup

Today is March 12, 2003. The world is a mess. Europe's economies are in total disarray with Germany leading the collapse, and all the major indices are hitting new 300-year lows every day. Japan remains mired in its mess and the Nikkei looks to be headed for triple digits. Venezuela is a pit. Argentina is left for dead. The dollar can't stop falling. Treasuries are through the roof. We've got a housing bubble to contend with, still. Serbia's PM is assassinated today. The UN is falling apart, and the US is burning all bridges. Consumers are over-leveraged and can't sustain the economy any longer.

President Bush has given Iraqi Dictator Saddam Hussein an ultimatum. A coalition of Allied troops will be invading Iraq. The reason for the invasion is to remove the current tyrannical Saddam Hussein Regime. The relations between the United States and Iraq have been deteriorating for months now. Back in October of last year, President Bush announced that the US would use armed forces to counter Iraq. Reportedly, Iraq has amassed weapons of mass destruction and has repeatedly threatened to attack US ally Israel. This move by the United States will definitely increase tension with many other Middle Eastern nations such as Iran and Turkey. Iraq has the fifth largest military in the world and a highly trained unit known as the Republic Guard. This is most likely going to be a much-extended war, and occupation of the country could run into next year.

General Electric (GE) is an American conglomerate that is typically very cyclical. How do you think this announcement will affect a company like GE? How will GE behave in this type of an economy? Obviously the US is going to spend a lot of money on this war and some of GE's products could possibly be in demand. Maybe this is a great buying opportunity. The stock has been volatile since the beginning of the year and could be positioned for some short-term price action.

General Electric

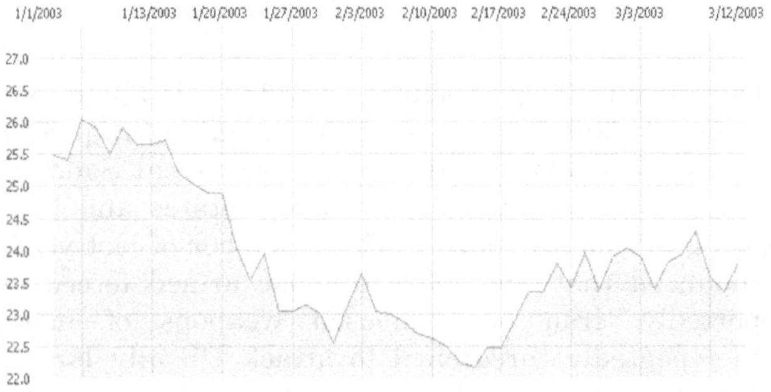

Source: MSN Money

If you are bullish and want to buy about $100,000 of GE common stock and hold it for the whole year, turn to page 49.

If you are bearish and want to short about $100,000 of GE common stock for the whole year, turn to page 50.

If you are bullish and want to buy about $50,000 of calls in GE for a short-term one month trade, turn to page 51.

If you are bearish and want to buy about $50,000 of puts in GE for a short-term one month trade, turn to page 52.

If you would rather find something else to trade this month, turn to page 46.

Operation Iraqi Freedom Stock Bullish Outcome

Congratulations, you just made a 30% return on your investment!

On the 19th, President Bush announced that the United States would invade Iraq. The announcement had little effect on the price of GE's stock. It seems like the beaten down bulls have some kind of restored confidence. Being the contrarian you are, you went long when everybody was selling out. This was a smart move. As with most cyclical companies this year, GE did very well. These stock prices are powering higher through a lot of bad news. The company grew its top line revenue growth by 10% as well as generating significant profits. It would be a stretch to say that this war has had a significant impact on General Electric's profits. The stock is up almost 30% from where you bought it.

General Electric

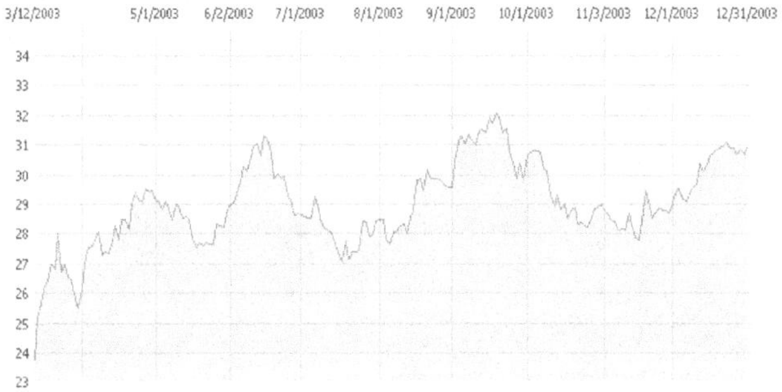

Source: MSN Money

If you would like to do more March trades, turn to page 46.

If you'd rather move onto the next month's set of trading options, turn to page 59.

Operation Iraqi Freedom Stock Bearish Outcome

Oops, you just lost 30% on your investment!

It seems that the war in Iraq has had little effect on the price of General Electric stock. You went with the flow and it cost you. Not long after you shorted the stock, President Bush announced that the United States would invade Iraq. This announcement did not do much for the stock but the headlines have quickly changed. Next time maybe you should try being a contrarian.

The corporation is continuing to grow their company, and they increased their top line by 10%. The broader markets are up for the year despite all of the horrifying news that was coming out earlier. The allied forces entered Iraq and conquered Baghdad within 21 days. The United States still occupies the country as a new democracy is set in place. Your poor logic has caused a sizable setback in your portfolio.

General Electric

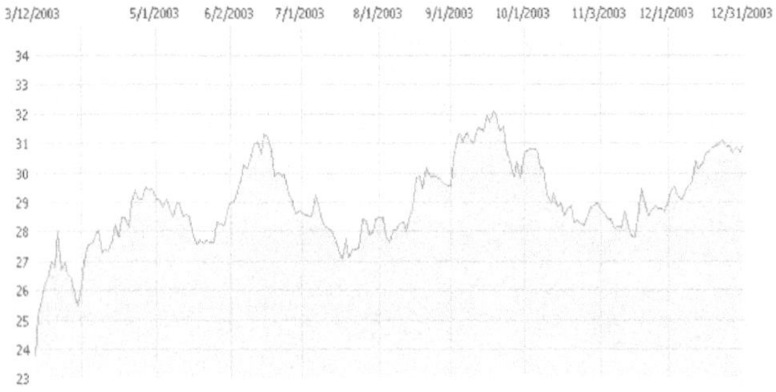

Source: MSN Money

If you would like to do more March trades, turn to page 46.

If you'd rather move onto the next month's set of trading options, turn to page 59.

Operation Iraqi Freedom Option Bullish Outcome

Congratulations, you just made a 15% return on your trade!

Well it seems that the headlines have changed since you bought the stock. Not long after you bought your call options, President Bush announced that a coalition of UN Nations would be invading Iraq. In the meantime, the GE stock has shot up 15%. It seems like the beat-down bulls finally have some confidence again and are rushing back into the market. It is not clear how this war will directly affect these stocks, if at all. The clear thing is that you bought a good company when nobody else wanted it and it paid off.

General Electric

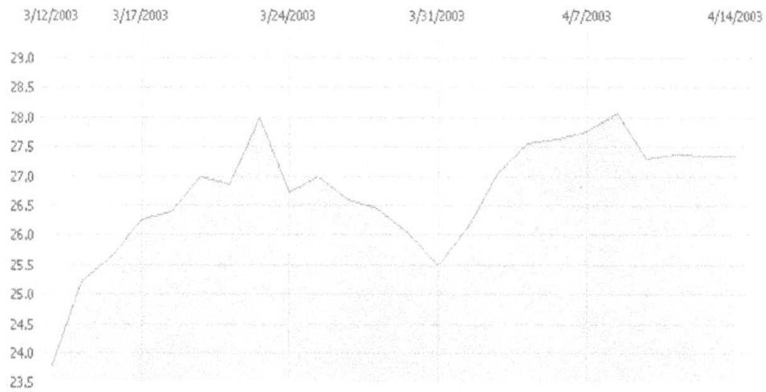

Source: MSN Money

If you would like to do more March trades, turn to page 46.

If you'd rather move onto the next month's set of trading options, turn to page 59.

Operation Iraqi Freedom Option Bearish Outcome

Oops, you just lost 15% on your trade!

Well it seems that the headlines have changed since you bought the put options. Not long after you bought your put options, President Bush announced that a coalition of UN Nations would be invading Iraq. In the meantime, the GE stock has shot up 15%. It seems like the beat-down bulls finally have some confidence again and are rushing back into the market. It is not clear how this war will directly affect these stocks, if at all. The clear thing is that you shorted a company just like everyone else–and it turned around on you.

General Electric

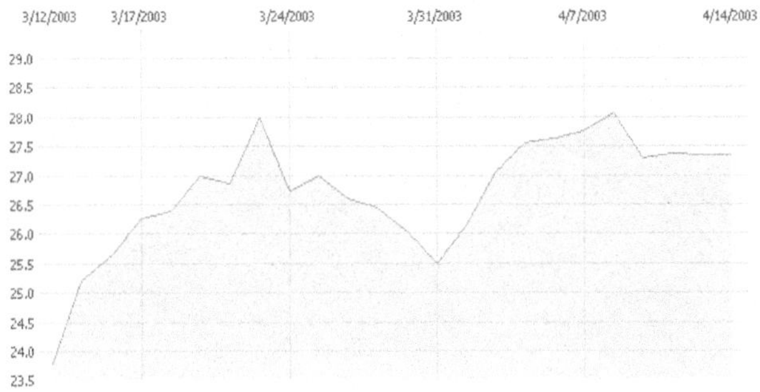

Source: MSN Money

If you would like to do more March trades, turn to page 46.

If you'd rather move onto the next month's set of trading options, turn to page 59.

Apple iTunes Rollout Setup

It's March 29th, 2003, and you're walking to the office. It's a particularly dreary morning; the indexes have been whipping around all year and are basically flat. To top it all off, the U.S. has just invaded Iraq to go and root out what the administration and the press call "Weapons of Mass Destruction" aka anthrax and nuclear material. Fun stuff.

As you get off the subway you notice that everyone is doing the same thing you are: bobbing their head with little white earbuds stuck into the side of their head. You look down at your own iPod which holds five to 20 GB, and cost you $299-$399:

When you get to the office you call up what Apple's stock has done since they introduced the iPod and basically killed off the competition:

AAPL

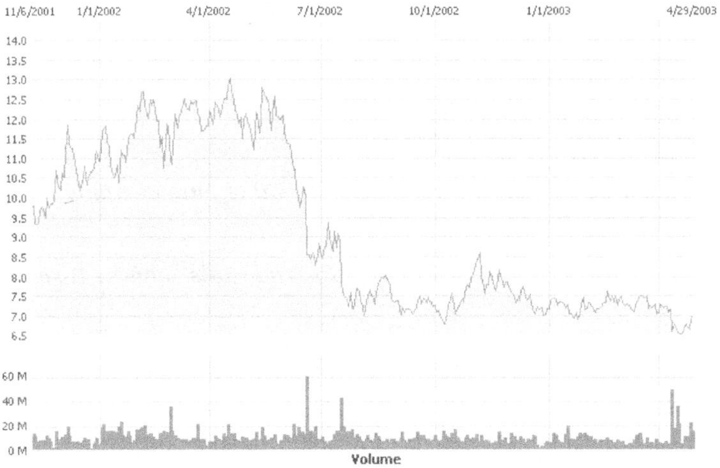

MSN Money

Not so hot. You look up the financials and you see a stock trading at about $7 per share with $8 in cash. Even after two successful consumer launches, the candy-colored iMac and the iPod, Apple is stuck in the muck and hated on Wall Street. There were rumors last week that Apple was about to buy a music label (namely Warner Music) but instead they launched an mp3 through their iTunes software.

Songs are 99 cents, so to legally fill your iPod would cost a couple hundred dollars. At this point you've purchased Bob Dylan's 'Blonde on Blonde" as a vinyl, an 8-track, a cassette, and a CD. You can also just keep ripping your CDs and uploading them as mp3s to your iPod, which takes hours. Most everyone chooses to go another route, downloading the music free via torrent and warez sites.

If you are bullish and want to buy about $100,000 of Apple common stock and hold it for the whole year, turn to page 55.

If you are bearish and want to short about $100,000 of Apple common stock for the whole year, turn to page 56.

If you are bullish and want to buy about $50,000 of calls in Apple for a short-term one month trade, turn to page 57.

If you are bearish and want to buy about $50,000 of puts in Apple for a short-term one month trade, turn to page 58.

If you would rather find something else to trade this month, turn to page 46.

Apple iTunes Rollout Stock Bullish Outcome

Congratulations, you just made a 50% return!

Wow, great timing. The stock immediately popped after you bought it and never looked back. The common stock is up almost 5o% and you really made a great trade here. There was really a lot of basis for this trade that you caught on to. First from a value perspective, Apple at $7 wasn't dirt cheap, it made dirt look good. In other words, if Apple were to liquidate, you would get more cash for each share than what you even paid for the share. That's not counting earnings and the other millions of dollars of assets that Apple owns. Next, Apple was a great growth play. You saw the platform that Apple was starting to build and you jumped on it. The iPod is the number one selling mp3 player in the world and the new iTunes just expounded on an already great product. Apple will continue to expand this platform and you really did good on this one.

Apple

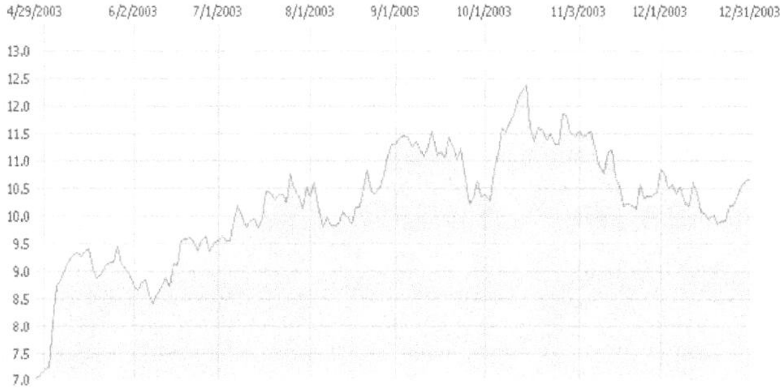

Source: MSN Money

If you would like to do more March trades, turn to page 46.

If you'd rather move onto the next month's set of trading options, turn to page 59.

Apple iTunes Rollout Stock Bearish Outcome

Oops, you just lost 50% on your investment!

It looks like you couldn't have picked a worse time to sell the Apple common stock. The combination of a number-one-selling mp3 player and the new iTunes is really starting to change the dynamics of Apple Computer. In fact it could be fair to say that sometime in the future, Apple won't even be known as a computer company. The dominance of the iPod is helping Apple to expand its platform and has given Apple more opportunities to generate profits. As Apple continues to expand this platform, we will see new products that are intertwined with other Apple products. From a value standpoint, you definitely should not have shorted Apple when it had more cash per share than what it cost to buy the share. You really blew this one.

Apple

Source: MSN Money

If you would like to do more March trades, turn to page 46.

If you'd rather move onto the next month's set of trading options, turn to page 59.

Apple iTunes Rollout Option Bullish Outcome

Congratulations, you just made a 30% return!

It seems like the constant flow of great new products coming from Apple is starting to pay off. The common stock has popped 30% since you bought your call options. iTunes is really taking hold of the music market–couple that with an mp3 player that is now the top-seller in the world and you have an extremely successful and profitable enterprise. It seems that investors are starting to see the massive potential for profits presented by this combination. Your call options have really paid off.

Apple 1 month

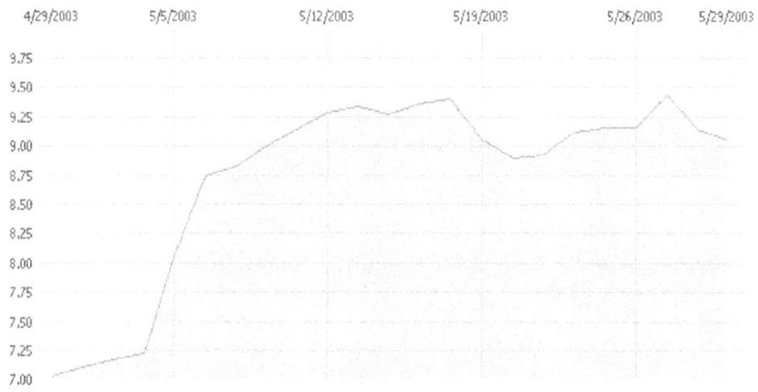

Source: MSN Money

If you would like to do more March trades, turn to page 46.

If you'd rather move onto the next month's set of trading options, turn to page 59.

Apple iTunes Rollout Option Bearish Outcome

Oops, you just lost 30% on your trade!

As more and more people continue to use iTunes to fill their iPod on their Mac computers, Apple is starting to show signs of recovery. The stock is up 30% in one month and the sentiment towards the computer company has changed. Apple's enterprise value (stock price-cash per share) is no longer negative and you called that one just right. For a long time, Apple has been viewed as a second-rate company compared to the dominating players in the computer world like Microsoft, Compaq, and HP. As Apple's focus shifts to music and personal devices like the iPod, we could see a new era for Apple Computer as they slip into new markets and take advantage of it like they did in music. The iPod and whatever else Apple has up its sleeve will continue to change the way we live our lives.

Apple 1 month

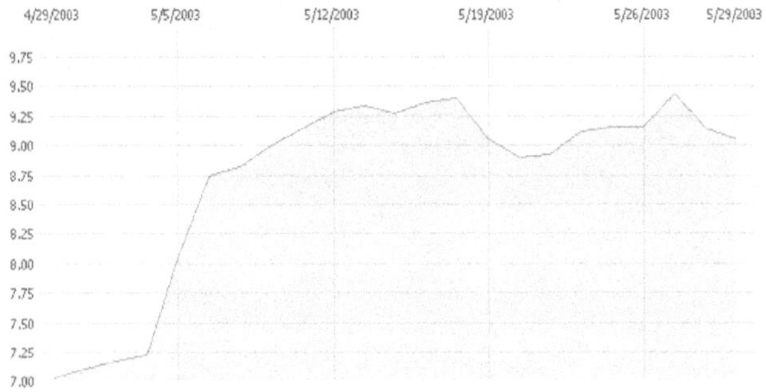

Source: MSN Money

If you would like to do more March trades, turn to page 46.

If you'd rather move onto the next month's set of trading options, turn to page 59.

Start trading April

You pull up a chart of the DJIA, the S&P 500, and the Nasdaq. You remember on that video how your Great Uncle Buster had turned almost angry when he'd talked about how he had barely beaten the major indices last year.

And here you are supposed to be getting 50% in a single year's timeframe.

If you want to trade a beverage company that has been a staple in American society just as they update their main product, turn to page 60.

If you want to trade a biotech company that just announced a new breakthrough, turn to page 66.

If you'd rather move onto the next month's set of trading options, turn to page 73.

If you've hit $1.5 million and are ready to cash in, turn to page 308.*

*(*PLEASE DO NOT GO TO PAGE 308 IF YOU HAVE NOT HIT $1.5 MILLION*

New Coke Setup

Today is April 19, 1985, and the Coca-Cola Corporation (KO) has announced that the Classic Coke formula will be replaced by a new, sweeter formula. This announcement comes as a response to the loss of market share experienced by Coca-Cola to Pepsi. Many drinkers prefer Pepsi due to the fact that it has a sweeter taste. Coca-Cola has been working on the project for several months, and they have a big marketing and sales plan ready to go. Coke has lost major ground in the area of supermarket sales and today only has 24% of the total market share for carbonated drinks. Coke is still the leader at fast food restaurants as well as in vending machine sales.

Coca-Cola stock is up nicely over the past year and appears to be on a steady climb. Pepsi has long been the leader in soft drinks and this new formula could possibly give Coke the chance to challenge that–although there is the possibility that traditional Coke drinkers will stop buying the product if they do not like the new formula.

Coca-Cola (KO)

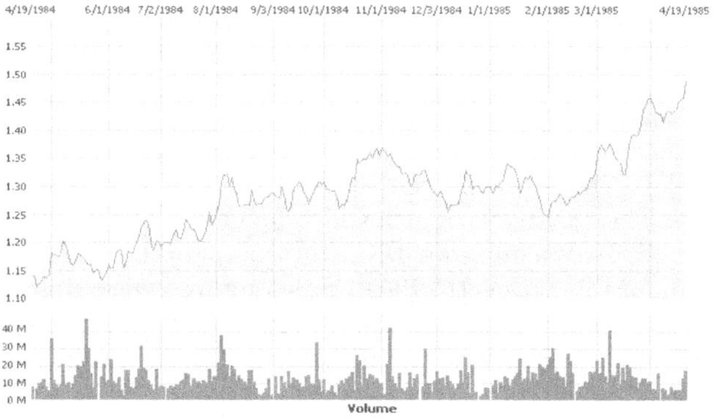

Source: MSN Money

If you are bullish and want to buy about $100,000 of Coca-Cola common stock and hold it for the whole year, turn to page 62.

If you are bearish and want to short about $100,000 of Coca-Cola common stock for the whole year, turn to page 63.

If you are bullish and want to buy about $50,000 of calls in Coca-Cola for a short-term one month trade, turn to page 64.

If you are bearish and want to buy about $50,000 of puts in Coca-Cola for a short-term one month trade, turn to page 65.

If you would rather find something else to trade this month, turn to page 59.

New Coke Stock Bullish Outcome

Congratulations, you just made a 15% return on your investment!

After the press conference, there were a lot of negative views towards the new formula. The scientists could not come up with a good explanation as to the difference between the new and the old formula. The marketing team also failed to explain the big reason as to why the corporation was switching formulas. This negative outlook caused to the stock to fall shortly after the announcement. Over a one month period, the stock was down a modest 3%.

Shorty after the selloff, the stock picked up into the end of the year rallying almost 20%. The extensive marketing scheme by the guys at Coke seemed to pay off. In Washington D.C., the company handed out free bottles to bystanders in Lafayette Park. Sales figures were up 8% in the first cities to receive the new formula, and people who have been life-long Coke drinkers said they would still be with the new formula. Coca-Cola has appeared to pull off a very successful launch.

Coca-Cola

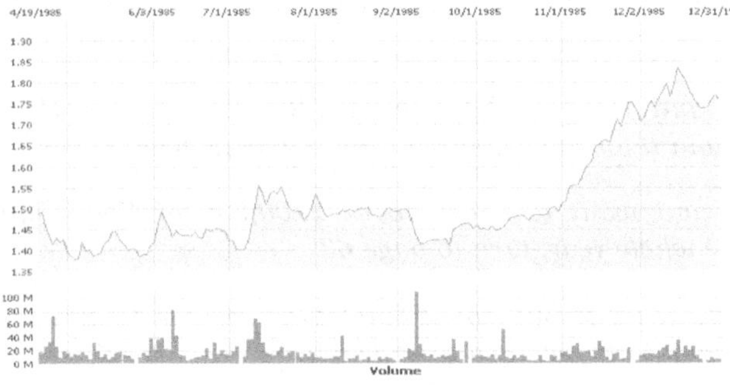

Source: MSN Money

If you want to do more April trades, turn to page 59.

If you'd rather move onto the next month's set of trading options, turn to page 73.

New Coke Stock Bearish Outcome

Oops, you just lost 16% on your investment!

After the official launch of the New Coke formula, there was a lot of negative outlook for the company. The marketing team failed to explain why they were switching formulas and the scientists struggled trying to explain the actual differences between the two. The stock was down slightly (-3%) the month after the announcement, but soon picked up and rallied almost 20% into the end of the year.

Once the New Coke formula hit the street, people really started liking it. "Classic" Coke drinkers said that they would buy more of the new formula. This new formula may pull in the people that used to like Pepsi while still keeping the current clientele. In the first cities that received the New Coke, sales were up 8%. This new formula may help keep Coca-Cola in the running for the leading soft drink in America. You take a loss on this investment. If you had gone short for the short-term, you would have had some nice gains–but the outlook on Coke changed into the course of the year and you lost money.

Coca-Cola

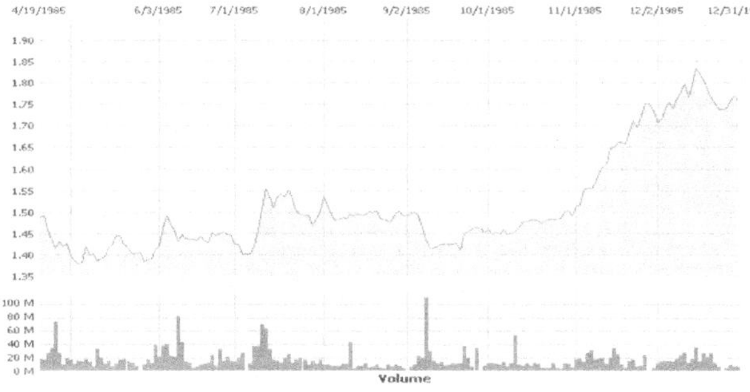

Source: MSN Money

If you would like to do more April trades, turn to page 59.

If you'd rather move onto the next month's set of trading options, turn to page 73.

New Coke Option Bullish Outcome

Oops, you just lost 3% on your trade!

Since its launch one month ago, the New Coke formula has had mixed response from consumers. In some geographic areas of the United States, New Coke was highly liked and sales were up by 8% in some of the first cities to try it, like New York and Washington D.C. In other areas like the South, the Coca-Cola company received highly negative feedback concerning the New Coke formula.

The company received thousands of letters urging the company to renew the classic formula. Who knows if Coke will actually go back to the original formula, but for now the stock is down 3% into the end of the month.

Coca-Cola

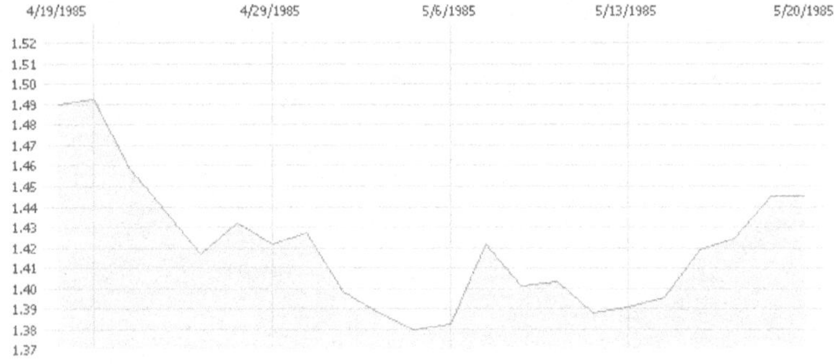

Source: MSN Money

If you would like to do more April trades, turn to page 59.

If you'd rather move onto the next month's set of trading options, turn to page 73.

New Coke Option Bearish Outcome

Congratulations, you just made a 3% return on your trade!

Since its launch one month ago, the New Coke formula has had mixed response from consumers. In some geographic areas of the United States, New Coke was highly liked and sales were up by 8% in some of the first cities to try it, like New York and Washington D.C. In other areas like the South, the Coca-Cola company received highly negative feedback concerning the New Coke formula. The company received thousands of letters urging the company to renew the classic formula. Who knows if Coke will actually go back to the original formula, but for now the stock is down 3% into the end of the month. Your put options are up nicely.

Coca-Cola

Source: MSN Money

If you would like to do more April trades, turn to page 59.

If you'd rather move onto the next month's set of trading options, turn to page 73.

Gilead setup

It's April of 2009 and you're looking for shelter from the storm. The stock market has been nothing but a heartache for the last two years. So you figure that lots of other people must be feeling ill and they'll need drugs too. You start looking at companies that sell blood pressure medication.

You land on Gilead, a biotech giant with a promising new hypertension drug, Darusentan. You see a press release with an image of the molecule:

You think back to Organic Chemistry, shudder, and need to take a break.

After a 30 minute pause to play Halo you're feeling well enough to start researching. Gilead is best known for making Tamiflu, the only thing that stopped the bird flu panic two years ago. Gilead is primarily in the business of treating HIV/AIDS–and what a lucrative business it is. The average HIV-positive patient can expect to live twenty years and will spend $600K over that time. And as the drugs get better, life expectancy will go up and so will that revenue stream. In 2008 Gilead's revenues were up 26% to $5.34 billion, with the profits in Q4 alone hitting $568.2 million.

Gilead's management wants to leverage their cash and know-how to crack into the lucrative blood pressure market. About 68 million people in the U.S. have high blood pressure and Gilead wants to sell them something. In 2006 Gilead bought Myogen Inc., the maker of ambrisentan (Letairsis in the U.S.) an endothelin receptor antagonist that works for pulmonary hypertension. While Letairsis will bring in about $184 million this year, that's not going to pay for the $2.6B acquisition costs without new drugs. That's where Darusentan comes in.

Myogen licensed Darusentan from Abott Labs (which was working on it for cancer treatments). Since then Darusentan has done very well in trials. In 2006 the drug was placed on its Phase III Fast Track. In 2005 Credit Suisse pegged the total Darusentan opportunity at $500M; the consensus now is that the drug would easily do $1B. One of the Phase III trials just completed and those results look great. The results will be presented next month at the American Society of Hypertension but the medical community is already buzzing. In a double-blind, placebo-controlled trial, 379 patients were given the drug. Fourteen weeks later, both systolic blood pressure (trough sitting SBP) and ambulatory blood pressure were down much more significantly in the patients taking Darusentan. Best of all, the most common side effects, peripheral edema and fluid retention, are very manageable. The results of the other, larger, Phase III trial will be announced in December. If that is also as successful, FDA approval for a full release isn't far behind.

Gilead is down 6% on the year and is down about 5% over the 52-weeks but that's nothing when compared to the broader market. The S&P is down 3.47% YTD and about 34% since April of 2008. Gilead just last month picked up CV Therapeutics for $1.4 billion. Gilead trades for about 22x earnings; for comparison, traditional drug maker Pfizer is selling for 11x earnings.

Gilead

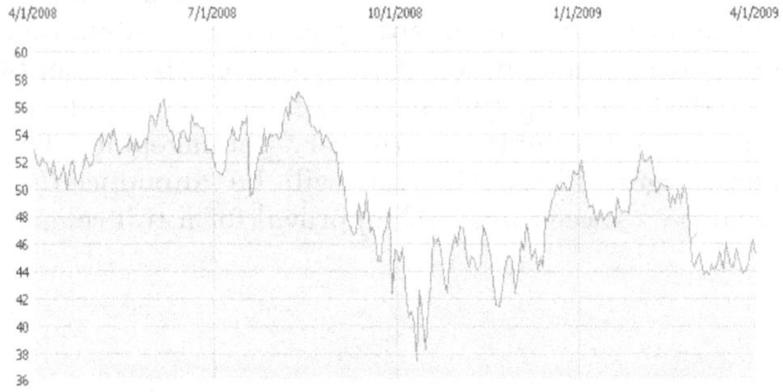

Source: MSN Money

If you are bullish and want to buy about $100,000 of common stock in Gilead and hold it for the whole year, turn to page 69.

If you are bearish and want to short about $100,000 of common stock in Gilead for the whole year, turn to page 70.

If you are bullish and want to buy about $50,000 of calls in Gilead for a short-term one month trade, turn to page 71.

If you are bearish and want to buy about $50,000 of puts in Gilead for a short-term one month trade, turn to page 72.

If you would rather find something else to trade this month, turn to page 59.

Gilead Stock Bullish

Oops, you just lost 5% of your investment.

You were up for most of the year on this trade, making money. But just when it looked like it was all yours as the year was about to end, on December 14, 2009, you see the following quote cross the wire:

"We are disappointed that darusentan did not achieve its primary endpoints in this study," said Norbert Bischofberger, PhD, Gilead's Executive Vice President, Research and Development and Chief Scientific Officer. "As a result, we think it would be challenging to define an expedient path forward. We would likely be required to initiate another Phase III study and would rather allocate our resources to other promising research and development opportunities in our pipeline."

Gilead Sciences Inc.

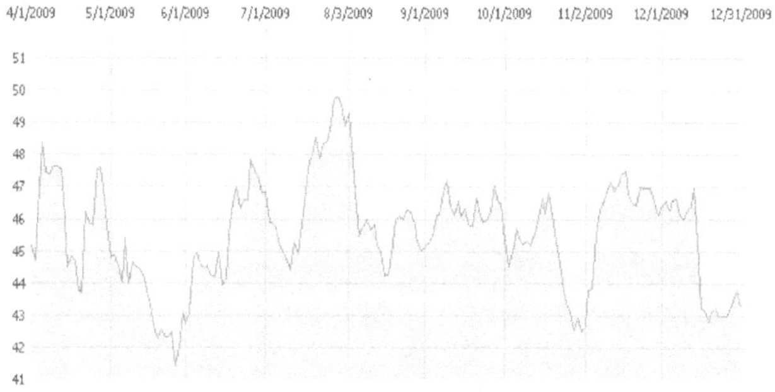

Source: MSN Money

If you would like to do more April trades, turn to page 59.

If you'd rather move onto the next month's set of trading options, turn to page 73.

Gilead Stock Bearish

Congratulations, you just made a 5% return on your investment.

You were down for most of the year on this trade, losing money. But just when it looked like all was lost as the year was about to end, on December 14, 2009, you see the following quote cross the wire: "We are disappointed that darusentan did not achieve its primary endpoints in this study," said Norbert Bischofberger, PhD, Gilead's Executive Vice President, Research and Development and Chief Scientific Officer. "As a result, we think it would be challenging to define an expedient path forward. We would likely be required to initiate another Phase III study and would rather allocate our resources to other promising research and development opportunities in our pipeline."

Gilead Sciences Inc.

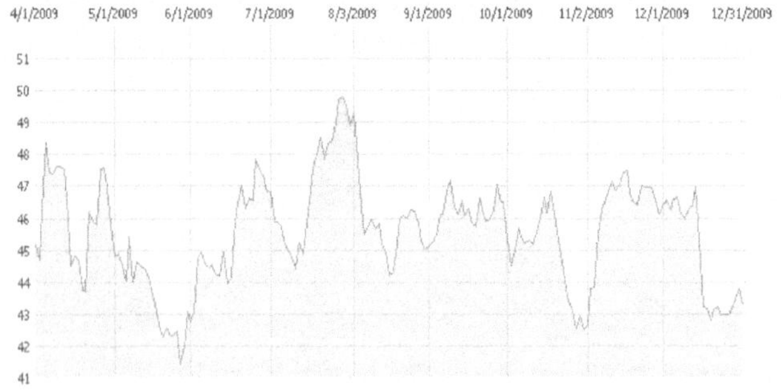

Source: MSN Money

If you would like to do more April trades, turn to page 59.

If you'd rather move onto the next month's set of trading options, turn to page 73.

Gilead Option Bullish

You broke even on your trade. There is no change to your portfolio value.

The stock popped just after you bought it, as the market liked the trends in the studies thus far. But without another catalyst to move it before month's end, you didn't make a dime on the Gilead option trade.

Gilead Sciences Inc.

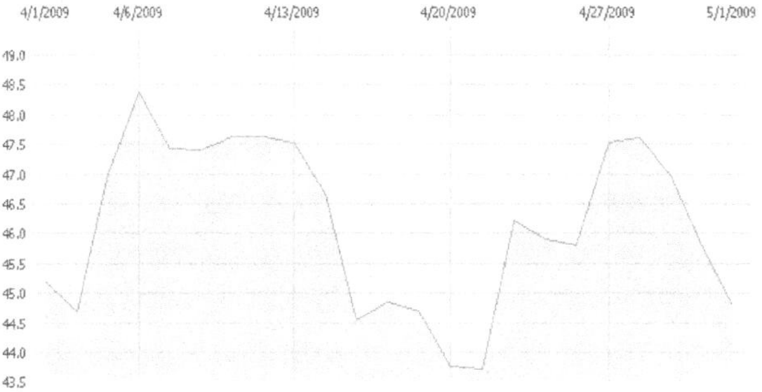

Source: MSN Money

If you would like to do more April trades, turn to page 59.

If you'd rather move onto the next month's set of trading options, turn to page 73.

Gilead Option Bearish

You broke even on your trade. There is no change to your portfolio value.

The stock popped just after you bought it, as the market liked the trends in the studies thus far. But without another catalyst to move it before month's end, you didn't make a dime on the Gilead option trade.

Gilead Sciences Inc.

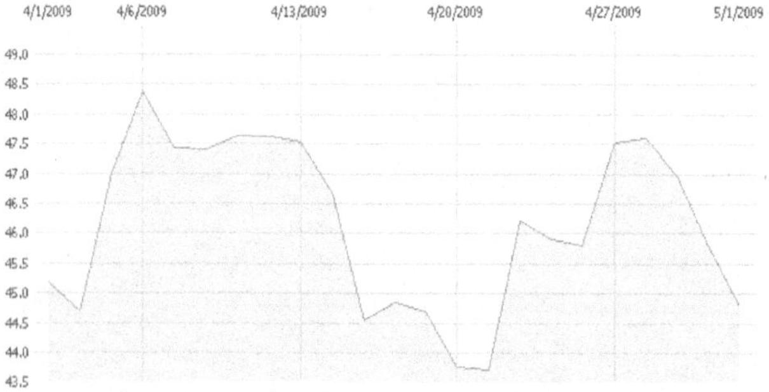

Source: MSN Money

If you would like to do more April trades, turn to page 59.

If you'd rather move onto the next month's set of trading options, turn to page 73.

Start trading May

You pull up a chart of the DJIA, the S&P 500, and the Nasdaq. You remember on that video how your Great Uncle Buster had turned almost angry when he'd talked about how he had barely beaten the major indices last year.

And here you are supposed to be getting 50% in a single year's timeframe.

If you want to trade a media company just as they release a new show, turn to page 74.

If you want to trade a clothing retailer with a new chain of stores, turn to page 80.

If you want to trade a high-end jewelry maker or a bargain retailer at a key moment in history, turn to page 88.

If you'd rather move onto the next month's set of trading options, turn to page 102.

If you've hit $1.5 million and are ready to cash in, turn to page 308.*

*(*PLEASE DO NOT GO TO PAGE 308 IF YOU HAVE NOT HIT $1.5 MILLION).*

American Idol Setup

It's May 2002, and next month, News Corporation's FOX Television stations will be airing a brand new series called *American Idol: The Search for a Superstar*. Simon Fuller will bring the show to the US from his native UK in a deal in which he is believed to be paid around $50m (£34.9m).

Fox will air 15 episodes of the show, which will be called *American Idol*, this summer with the hope that it will emulate the success of the show in the UK, where as many as 8.7 million viewers voted in the final show.

Fuller, who was the former manager of the Spice Girls, will, in addition to selling the News Corporation-owned station the format, also benefit from lucrative sponsorship and telephone revenue-sharing deals.

In its most recent quarter, Rupert Murdoch's News Corporation has posted a quarterly loss of more than $3 billion after writing down the value of its stake in Gemstar-TV Guide International.

Shares in Gemstar, which provides on-screen TV program guides, have lost more than two-thirds of their value since last year, leading to the massive write-down. News Corp owns 38% of Gemstar.

However, News Corp's revenues for the first three months of 2002 rose 18% to more than $3.5 billion as its 20th Century Fox movies *Moulin Rouge* and *Ice Age* boomed at the box office. Without the effect of the $4.23b write-off in Gemstar and other one-time effects, profits nearly doubled to $236m from $127m a year ago.

News Corp also owns the Fox TV network, StarTV in Asia and the News International newspapers in the UK, which include *The Sun* and *The Times*.

Operating income at the UK newspapers was in line with expectations, but higher circulation revenues and savings on newsprint prices could not offset a drop in advertising revenue, which was 16% down on the first three months of last year.

In its third quarter statement News Corp said the advertising slump was affecting all categories.

"The advertising weakness was principally the result of lower volumes and yields across all major advertising categories," it said.

News Corp owns 36% of BSkyB and last week's draft communications bill lifted the barrier preventing it from buying Channel 5 or a commercial radio station.

News Corp (NWS)

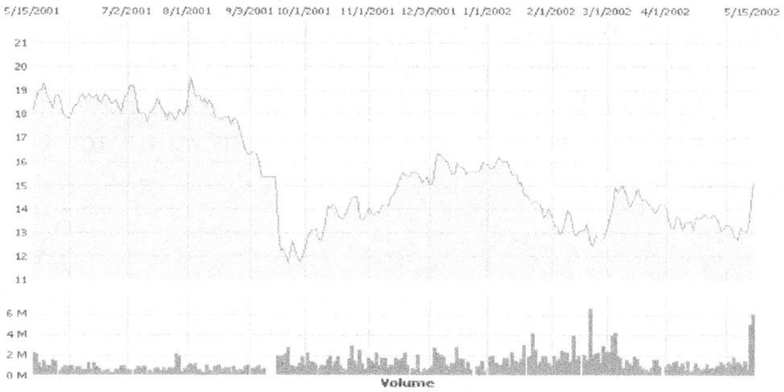

Source: MSN Money

If you are bullish and want to buy about $100,000 of common stock in NWS and hold for the whole year, turn to page 76.

If you are bearish and want to short about $100,000 of NWS common stock for the whole year, turn to page 77.

If you are bullish and want to buy about $50,000 of calls in NWS for a short-term one month trade, turn to page 78.

If you are bearish and want to buy about $50,000 of puts in NWS a short-term one month trade, turn to page 79.

If you would rather find something else to trade this month, turn to page 73.

American Idol Stock Bullish Outcome

Oops, you just lost 15% on your trade!

As you look back at the chart, you are happy to sell your stock at a 15% loss. Your shares were down almost 50% at one point but now have bounced back significantly. The first episode of *American Idol* aired on June 11 with around 9.85 million viewers. After watching the show, you decide that you really like it and this could definitely be a growth driver in the future. One neat part about the show is that it locks the viewer into it, thus providing a steady audience throughout the course of the show. People have their favorites and they want to see how they do. However, it looks like it's going to take some more time for the stock to really grow from here.

News Corp (NWS)

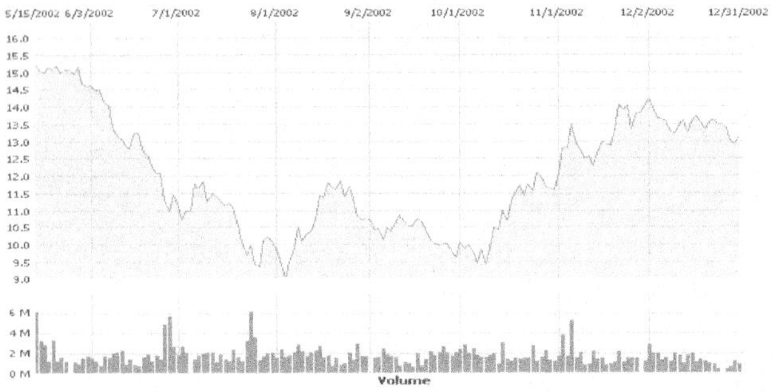

Source: MSN Money

If you would like to do more May trades, turn to page 73.

If you'd rather move onto the next month's set of trading options, turn to page 102.

American Idol Stock Bearish Outcome

Congratulations, you just made a 15% return!

The first episode of *American Idol* aired on June 11 and had around 9.85 million viewers. The show turned out to be pretty good watching and you already have your favorite singers. The show really locks people into it as they become more and more attached to the singer. This could provide a steady audience as people continue to see how their favorite singer does. Until this money really starts rolling in, NWS will likely remain steady-to-lower. As you look at the chart into the end of the year, you see that the stock is starting to make some sort of a comeback. You have lost some of your gains but you cover your sell, locking in a 15% gain.

News Corp (NWS)

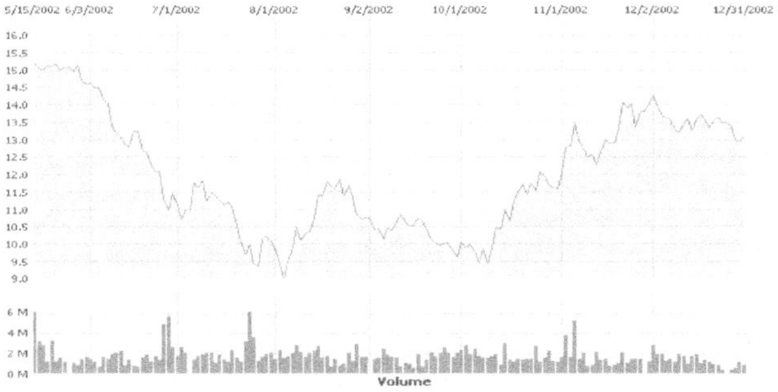

Source: MSN Money

If you would like to do more May trades, turn to page 73..

If you'd rather move onto the next month's set of trading options, turn to page 102.

American Idol Option Bullish Outcome

Oops, you just lost 16% on your trade!

Man, this one's going to hurt. *American Idol* aired on June 11 with 9.85 million viewers. Not bad for a premier. You obviously watched the show to support your new News Corp Stock (1 in 9.85 million obviously increases ad revenue) and you already have favorites. You decided to finish the season to see who wins the record deal. The show is really good and will probably be a big hit someday. For now, you got the wrong end of the stick and it's going to cost you. The common stock has fallen 15% and your calls are down more than that.

News Corp 1 Month

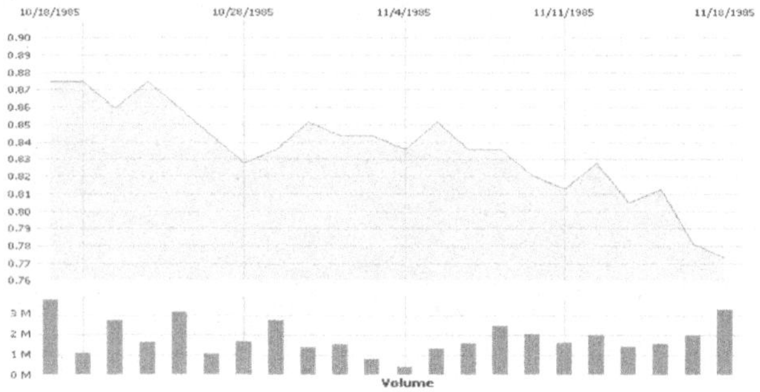

Source: MSN Money

If you would like to do more May trades, turn to page 73.

If you would like to skip to next month's set of trading options, turn to page 102.

American Idol Option Bearish Outcome

Congratulations, you just made a 16% return!

The first episode of *American Idol* aired on June 11 with 9.85 million viewers. The show ran well, and after watching it you already have favorites and are planning on watching the whole season to see who wins. Although the show has been a success, the stock price of parent company News Corp has continued to fall. As more and more viewers are sucked into the drama of *American Idol*, ad revenue will increase but this will certainly take time. You called this one right. The common stock is down 16% and your puts are well in the money.

News Corp Month

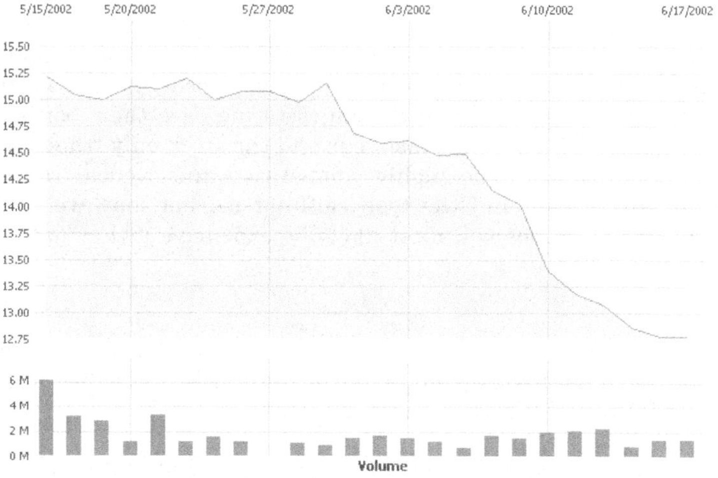

Source: MSN Money

If you would like to do more May trades, turn to page 73.

If you would like to skip to next month's set of trading options, turn to page 102.

Hollister Co. Setup

It is May 2000, and next month Abercrombie & Fitch is going to launch a new brand of stores known as Hollister Co. These stores are based on a So-Cal theme of trendy/colorful clothes, and targets 14-18-year-olds. The lineup will include graphic tees, polo shirts, long and short sleeve collared shirts, jeans, cologne/perfume, and bath products, among other things. The clothes are likely to be very trendy coming from higher-end clothing retailer Abercrombie & Fitch. Abercrombie & Fitch states that their main target age is college level 18-22-year-olds. This new brand will give them exposure to a demographic that they have yet to reach. This new brand will face significant competition from existing teen retail outlets like American Eagle, Aéropostale, and Old Navy.

Management at A&F has continued to do well even in a struggling retail environment. The company has reported record revenue each year over the past five years, and continues to increase their bottom line. The stock is off 75% over the last year and the stock only trades at 5.6x this year's earnings. The highly competitive and cyclical retail stores are always a risk–and the teen clothing market may well be saturated. Hollister clothes will most likely be expensive if they follow suit with A&F.

"Abercrombie's been the most profitable in the industry, but I don't see where it has room to grow," said Deutsche Banc Alex. Brown retail analyst Marcia Aaron recently in an interview.

Although the company reported profits rose 27% in the last quarter, mark-downs cut into the hip retailer's sales growth, which has consistently been slowing the past two years.

Marino-Nachison with Lonnie Fogel, Investor Relations and Communications Director for Abercrombie, said on the most recent earnings report:

"It's a very simple profitability model. The general idea is to open new stores at the approximate rate of 20% per year to achieve comparable-store sales in the range of 5% to 6% and with leverage on your fixed expense base you can achieve 30% EPS growth. Now, clearly the kids' business now is above and beyond the 20% profitability model so there's some upside to that, but in terms of a long-term profitability model that's our focus.

"Now, we have nearly 200 Abercrombie & Fitch stores at this point in time. Conservatively, our thinking is that 400 domestically is pretty much where we max out, although some people on Wall Street are arguing that there's more room. For us, we're feeling conservative. So we figure at some point you become close to at least theoretical saturation domestically. We haven't even really begun to seriously consider anything international."

The projections are still that the company will be growing at an earnings per share rate of 30%, and comp-store sales are targeted for a range of perhaps 3-6%.

Abercrombie & Fitch Co. (NYSE: ANF)

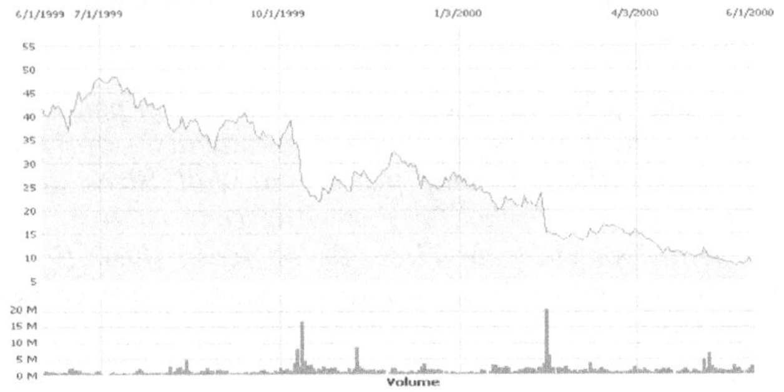

Source: MSN Money

If you are bullish and want to buy about $100,000 of common stock in ANF and hold it for the whole year, *turn to page 83.*

If you are bearish and want to short about $100,000 of common stock in ANF for the whole year, *turn to page 85.*

If you are bullish and want to buy about $50,000 of calls in ANF for a short-term one month trade, *turn to page 86.*

If you are bearish and want to buy about $50,000 of puts in ANF for a short-term one month trade, *turn to page 87.*

If you would rather find something else to trade this month, *turn to page 73.*

Hollister Co. Stock Bullish Outcome

Congratulations, you just made a 300% return on your investment.

People are really excited about this new line-up of clothes. The first store, which opened in Columbus, Ohio, was followed by four more stores in the next two weeks. The CEO of A&F said that the performance of the five Hollister stores continues to exceed expectations. All of this has happened without marketing or advertising support, and he sees the brand as a key driver for growth in the future.

These stores are all going to be located within malls and the theme is very much like a west coast beach house. The stores present a feel that is very different from any other existing retail outlets. With the great success of the brand, we can expect that A&F will expand these outlets more and more. The common stock popped as soon as you bought it, and it went on to more than double in price into the end of the year. This has turned out to be a great investment and it looks like A&F will be doing great for some time now due to the success of Hollister Co.

ANF

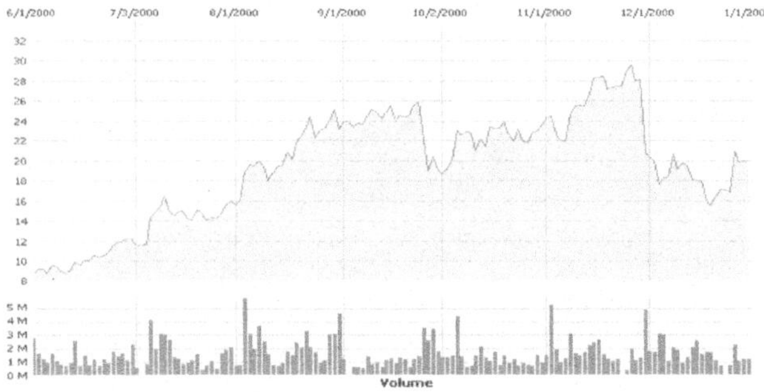

Source: MSN Money

If you would like to do more May trades, turn to page 73.

If you'd rather move onto the next month's set of trading options, turn to page 102.

Hollister Co. Stock Bearish Outcome

Oops, you just 75% of your investment.

The Hollister stores are a big hit. After the first store opened in Columbus, Ohio, A&F proceeded to open another five stores in the following two weeks. The CEO of A&F said that the performance of the Hollister brand continues to outperform all expectations and that the brand will likely by a key growth driver in the coming years. The trendy and relatively cheap (compared to A&F) Hollister clothes are a hit among young people. Even in a place like Columbus, Ohio where there is virtually no West Coast presence, teenagers are buying all of the Hollister clothes they can get their hands on.

The general prosperity of today has led buyers to buy higher end designer clothes that were previously considered too expensive. We will likely see A&F expand the Hollister brand as it continues to be a growth driver. You were dead wrong on this trade and it is has wiped out a lot of your gains.

ANF

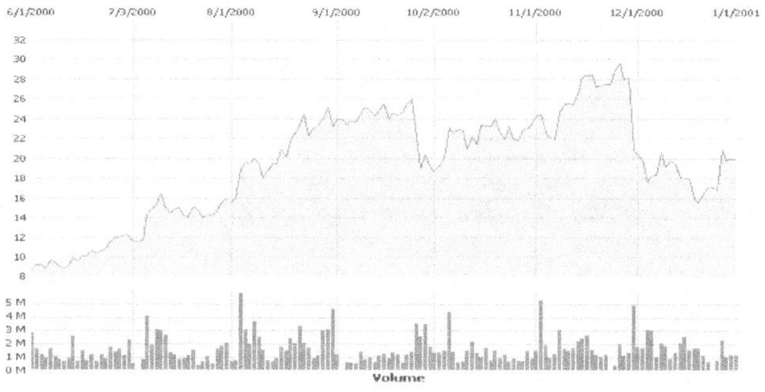

Source: MSN Money

If you would like to do more May trades, turn to page 73.

If you'd rather move onto the next month's set of trading options, turn to page 102.

Hollister Co. Option Bullish Outcome

Oops, you lost 20% on your trade.

You lost out on this one. Although the Hollister openings were a success, it was not enough of a catalyst to bring the stock out of free fall. The common stock is down almost 20% over one month, and your call options are down more than that. The Hollister brand will most likely be a growth driver for Abercrombie & Fitch; however, it will take a few quarters of solid growth before the stock drives higher.

Abercrombie & Fitch Co. (NYSE: ANF)

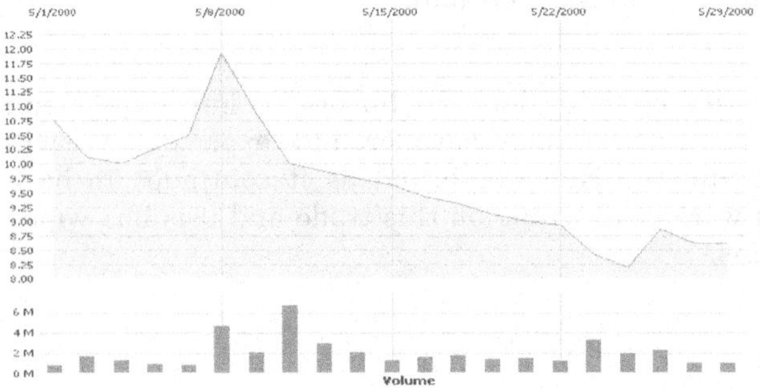

Source: MSN Money

If you would like to do more May trades, turn to page 73.

If you'd rather move onto the next month's set of trading options, turn to page 102.

Hollister Co. Option Bearish Outcome

Congratulations, you just made 20% on your trade.

Good job–the common stock is down almost 20% in just one month. Although the Hollister opening went very well, the stock is still falling. The stores have been met with great success and in the long run will probably drive the stock higher. The general prosperity is increasing the demand for higher quality, more stylish, and more expensive clothes. Your timing was dead on with this one, and you have some nice returns.

Abercrombie & Fitch Co. (NYSE: ANF)

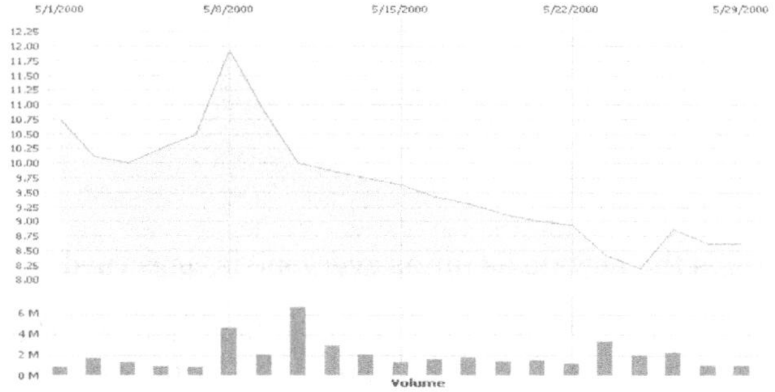

Source: MSN Money

If you would like to do more May trades, turn to page 73.

If you'd rather move onto the next month's set of trading options, turn to page 102.

Tiffany's vs Wal-Mart setup

It's May of 2009 and you are just plain tired. The last two years have been brutal; all-time highs in the market just before the crash, a financial crisis that nearly wiped out the banking system, and a never-ending stream of foreclosures. You pull up a chart of the market, YTD.

Source: MSN Money

Flat (or slightly down) is the new up as far as everyone is concerned.

And the epidemic is nationwide. The total number of foreclosures is the third highest on record, up 18% year-over-year. 40, 870 foreclosures notices were sent out this month to Californians alone. When lenders do decide to sell a foreclosed home in California they're only getting about 60% of the *loan amount*. You start working out the hypothetical numbers and see just how bad the problem is. A house purchased for $500K (with a 20% down payment) is now selling for $240K. And all those loans are bundled and collateralized and spread in banks all over the world.

Unemployment is at 9.4%. The government just keeps handing out bailout cash, even to foreign corporations. Fiat is close to buying Chrysler. The bailout for Main Street isn't quite on the same scale but it's not nothing. A tax-credit along with a payroll tax-cut is already juicing consumer spending, which was up 2.2% in the first quarter.

If this is the new normal, a perma-poorer consumer that doesn't have a house, you want to know about both ends of the spectrum. You pull up a YTD chart of Wal-Mart vs Tiffany's:

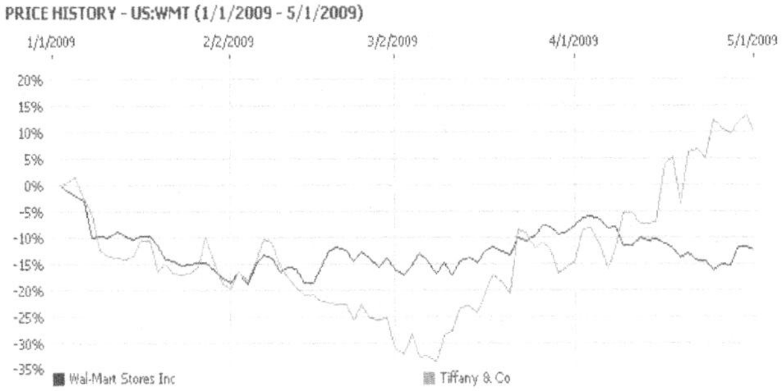

Source: MSN Money

Whoa, Tiffany's is totally beating the Wrangler-pants off Wal-Mart. You look back over a year and the situation looks much different:

Source: MSN Money

Do you bet on the trade down of the average consumer or the resillency of the rich? Is Wal-Mart the bargain or is Tiffany's the one on rollback special?

If you are bullish and want to buy about $100,000 of Tiffany common stock and hold it for the whole year, turn to page 91.

If you are bullish and want to buy about $100,000 of Wal-Mart common stock and hold it for the whole year, turn to page 92.

If you are bearish and want to short about $100,000 of Tiffany common stock for the whole year, turn to page 94.

If you are bearish and want to short about $100,000 of Wal-Mart common stock for the whole year turn to page 96.

If you are bullish and want to buy about $50,000 of calls in Tiffany for a short-term one month trade, turn to page 98

If you are bullish and want to buy about $50,000 of calls in Wal-Mart for a short-term one month trade, turn to page 99.

If you are bearish and want to buy about $50,000 of puts in Tiffany for a short-term one month trade, turn to page 100.

If you are bearish and want to buy about $50,000 of puts in Tiffany for a short-term one month trade, turn to page 101.

If you would rather find something else to trade this month, turn to page 73.

Tiffany's vs Wal-Mart TIF Stock Bullish Outcome

Diamonds are a trader's best friend, apparently, and you're up 57% on the trade!

Tiffany's stock is up a whopping 57% since you bought the stock in May. This has definitely been an outperformer and has blown everyone's mind. This stock continues to climb and lead the way out of recession. Fighting all of the bad news coming from the leading financial broadcasters paid off.

You are the kind of value investor that Warren Buffet would be proud of. Trading at only 11 times earnings, TIF was a great buy. Remarkably, TIF has even outperformed Walmart, the low end retailer that would typically benefit off of lower incomes. Even as Tiffany's earnings fell 25% year over year, the stock continues to climb. Over the same time period, Walmart was up only 7%.

TIF

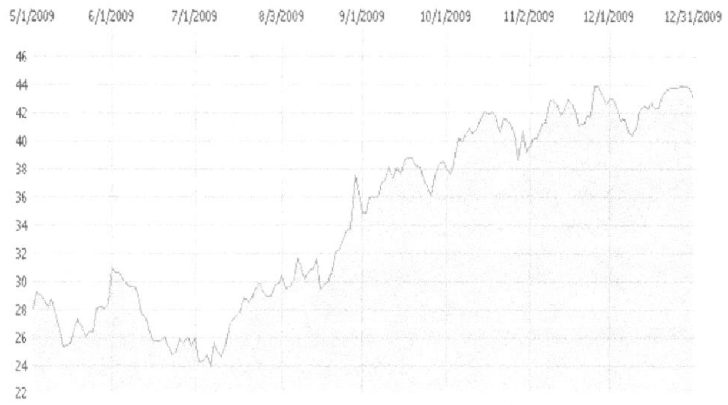

Source: MSN Money

If you would like to do more May trades, turn to page 73.

If you'd rather move onto the next month's set of trading options, turn to page 102.

Tiffany's vs Wal-Mart WMT Stock Bullish Outcome

Not bad, you just made a 7% return on trade!

Since you bought Wal-Mart back in May, the common stock has risen 7%. This stock is starting to gain traction as consumer spending continues to increase and that profit is returned to shareholders. All retailers are reaping the benefit of this business. Even as Wal-Mart faces competition from online retailers like Amazon, Ebay, Buy.com, and others, the company continues to do well.

This was a great time to buy. Wal-Mart was trading 14.9 times earnings which is the lowest multiple for the stock since 2000. Although the economy is still under the effects of the Financial Crisis from late last year, it looks like you may have caught the bottom of this market. You bought the stock from the pessimists/bears who thought that the American economy was doomed. Those headlines stating how the end wasn't in sight and how the market was headed lower were just signs telling you to buy. Your buy the weakness strategy has paid off on this one and you have some nice gains going into the end of the year.

Wal-Mart

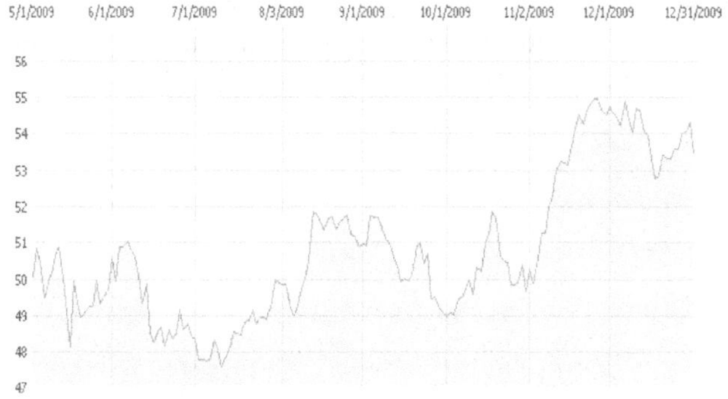

Source: MSN Money

If you would like to do more May trades, turn to page 73.

If you'd rather move onto the next month's set of trading options, turn to page 102.

Tiffany's vs Wal-Mart TIF Stock Bearish Outcome

Diamonds are a trader's best friend, apparently, and you're down 57% on the trade!

Tiffany's stock is up a whopping 57% since you shorted the stock in May. This has definitely been an outperformer and has blown everyone's mind. This stock continues to climb and lead the way out of recession. Fighting all of the bad news coming from the leading financial broadcasters paid off.

Even though all of the news said that high end retailers would tank, Tiffany's has topped all expectations. The stock was only trading at 11 times earnings when you shorted it which was the lowest multiple for the stock in the past 10 years. As the stock has continued to climb and the markets enter recovery mode, the doom and gloom has faded away.

The government has stepped in and saved the financial industry, well kind of, cause Lehman Brothers went under, but Bear Stearns and AIG got bailed out, and everything's corrupt, but it's all legal, and well who knows! This financial situation will probably never be entirely unveiled but regardless you lost your butt on this trade. Even as TIF net income fell 25%, the stock continues to skyrocket.

TIF

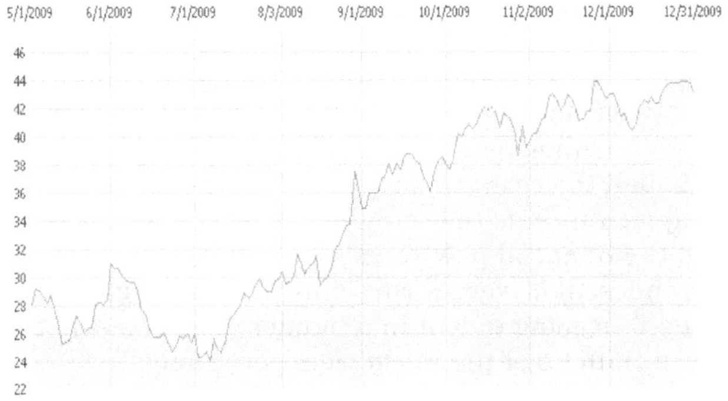

Source: MSN Money

If you would like to do more May trades, turn to page 73.

If you'd rather move onto the next month's set of trading options, turn to page 102.

Tiffany's vs Wal-Mart WMT Stock Bearish Outcome

Oops, you lost 7% on the trade!

Since you shorted Wal-Mart back in May, the common stock has risen 7%. This stock is starting to gain traction as consumer spending continues to increase and that profit is returned to shareholders. All retailers are reaping the benefit of this business. Even as Wal-Mart faces competition from online retailers like Amazon, Ebay, Buy.com, and others, the company continues to do well.

This was not the best time to go short in the markets as companies were trading extremely cheap relative to historical prices. Wal-Mart was trading 14.9 times earnings which is the lowest multiple for the stock since 2000. Although the economy is still feeling the effects of the financial crisis, it appears that the broader markets are on the rebound. You turn on the financial news and you don't see any of those doom and gloom headlines that were airing only 8 month ago saying the American economy was going to hell in a handbasket. You sold the stock when the Warren Buffetts of the world were going long.

This one cost you slightly and have definitely learned a lesson on this trade. Buy the panic, sell the hype.

Wal-Mart

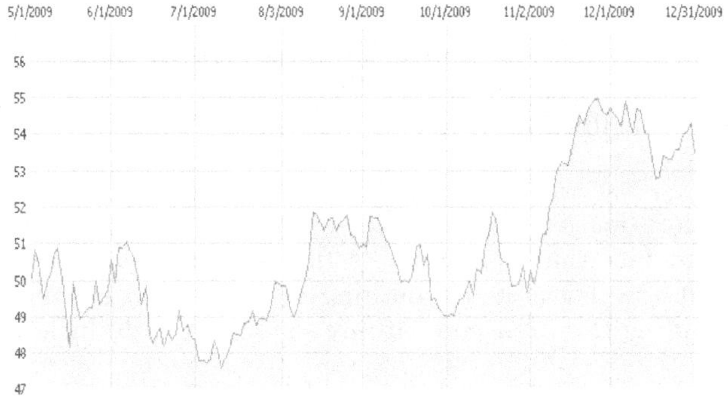

Source: MSN Money

If you would like to do more May trades, turn to page 73.

If you'd rather move onto the next month's set of trading options, turn to page 102.

Tiffany's vs Wal-Mart TIF Option Bullish Outcome

Congratulations, you just made a 10% return on your trade!

Tiffany's was flat to lower over the first part of the month and suddenly in the last 1-2 days of trading, the stock popped 10%. Your call options are now worth good money and you lock in some nice returns today. The retail market is steadily on the comeback and remarkable Tiffany's is bouncing back.

Sometimes the market doesn't always behave like we think it would. Even stranger is the fact that Wal-Mart is flat over the same time period! The discount retailer is doing nothing while for some reason investors are demanding the high end Tiffany's stock. A little luck on this one perhaps?

TIF

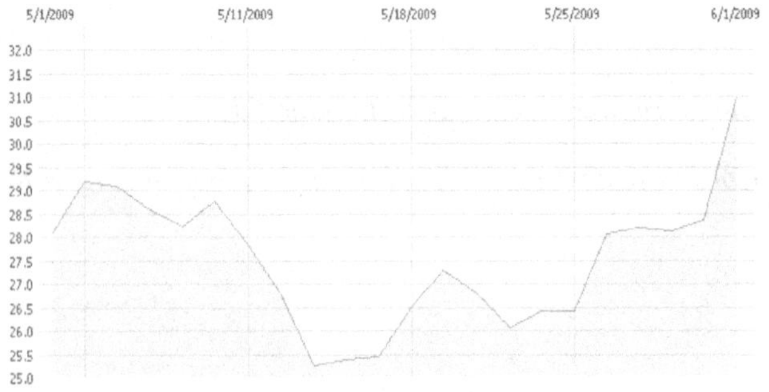

Source: MSN Money

If you would like to do more May trades, turn to page 73.

If you'd rather move onto the next month's set of trading options, turn to page 102.

Tiffany's vs Wal-Mart WMT Option Bullish Outcome

You broke even. At least you didn't lose money on the trade!

After a month of fairly volatile trading, the Walmart stock is up just $0.50 from where you bought it. The economy is still lagging after the financial crisis of last year and it is going to take a big catalyst to really make this stock go significantly higher over the course of a month.

Although you didn't lose money, this trade shows that aggressive options are not always the right trade. In a case like this without an expected catalyst for the stock to move significantly, it might be better to simply go long via common stock. Luckily you are going to get your money back and you live to trade another day.

Wal-Mart

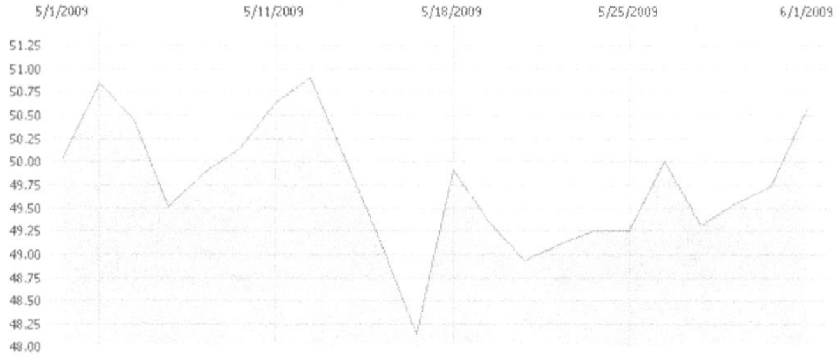

Source: MSN Money

If you would like to do more May trades, turn to page 73.

If you'd rather move onto the next month's set of trading options, turn to page 102.

Tiffany's vs Wal-Mart TIF Option Bearish Outcome

Don't have a tiff, but you lost 10% on TIF!

Tiffany's was flat to lower over the first part of the month and suddenly in the last 1-2 days of trading, the stock popped 10%.Your put options were in the money till now. Today you take a loss on this trade. The retail market is steadily on the comeback and remarkable Tiffany's is bouncing back.

Sometimes the market doesn't always behave like we think it would. Even stranger is the fact that Wal-Mart is flat over the same time period! The discount retailer is doing nothing while for some reason investors are demanding the high end Tiffany's stock. A little bad luck on this one perhaps?

TIF

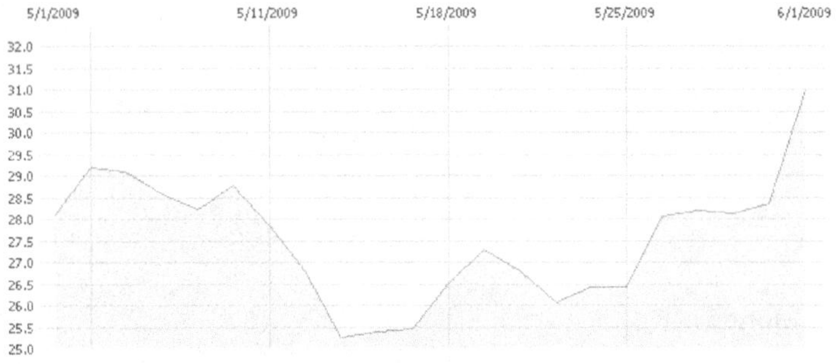

Source: MSN Money

If you would like to do more May trades, turn to page 73.

If you'd rather move onto the next month's set of trading options, turn to page 102.

Tiffany's vs Wal-Mart WMT Option Bearish Outcome

You broke even. At least you didn't lose money on the trade!

After a month of fairly volatile trading, the Walmart stock is up just $0.50 from where you shorted it. The economy is still lagging after the financial crisis of last year and it is going to take a big catalyst to really make this stock go significantly lower over the course of a month.

Although you didn't lose money, this trade shows that aggressive options are not always the right trade. In a case like this without an expected catalyst for the stock to move significantly, it might be better to simply go long/short via common stock. Luckily you are going to get your money back and you live to trade another day.

Wal-Mart

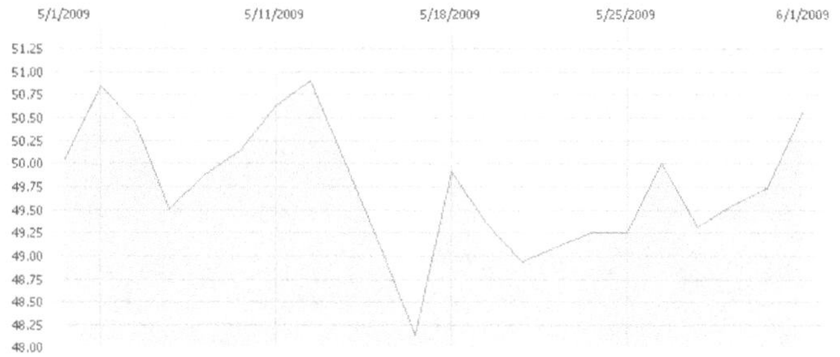

Source: MSN Money

If you would like to do more May trades, turn to page 73..

If you'd rather move onto the next month's set of trading options, turn to page 102.

Start trading June

You pull up a chart of the DJIA, the S&P 500, and the Nasdaq. You remember on that video how your Great Uncle Buster had turned almost angry when he'd talked about how he had barely beaten the major indices last year.

And here you are supposed to be getting 50% in a single year's timeframe.

If you want to trade a hot forestry stock just as a new report is released on them, turn to page 103.

If you want to trade oil at a key moment in history, turn to page 109.

If you'd rather move onto the next month's set of trading options, turn to page 113.

If you've hit $1.5 million and are ready to cash in, turn to page 308.*

*(*PLEASE DO NOT GO TO PAGE 308 IF YOU HAVE NOT HIT $1.5 MILLION).*

Sino-Forest Setup

Today is June 2, 2011, and Muddy Waters Research just released a report that Canadian forestry company Sino-Forest has expanded–and lied about their assets and income. Sino-Forest claims to own major stakes in Chinese forests and this report claims that it was all one big lie.

The company has become a favorite of investors, both because it offers exposure to China and because it is one of the only successful forestry companies of the last decade. Unlike its rivals, it has reported consistent revenue and earnings growth and constantly expanded its operations. For 2010, Sino-Forest reported a net income of US$170.9-million, up 52% from 2009.

The company had a market value of almost $5 billion, but the stock has fallen 60% today after Muddy Waters Research last night released an extensive report by a short-seller that called the operation an "established institutional fraud."

The Muddy Waters report claims that Sino-Forest was a "multi-billion-dollar Ponzi scheme" that was "accompanied by substantial theft."

Sino-Forest is fighting back against the report though: "It is important that our independent committee thoroughly address Muddy Waters' allegations, and they will have my full support and those of the management team in doing so," chairman and chief executive Allen Chan said in a statement.

"However, let me say clearly that the allegations contained in this report are inaccurate and unfounded."

Sino-Forest noted that Muddy Waters held a short position in the company. A short position allows an investor to profit when a share falls in price.

"Muddy Waters' shock-jock approach is transparently self-interested and we look forward to providing our investors and other stakeholders with additional information to rebut these allegations," Chan said.

Sino-Forest Corp.

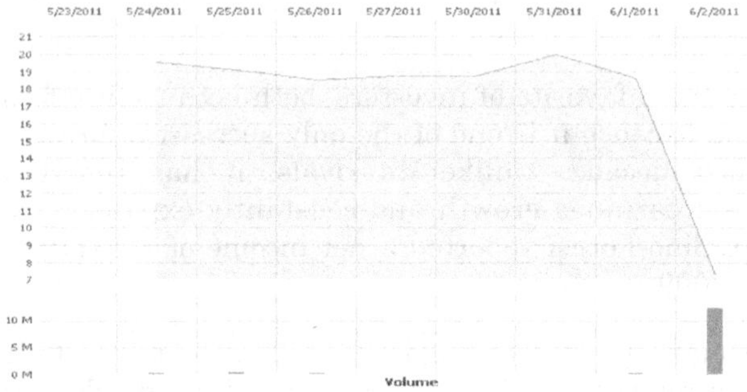

Source: MSN Money

If you are bullish and want to buy about $100,000 of Sino common stock and hold it for the whole year, turn to page 105.

If you are bearish and want to short about $100,000 of Sino common stock for the whole year, turn to page 106.

If you are bullish and want to buy about $50,000 of calls in Sino for a short-term one month trade, turn to page 107.

If you are bearish and want to buy about $50,000 of puts in Sino for a short-term one month trade, turn to page 108.

If you would rather find something else to trade this month, turn to page 102.

Sino-Forest Stock Bullish Outcome

Man, this sucks. You just lost every dollar you invested in this stock!

This trade is going down as one of the worst you've ever done as a trader. Turns out that the report hit the nail on the head. Sino-Forest lied about their assets, income, and debt in a disgusting statement of fraud. The company was essentially a giant Ponzi-Scheme and you took the bait. Sino-Forest stock was suspended from trading on August 26, 2011, by the Ontario Securities Commission.

Canadian authorities are currently investigating the company to find out what exactly is going on. Until the stock is allowed to trade again, you are out 100%. That's right, you lost everything you put in this stock (10% of your portfolio). Someday the stock will trade again after the authorities release it and you might get lucky and sell the stock for a few pennies a piece. This was a horrible trade and it looks like the report by the Muddy Waters Research was true.

Sino-Forest Corp

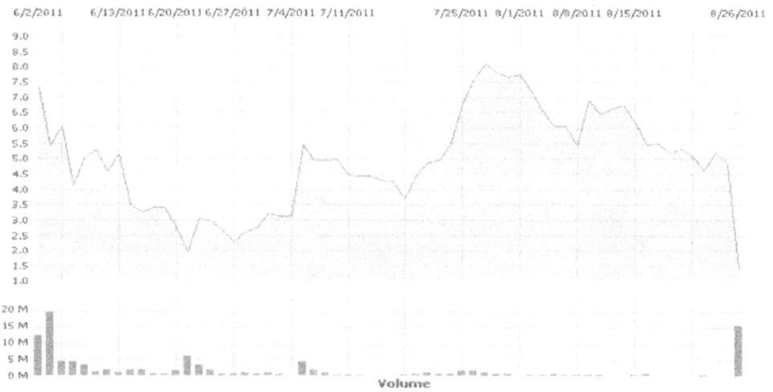

Source: MSN Money

If you would like to do more June trades, turn to page 102.

If you'd rather move onto the next month's set of trading options, turn to page 113.

Sino-Forest Stock Bearish Outcome

Man, this rocks. You just made a 100% gain by shorting this stock!

This trade is going down as one of the best you've ever done as a trader. Turns out that the report hit the nail on the head. Sino-Forest lied about their assets, income, and debt in a disgusting statement of fraud. The company was essentially a giant Ponzi Scheme and you saw right through that. Sino-Forest stock was suspended from trading on August 26, 2011, by the Ontario Securities Commission.

Canadian authorities are currently investigating the company to find out what exactly is going on. You sold the stock and someday you will be able to buy it back for pennies, literally. The worthless company's stock will be allowed to trade again some time in the future but for now, you have some sweet gains. You will experience close to or exactly 100% gains on the shorting of Sino-Forest once you cover your sale. Turns out that the report by Muddy Waters was right.

Sino-Forest Corp

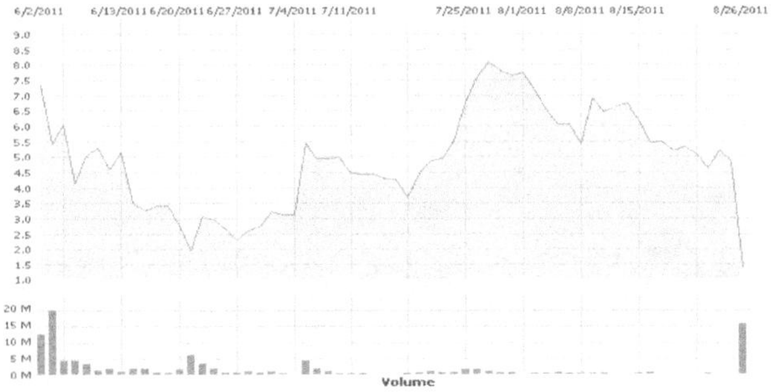

Source: MSN Money

If you would like to do more June trades, turn to page 102.

If you'd rather move onto the next month's set of trading options, turn to page 113.

Sino-Forest Option Bullish Outcome

Not good. You just lost 57% on this trade!

Well, this has been a losing trade for you. The stock has continued to sink every day since you bought it. The executives at Sino-Forest have denied the claims and have even provided information on cash and income to try and support the stock. Although the allegations have still not been proven to be true, it looks like investors believe the news coming from Muddy Waters.

The Muddy Waters researchers have made a business out of shorting fraudulent Chinese companies and actually have a lot of credibility when it comes to subjects like this. Famous investor John Paulson closed his long position in Sino-Forest for a $720 million dollar loss. Today, you sell your call options while the common stock is down 56% from where you bought it.

Sino-Forest Corp

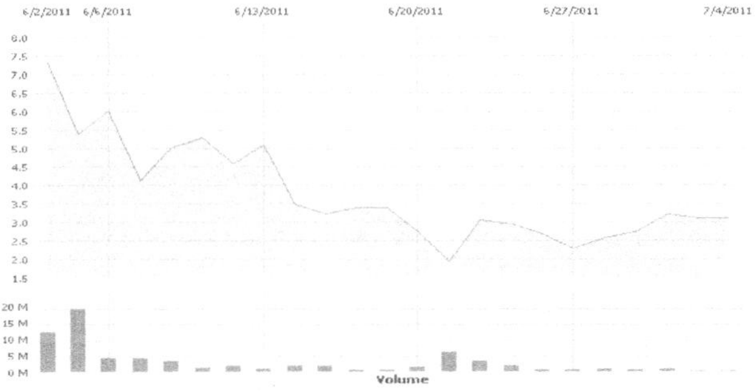

Source: MSN Money

Sino-Forest was suspended from trading on August 26,2011 by the Ontario Exchange Commission.

If you would like to do more June trades, turn to page 102.

If you'd rather move onto the next month's set of trading options, turn to page 113.

Sino-Forest Option Bearish Outcome

Awesome. You just made 57% on this trade!

This has been a great trade for you. Your put options have gained significant value as the common stock has fallen 56% over the course of one month. The management at Sino-Forest says that the allegations made by the Muddy Waters researchers is based on insider motives. The research firm is short the stock and have made significant money off of the crash.

Sino-Forest has also provided documentation on their cash and income, and continues to claim that they are operating a strong business. However investors aren't buying it. Muddy Waters has made a business out of shorting fraudulent Chinese companies, and they have a lot of respect when it comes to this subject. The stock has moved nearly straight down since you bought the put options and today you lock in some really nice gains.

Sino-Forest Corp

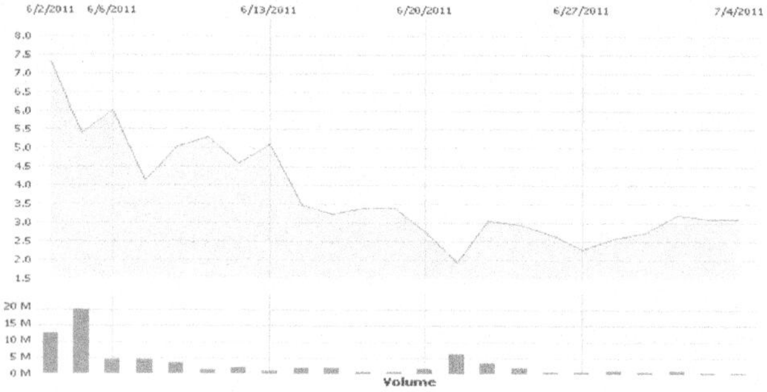

Source: MSN Money

Sino-Forest stock was suspended from trading on August 26, 2011 by the Ontario Securities Commission.

If you would like to do more June trades, turn to page 102.

If you'd rather move onto the next month's set of trading options, turn to page 113.

WTI Crude Oil setup

It's late June, 2008. West Texas Intermediate Crude Oil August contracts just hit a record high of $142 as the supply of oil seems to be dwindling. Everybody on TV is talking about how strong the economy is. It seems like every investor, hedge fund manager, and investment banker you know is leveraging everything they have to get as much exposure to oil, gold and silver as they can. Even your neighbor, a premium car salesman, is so proud of his commodity investments that you can't get him to stop talking about all the money he's been making on them.

The President of OPEC has been quoted all over saying that oil could easily reach $170 a barrel in the next few months if Libya threatened to cut output. You are looking at the July contracts that expire in a month, or looking at December Contracts and you can choose to buy them, or sell them short today hoping the price will fall.

If you are bullish and want to buy about $100,000 of December Contracts and hold them, turn to page 110.

If you are bearish and want to short about $100,000 of December Contracts, turn to page 111.

If you would rather find something else to trade this month, turn to page 102.

WTI Crude Oil Bullish Outcome

Oops, you just lost 61% on your investment.

You have sat back and watched the value of your December contracts dwindle away to nothing. The NYMEX is giving you a margin call and you don't have the capital to meet it. Like so many other commodities traders, you have to sell your contracts in order to meet the margin call. Every investment traded on the open market is falling rapidly. Equities, commodities, ETFs, you name it, this market is going down.

As everyone who was so highly leveraged has to liquidate to meet margin calls, these markets seem to be in free fall mode. Investment banks are taking a huge hit and Lehman Brothers filed for Chapter 11 bankruptcy protection on September 25. The housing market is tanking as well as this mass liquidation is spreading across the board and around the world. It appears that the price of oil was based solely on speculation as even a massive drop in demand could not have caused such a swift drop in price. This one hurt.

WTI since 2008

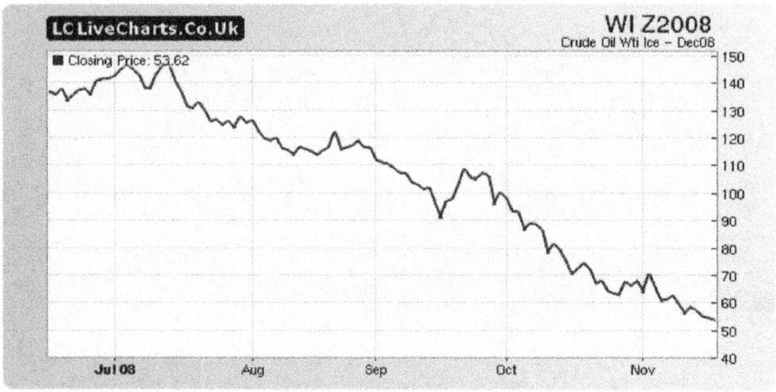

Souce: Simple RNA

If you would like to do more June trades, turn to page 102.

If you'd rather move onto the next month's set of trading options, turn to page 113.

WTI Crude Oil Bearish Outcome

Congratulations, you just made a 154% return on your investment.

This market is done. Panic has spread across the world as one of the worst crashes is stock market history has crushed the value of equities, commodities, and virtually everything else traded on the public markets. Oil is now half of what it was when you sold it. The housing market has tanked as the endless fraud and cheating is starting to come to the light. Lehman Brothers recently filed for chapter 11 bankruptcy protection and it seems like all confidence has been lost in the American financial system. The almost $700 billion dollar bankruptcy is the biggest in history by far.

All of those traders who were leveraging so much are having to liquidate everything in order to meet margin calls. You, however, are looking at huge returns as you buy back your contract for half of what you paid for it. In the grander scheme of things, this could be the end of the major American financial institutions and the beginning of another great depression.

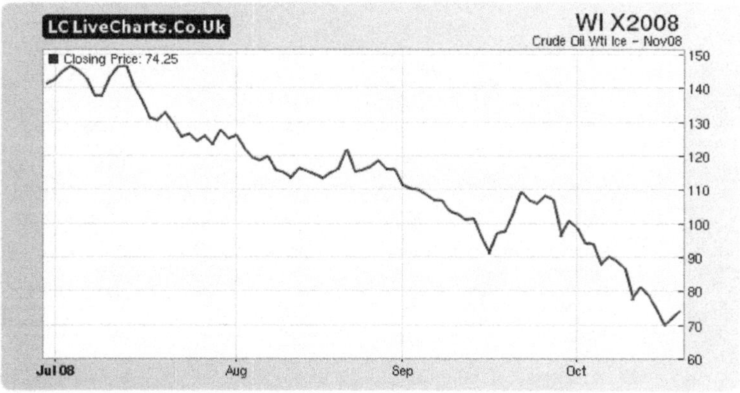

WTI Crude Oil since 2008

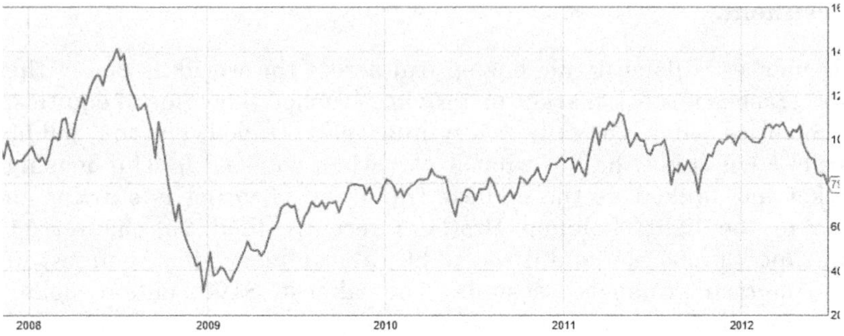

Source: Simple RNA

If you would like to do more June trades, turn to page 102.

If you'd rather move onto the next month's set of trading options, turn to page 113.

Start trading July

You pull up a chart of the DJIA, the S&P 500, and the Nasdaq. You remember on that video how your Great Uncle Buster had turned almost angry when he'd talked about how he had barely beaten the major indices last year.

And here you are supposed to be getting 50% in a single year's timeframe.

If you want to trade an agricultural company just as a favorable law is passed, turn to page 114.

If you want to trade a technology company just as their founder returns, turn to page 123.

If you'd rather move onto the next month's set of trading options, turn to page 129.

If you've hit $1.5 million and are ready to cash in, turn to page 308.*

*(*PLEASE DO NOT GO TO PAGE 308 IF YOU HAVE NOT HIT $1.5 MILLION).*

Ethanol Mandate Setup

It's August and President George W. Bush has just signed the Energy Policy Act of 2005 in Albuquerque, NM. You go to the website of Rep. Joe Barton (R) from the Texas 6th, sponsor of the Bill. The table of contents is eleven pages long. You're gonna need some energy of your own, so you down that second can of sugar-free Red Bull.

You start by reading all the subsections in the TOC. The very first one makes you laugh out loud:

Sec. 101. Energy and water saving measures in congressional buildings.

Nice to see that Congress is learning about personal conservation–odd to see it in federal legislation. A kindergarten refresher or a Home Depot visit couldn't do. You wonder if Senators are being told "If it's yellow, let it mellow..." No matter, you move on.

The bill is chock-full of seemingly every energy idea every think tank has ever had. There's a re-consideration of daylight savings and a study about elevator efficiency. But the real pattern you pay attention to is all the ink given over to energy technologies.

Sure there's stuff for nuclear, wind, coal, hydroelectric, fuel cells, natural gas and methane (how come no one ever just says cow farts?) but the big daddy king kahuna in the bill is ethanol.

Some company named Pacific Ethanol went public earlier this year. You've seen at least ten pitch decks in the past year from ethanol companies looking for VC mezzanine funding. You start searching around your room and you find one with Sequoia as the lead investor under an unholy pile of papers and notebooks. The company is based in Iowa and you realize why Congress is lavishing so much attention on ethanol; you need corn to make this stuff and Iowa is the first presidential primary, so any money for ethanol is money for Iowa. What politician wouldn't want to make that trade?

Now you get excited and start digging into the scale of the mandates. 7.5 *billion* barrels of ethanol and bio-diesel to be used by 2012. Wait, what? You start checking the math. Last year (2004) saw 1.26 billion bushels of domestic corn production go towards ethanol production. These mandates would mean that eventually 40% of the corn crop would go towards ethanol.

You lean back in your chair. Then you lean forward and re-check the math. Yeah, looks like a huge chunk of the corn crop is about to be diverted to making fuel. Now what you really want to know is how this will impact corn prices. International demand for American corn has been ticking up. You know that most corn is fed to livestock and processed into sugar, neither of which seem to be slowing down, but aren't really going up either. Americans ate 27.8 billion pounds of beef last year and that's probably going to stay the same this year. So if other sources of demand for corn will likely be flat over the next half-decade as ethanol ramps up, what does that mean for prices? And if corn prices go up because of ethanol, won't that make Americans eat chicken instead of beef, which will put downward pressure on corn? You remember your mentor's saying about commodities: "The cure for high prices is high prices."

You go back to your original premise, that corn is all about Iowa, and you consider the supply side of corn prices. 2004 was a pretty good year for corn; prices were the best in a couple years and the crop yielded about 142 bushels per acre. What didn't go up that much were new acres for planting, only about 800K came on line. Farmers are predicting $2.90/bushel for this year, a big spike from today, unless almost another 50% or 1.2M acres comes online. With land prices going up as fields are plowed over for housing, you doubt that will happen. Ethanol already accounts for one out of every ten acres of corn. The weather has been pretty good and advances in crop technologies have meant better yields so maybe farmers will do more with less.

You're not about to start trading the futures in any scenario (you've learned from the last time) so you start looking for derivative plays on ethanol and corn. You consider Archer Daniels Midland but think that the company just has too many moving parts. Then you start thinking about what it takes to make corn...water, a little sun, luck, fertilizer, more luck, seed and...farming equipment!

There's only one farming equipment name to consider and that's John Deere, which you discover goes by the corporate name Deere & Co. You think about the riding mower your parents had and regret that you can't drink a beer and mow Central Park for a couple hours. You punch up a one year chart and see that it's up about 14% since last August; YTD mighty Deere is down slightly. You dig into the financials and see that Deere earned $1.4 billion in 2004, almost double 2003. Revenues were up 29% to almost $20 billion (seriously almost, just $14 million short). You see that the manufacturing side takes huge capital investment, with Deere managing 29.4 million square feet of factory space! Deere has upped the dividend every year since 1982. All this adds up to a market cap around $17 billion trading about 12x earnings.

So what do you do?

Deere & Co.

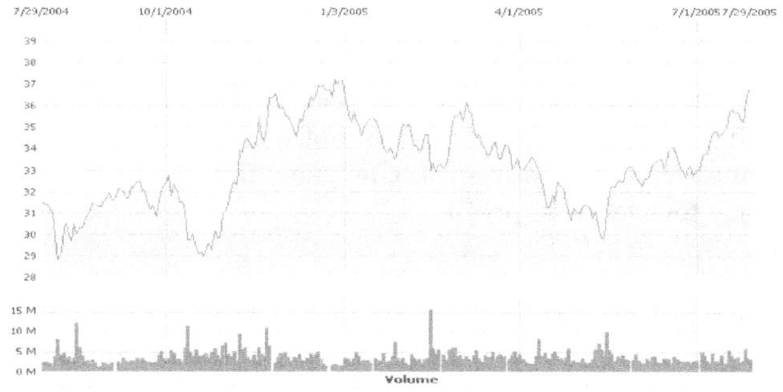

Source: MSN Money

If you are bullish and want to buy about $100,000 of DE common stock hold it for the whole year, turn to page 118.

If you are bearish and want to short about $100,000 of DE common stock for the whole year, turn to page 119.

If you are bullish and want to buy about $50,000 of calls in DE for a short-term one month trade, turn to page 121.

If you are bearish and want to buy about $50,000 of puts in DE for a short-term one month trade, turn to page 122.

If you would rather find something else to trade this month, turn to page 113.

Ethanol Mandate Stock Bullish Outcome

Oops, you just lost 5% on your investment.

It looks like you were a little off on your timing. The stock fell hard in the first few months after you bought it. You were down 20% at one time but in the last month and one half of the year, the stock rallied. It seems that the signing of the bill into law was not a direct catalyst for the stock to pop, but over the course of the year investors started seeing the opportunity for Deere to profit.

Your analysis seemed to be right and if you would have had a little better timing, you could have profited on the trade. Too bad you have to sell this stock at the end of the year, it could actually turn into a great investment if you could hold it longer.

Deere & Co

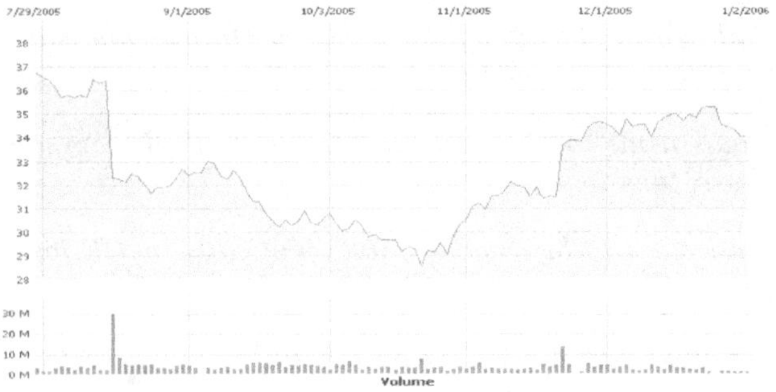

Source: MSN Money

If you would like to do more July trades, turn to page 113.

If you'd rather move onto the next month's set of trading options, turn to page 129.

Ethanol Mandate Stock Bearish Outcome

Congratulations, you just made a 5% return on your investment.

The stock has fallen sharply since you shorted the common stock. You were really sitting on some big gains, but in the last month and a half of the year, the stock came back hard. The signage of the bill provided no upside catalyst for the stock and it fell for several months. Now the stock is starting to pick up as the effects of this bill are starting to kick in.

This is one piece of legislation that actually has strenuous time constraints on it. Corn producers and gasoline mixers are going to have to get right at work at making the mandate for ethanol. You cover your short sell for some nice gains.

Deere & Co since Ethanol Mandate

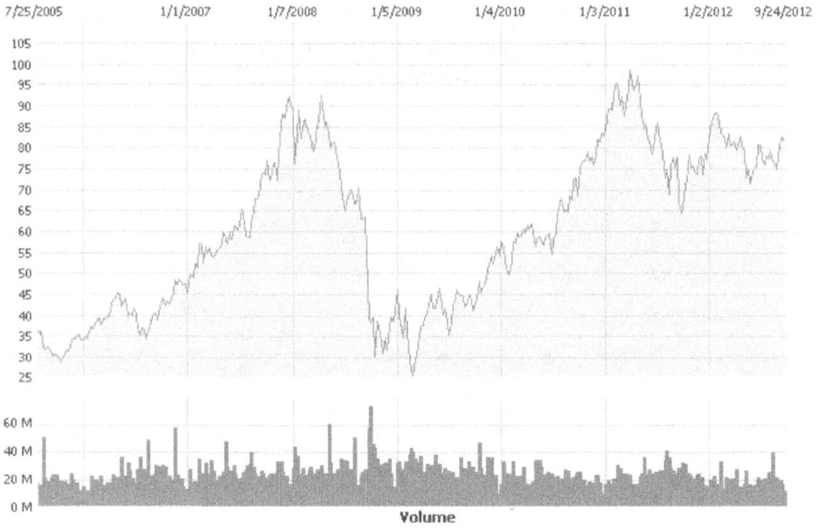

MSN: Money

If you would like to do more July trades, turn to page 113.

If you'd rather move onto the next month's set of trading options, turn to page 129.

Ethanol Mandate Option Bullish Outcome

Oops, you just lost 14% on your trade.

Well it looks like this new legislation wasn't enough to get Deere off the ground. The common stock fell a little over 10% since you bought your call options and you are going to take a loss on this trade. I guess the lesson to be learned here is that sometimes things we think might be catalysts don't always turn out that way.

It is going to take awhile for the bureaucracy of our federal government to actually implement this gigantic bill. When this happens, Deere & Co will likely profit from the expansion of corn demand but for now things are looking down.

Deere & Co

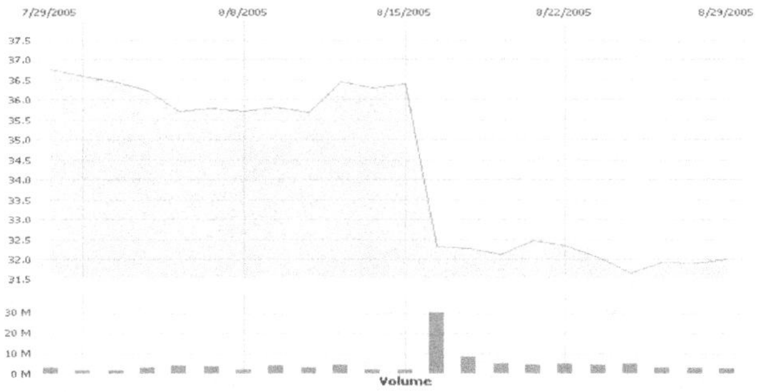

Source: MSN Money

If you would like to do more July trades, turn to page 113.

If you would like to skip to next month's set of trading options, turn to page 129.

Ethanol Mandate Option Bearish Outcome

Congratulations, you just made 14% on your trade.

It looks like the stock hasn't caught the news yet (or has it?). John Deere traded lower the month after you bought your put options and you are now sitting on some nice gains.

At this point in time it looks like investors are not saying that this new legislation is going to effect Deere's bottom line. The stock is continuing to trade lower and it appears that the signage of the bill has had no positive effect on DE's stock price.

Deere & Co

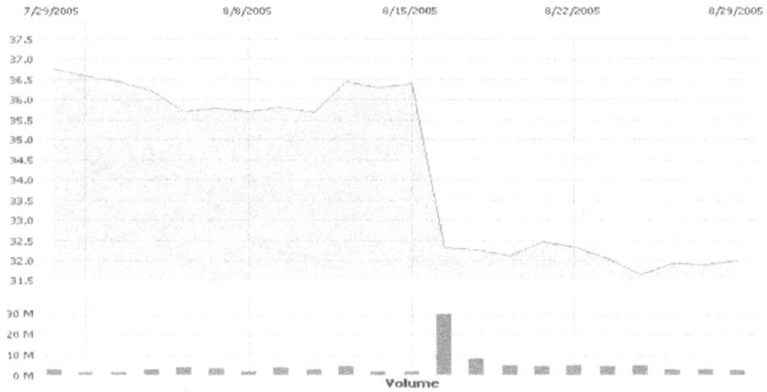

Source: MSN Money

If you would like to do more July trades, turn to page 113.

If you would like to skip to next month's set of trading options, turn to page 129.

Return of Steve Jobs setup

It's July 9, 1997. Apple Computers announced today that founder and former CEO Steve Jobs is going to replace current CEO Gil Amelio. The struggling company has lost some of its momentum and this visionary may just be what the company needs. Since he left Apple, Jobs has been very successful with his ventures at Pixar and NeXT Computers.

The tech industry is booming. Personal computers are now cheaper and more powerful than ever. The internet is really starting to take off and it seems that any stock having to do anything with the internet is going sky-high. If Steve Jobs can capitalize on this, then maybe this could be the comeback story of the century. Then again, Apple is not even in the top five computer makers by market share. Apple faces serious competition from other computer makers like Compaq, IBM, and Hewlett-Packard. Also, Steve Jobs is known to be a sporadic and harsh manager.

Apple Inc.

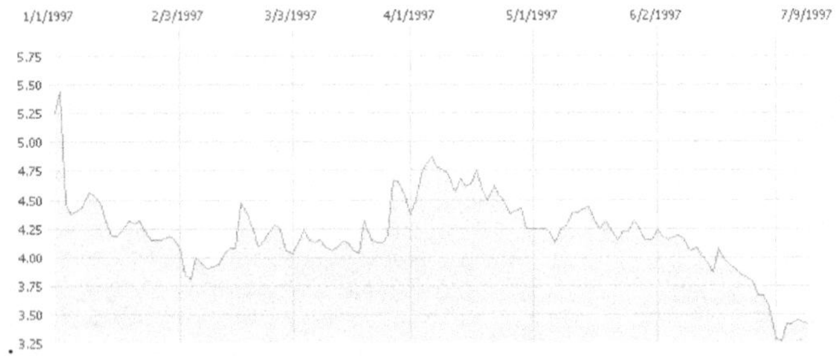

Source: MSN Money

If you are bullish and want to buy about $100,000 of AAPL common stock and hold it for the whole year, turn to page 125.

If you are bearish and want to short about $100,000 of AAPL common stock for the whole year, turn to page 126.

If you are bullish and want to buy about $50,000 of calls in AAPL for a short-term one month trade, turn to page 127.

If you are bearish and want to buy about $50,000 of puts in AAPL for a short-term one month trade, turn to page 128.

If you would rather find something else to trade this month, turn to page 129.

Return of Steve Jobs Stock Bullish Outcome

You broke even on your investment. There is no change to your portfolio value.

The stock rallied the month after you bought it as everyone was caught up in the charisma and charm that Steve Jobs brought to the table. He definitely could turn this company around. He is an incredible visionary and no one exactly can say what he might have up his sleeve. Unfortunately, the same problems still exist and Apple is not entirely out of the hole yet. The stock fell back to just above your purchase price by the end of the year. Your bullish outlook was not entirely wrong, but it may take more time for this stock to play out like you want.

Apple

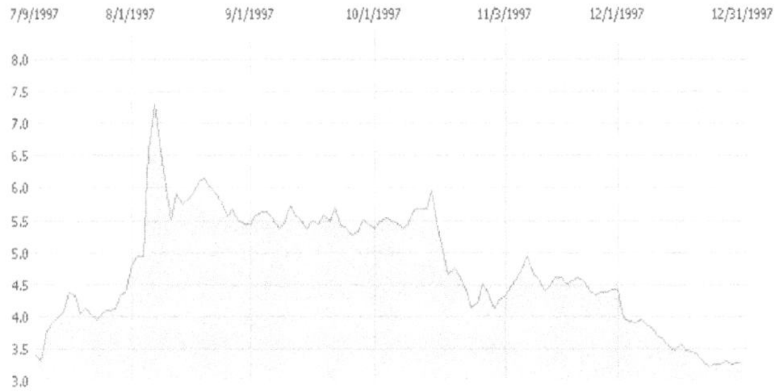

Source: MSN Money

If you would like to do more trades in July, turn to page 113.

If you'd rather move onto the next month's set of trading options, turn to page 129.

Return of Steve Jobs Stock Bearish Outcome

You broke even on your investment. There is no change to your portfolio value.

The stock rallied the month after you bought it as everyone was caught up in the charisma and charm that Steve Jobs brought to the table. He is truly a visionary and this could be a new era for Apple. However, Apple still faces the same problems as it did before Jobs returned. If Apple does not make some serious changes to its current business, it could be done. The common stock closed the year at just below your selling price. Apple may be making a comeback, but it will take some time to find out just how this story will play out.

Apple

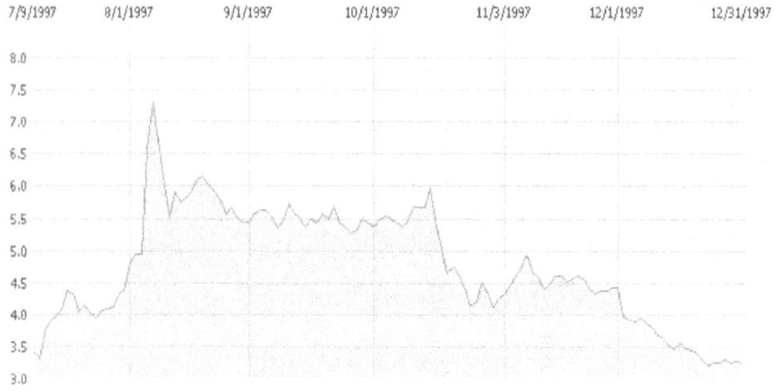

Source: MSN Money

If you would like to do more trades in the month of July, turn to page 113.

If you'd rather move onto the next month's set of trading options, turn to page 129.

Return of Steve Jobs Option Bullish Outcome

Congratulations, you just made a 100% return on your trade!

The thought of Steve Jobs running Apple computer has really pumped up investors. In many people's minds, Steve Jobs is Apple. With the man and his creation back together, the possibilities are endless. Hopefully, Apple can ramp up its computer business and get the ball rolling again.

If Steve Jobs can take advantage of all of the potential with today's internet, networking, and other technological advances, Apple could really become something great. For now, it seems that this announcement has really paid off for you! You sell your calls for great money as the common stock almost doubles over the course of one month.

Apple

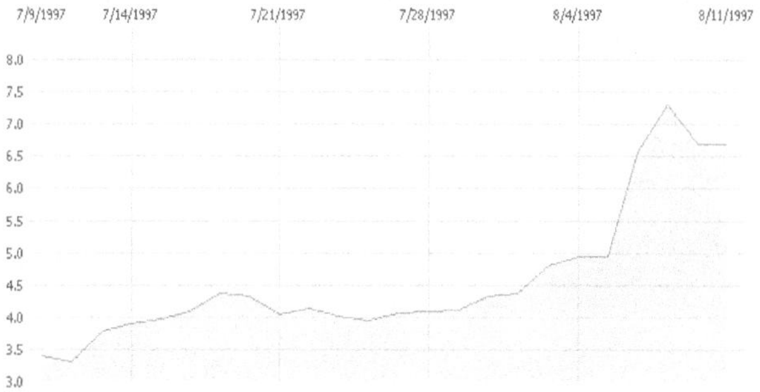

Source: MSN Money

If you would like to do more trades in the month of July, turn to page 113.

If you'd rather move onto the next month's set of trading options, turn to page 129.

Return of Steve Jobs Option Bearish Outcome

Oops, you just lost 100% on your trade!

The thought of Steve Jobs running Apple computer has really pumped up investors. In many people's minds, Steve Jobs is Apple. With the man and his creation back together, the possibilities are endless. Hopefully, Apple can ramp up its computer business and get the ball rolling again.

If Steve Jobs can take advantage of all of the potential with today's internet, networking, and other technological advances, Apple could really become something great. For now, it seems that this trade is going to cost you big time. By going short Apple via put options, you have lost more than if you had simply purchased common. Over the course of this last month, Apple stock has doubled. It probably wasn't a great idea to short the man that will someday be named one of the top 20 most influential Americans of all time.

Apple

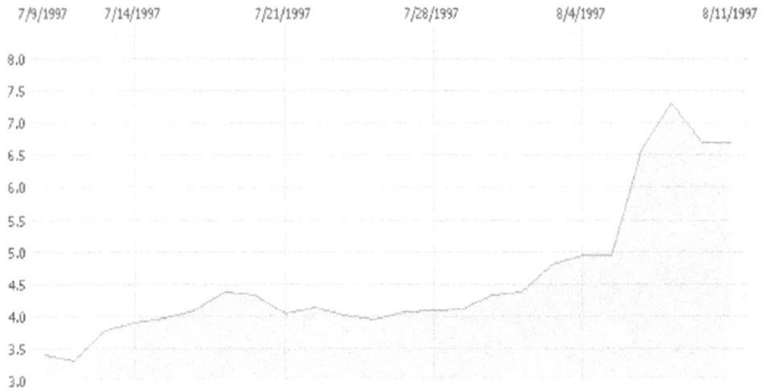

Source: MSN Money

If you would like to do more trades in the month of July, turn to page 113.

If you'd rather move onto the next month's set of trading options, turn to page 129.

Start trading August

You pull up a chart of the DJIA, the S&P 500, and the Nasdaq. You remember on that video how your Great Uncle Buster had turned almost angry when he'd talked about how he had barely beaten the major indices last year.

And here you are supposed to be getting 50% in a single year's timeframe.

If you want to trade an influential technology company just after they IPO, turn to page 130.

If you want to trade search engine giant just after they IPO, turn to page 135.

If you'd rather move onto the next month's set of trading options, turn to page 142.

If you've hit $1.5 million and are ready to cash in, turn to page 308.*

*(*PLEASE DO NOT GO TO PAGE 308 IF YOU HAVE NOT HIT $1.5 MILLION).*

Netscape IPO Setup

It's August 9,1995. A lot of new technology is starting to change the way that we live our lives. Mobile phones allow us to instantly contact each other, and along with the internet and email, communication has increased to a new level. One of the companies that is helping to expand on the capabilities of the internet is Netscape. Ninety percent of web users are using the Netscape internet browser, and now the company is coming public.

The stock came public today–there was so much demand for the stock that the NYSE had to stop trading by request of one of the underwriters (Morgan Stanley). When trading began, the stock skyrocketed to $75, more than 2.5x the IPO price of $28. It's later in the day now and the stock has sold off to $50. Is this a short-term buying opportunity? This company is changing the way we use computers. Maybe common stock is the way to go. The stock is now trading at 126 times its earnings. Maybe it is all hype. Microsoft will soon be releasing their own browser called "Internet Explorer."

If you are bullish and want to buy about $100,000 of Netscape common stock and hold it for the whole year, turn to page 131.

If you are bearish and want to short about $100,000 of Netscape common stock for the whole year, turn to page 132.

If you are bullish and want to buy about $50,000 of calls in Netscape for a short-term one month trade, turn to page 133.

If you are bearish and want to buy about $50,000 of puts in Netscape for a short-term one month trade, turn to page 134.

If you would rather find something else to trade this month, turn to page 129.

Netscape Stock Bullish Outcome

Congratulations, you just made a 180% return on your investment!

Netscape ended up falling the month after you bought it. The common stock was down 10%. A bit of the euphoria faded away as the realization of just how expensive this stock was hit the market. However, the stock rebounded into year-end like non other.

More and more companies are now following in Netscape's path as tech IPOs are going through the roof. This may be the beginning of the next great bubble. Your stock has appreciated massively. This may have been a once-in-a-lifetime kind of trade. The stock is up 180% from your $50 cost basis. Congratulations.

Netscape Communications

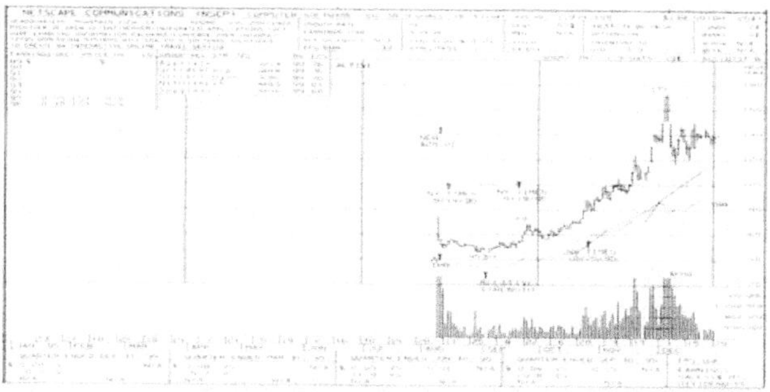

If you want to do more August trades, turn to page 129.

If you'd rather move onto the next month's set of trading options, turn to page 142.

Netscape Stock Bearish Outcome

Oops, you just lost 180% on your investment!

It seems like the euphoria of the IPO has seriously faded away as the stock has fallen 10% over the time of one month.

After its one month downturn, the stock ran to the top of the chart as people started getting wrapped up in the internet all over again. Turns out that the internet is the way of the future. You sold the stock at $50 and today you had to cover at $140. That's a massive hit to your portfolio–not only that, your negative outlook on internet companies has caused you to miss out on one of the biggest rallies in history. You fall into a state of slight depression as you see amateur traders double their accounts in one month while you sit back and look at a sheet full of red numbers. Better luck next time.

Netscape Communications

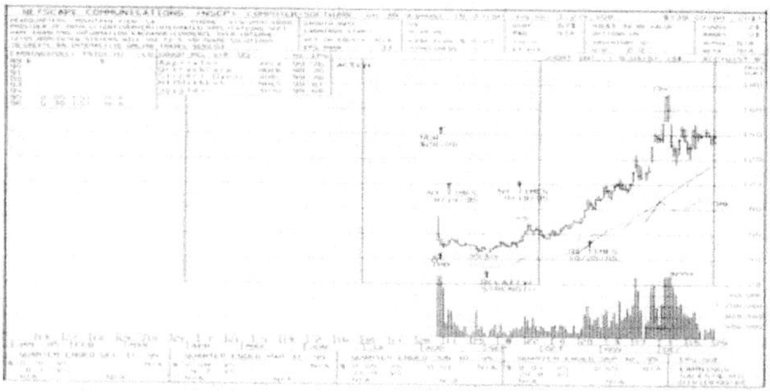

Source: Bloomberg

If you want to do more August trades, turn to page 129.

If you'd rather move onto the next month's set of trading options, turn to page 142.

Netscape Option Bullish Outcome

Oops, you just lost 10% on your trade!

Netscape ended up falling the month after you bought it. The common stock was down 10%. A bit of the euphoria faded away as the realization of just how expensive this stock was hit the market. Today your call options have lost some of their value. The future of the internet and technology in general is looking to be very exciting and your bullish outlook will probably pay off sometime in the near future.

Netscape Communications

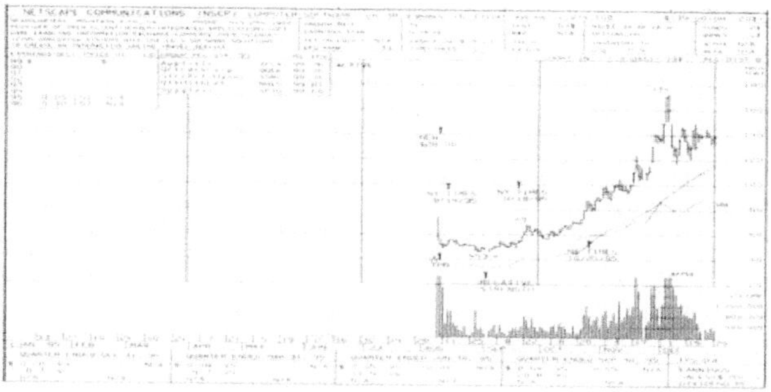

Source: Bloomberg

If you want to do more August trades, turn to page 129.

If you'd rather move onto the next month's set of trading options, turn to page 142.

Netscape Option Bearish Outcome

Congratulations, you just made a 10% return on your trade!

Netscape ended up falling the month after you bought the put options. The common stock was down 10%. A bit of the euphoria faded away as the realization of just how expensive this stock was hit the market. Today your put options have risen in value significantly. The future of the internet and technology in general is looking to be very exciting and your bearish outlook might cost you in the near future.

Netscape Communications

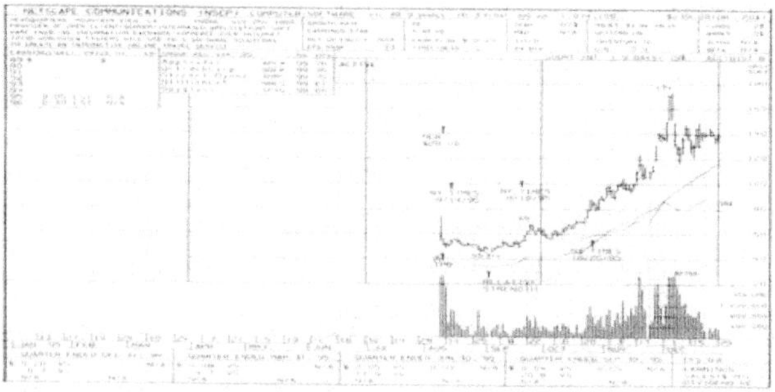

Source: Bloomberg

If you want to do more August trades, turn to page 129.

If you'd rather move onto the next month's set of trading options, turn to page 142.

Google IPO Setup

It's August 19, 2004, and the SEC requires that companies make their information public "20 days after the close of the year in which the company reaches $10 million in assets and/or 500 shareholders, including people with stock options." At that point most companies figure they might as well raise capital, and Google is not an exception. Nerds that they are, Google is seeking to raise up to $2,718,281,828, or the mathematical constant "e" to the 10th-digit.

Google has replaced every other search engine for you and it's now your homepage. And on April Fool's Day earlier this year, Google released Gmail as beta, a free web email service with a whole gigabyte of free storage; you immediately switch over from Microsoft's Hotmail when you're friend gets you in as a beta-tester. Google gives you five Gmail invites which are a hot commodity and are trading for $150 on Ebay.

You call around to other investors and bankers and you hear something you can't even believe: Google is going to cut Wall Street out of the IPO process altogether and use a 'Dutch Auction" to go publicly directly. Time to dig into the S-1.

Even though it was just founded in 1988, Google already has $961.9 billion in revenue for 2003, and a profit of $106.5 million. So if the IPO prices at about 20x earnings, that would make Google worth about $20 billion on the first day. You scratch your head and look at previous tech IPOs from the tech bubble that are now trading at market caps about 95% lower. Google is a great business but there are some things that worry you in the S1. You take out your highlighter and mark the following:

If opportunities arise that might cause us to sacrifice short term results but are in the best long term interest of our shareholders, we will take those opportunities. We will have the fortitude to do this. We would request that our shareholders take the long term view **(Umm, how long is this "long-term?" Founders can convince themselves of a lot, and while you want to buy into a long-term business, the IPO is at a pretty large market cap so the short-term does matter.).**

We aspire to make Google an institution that makes the world a better place. With our products, Google connects people and information all around the world for free.

(So your capital will be used to make things that are given away?)

We provide advertising, web search and other services to members of our Google Network. The net revenues generated from the fees advertisers pay us when users click on ads that we have delivered to our Google Network members' web sites represented approximately 15% of our net revenues in 2003, and approximately 21% of our net revenues for the three months ended March 31, 2004, and we expect this percentage to increase in the future. We consider this network to be critical to the future growth of our net revenues. However, some of the participants in this network may compete with us in one or more areas. Therefore, they may decide in the future to terminate their agreements with us. If our Google Network members decide to use a competitor's or their own web search or advertising services, our net revenues would decline.

(A fifth of revenues are from direct competitors?)

Advertising revenues made up 77%, 92%, 95% and 96% of our net revenues in 2001, 2002, 2003 and in the three months ended March 31, 2004.

(So this is an advertising company? You consider the stocks of ad companies and the total pie of ad spending.)

iShares S&P Global Technology (IXN)

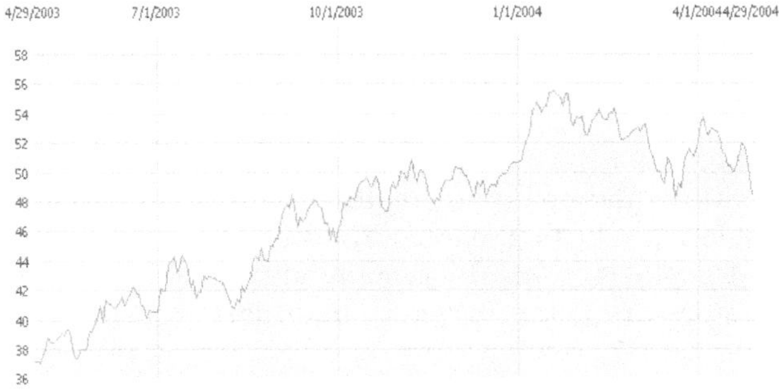

Source: MSN Money

If you are bullish and want to buy about $100,000 of common stock in Google and hold it for the whole year, turn to page 138.

If you are bearish and want to short about $100,000 of common stock in Google for the whole year, turn to page 139.

If you are bullish and want to buy about $50,000 of calls in Google for a short-term one month trade, turn to page 140.

If you are bearish and want to buy about $50,000 of puts in Google for a short-term one month trade, turn to page 141.

If you would rather find something else to trade this month, turn to page 129.

Google IPO Stock Bullish Outcome

Congratulations, you have made a 123% return on your investment.

Since its IPO, Google has gone up 123% into the end of the year. Google has a great search engine and from that they are creating a magnificent platform. Google is by far the most widely-used search engine on the web.

This user base gives them the power to create an ecosystem that ties together all of Google's products (Search, Youtube, Docs, etc.) and profit off of them. Google is going to remain at the head of web innovation and investors are going to get to take part in a big new trend.

By buying the common stock, you made more money than you could have using the short term call options. Google is a great investment and has the opportunity for huge growth in the future. This has really been a fun trade.

Google

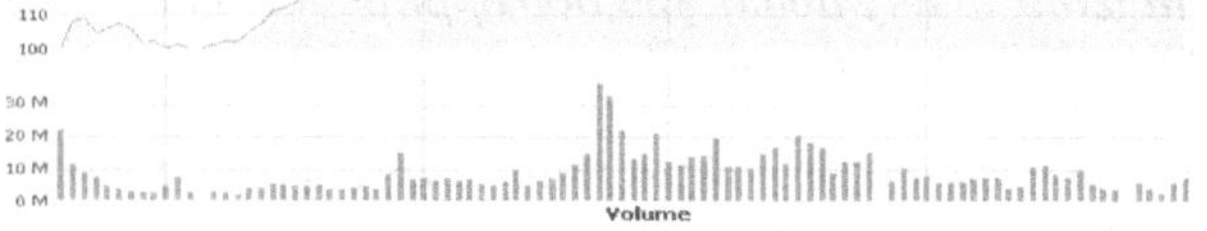

Source: MSN Money

If you would like to do more August trades, turn to page 129.

If you would rather skip to next month's set of trading options, turn to page 142.

Google IPO Stock Bearish Outcome

Oops, you have lost 123% on your investment.

Since its IPO, Google has gone up 123% into the end of the year. Google has a great search engine and from that they are creating a magnificent platform. Google is by far the most widely-used search engine on the web. This user base gives them the power to create an ecosystem that ties together all of Google's products (Search, YouTube Docs, etc.) and profit off of them. Shorting the common stock has really cost you. Google continues to innovate and as they do, they will continue to increase their top-line. Google already operates at great margins and the more revenue they can put through their profit engine, the better. Your poor analysis of this company has really cost you.

Google

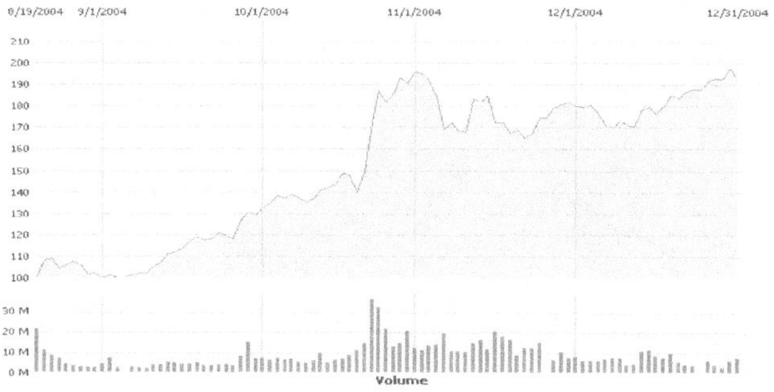

Source: MSN Money

If you would like to do more August trades, turn to page 129.

If you would rather skip to next month's set of trading options, turn to page 142.

Google IPO Option Bullish Outcome

Congratulations, your have a 38% return on your trade.

The Google IPO was a big success. The stock is up 38% from the IPO price of $85. Google has built a great platform and will continue to do so through acquisitions and innovation within the company. Google is by far the standard in internet search and this will be the basis for the Google ecosystem. A new era is emerging as companies like Apple and Google expand their platforms and lock in users. This large user base provides a large revenue base and also gives each company a great opportunity to grow. Your call options are up big. Good move on Google.

Google

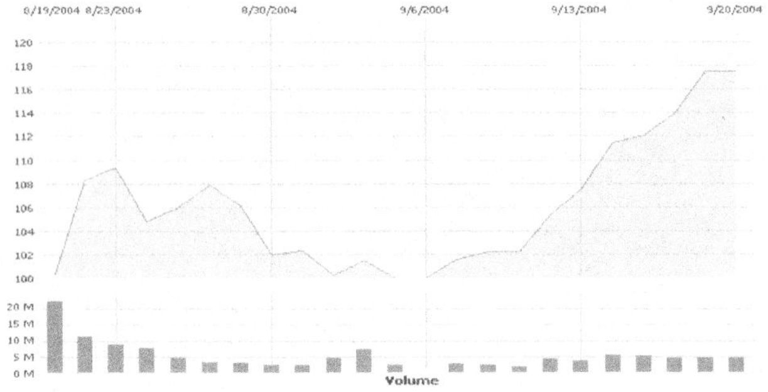

Source: MSN Money

If you would like to do more August Trades, turn to page 129.

If you would rather skip to next month's set of trading options, turn to page 142.

Google IPO Option Bearish Outcome

Oops, you lost 38% on your trade.

Ouch! The Google IPO was a big success. The stock is up 38% from the IPO price of $85. Google has built a great platform and will continue to do so through acquisitions and innovation within the company. Google is by far the standard in internet search and this will be the basis for the Google ecosystem.

A new era is emerging as companies like Apple and Google expand their platforms and lock in users. This large user base provides a large revenue base and also gives each company a great opportunity to grow. You messed up shorting a company that is showing this kind of growth. Although the IPO was the biggest in history, it was a big hit. Your puts are down big time.

Google Inc.

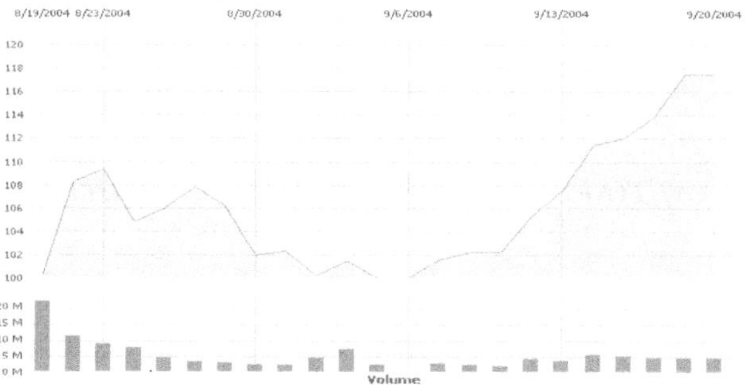

Source: MSN Money

If you would like to do more August Trades, turn to page 129.

If you would rather skip to next month's set of trading options, turn to page 142.

Start trading September

You pull up a chart of the DJIA, the S&P 500, and the Nasdaq. You remember on that video how your Great Uncle Buster had turned almost angry when he'd talked about how he had barely beaten the major indices last year.

And here you are supposed to be getting 50% in a single year's timeframe.

If you want to trade an auto manufacturer after a bailout was requested, turn to page 143.

If you want to trade a smart phone manufacturer just after a new product is announced, turn to page 148.

If you'd rather move onto the next month's set of trading options, turn to page 154.

If you've hit $1.5 million and are ready to cash in, turn to page 308.*

*(*PLEASE DO NOT GO TO PAGE 308 IF YOU HAVE NOT HIT $1.5 MILLION).*

Chrysler Bailout 1979 Setup

Today is September 7, 1979. Today the CEO of Chrysler Lee Iacocca asked congress for $1.5 billion in loan guarantees to keep the company from filing bankruptcy. How will this affect Ford?

Ford Motor Company (F)

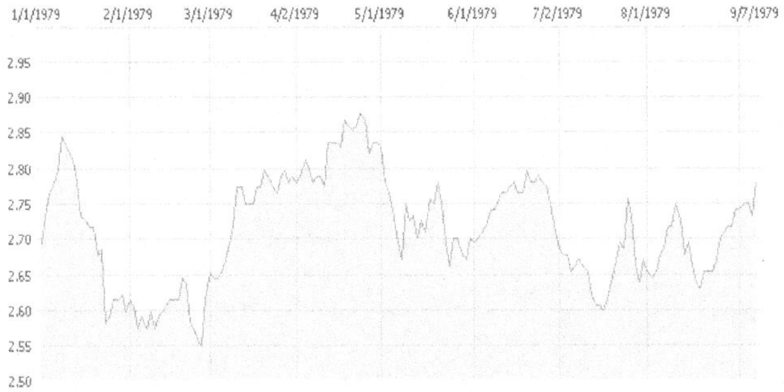

Source: MSN Money

If you are bullish and want to buy about $100,000 of Ford common stock and hold it for the whole year, *turn to page 144.*

If you are bearish and want to short about $100,000 of Ford common stock for the whole year, *turn to page 145.*

If you are bullish and want to buy about $50,000 of calls in Ford for a short-term one month trade, *turn to page 146.*

If you are bearish and want to buy about $50,000 of puts in Ford for a short-term one month trade, *turn to page 147.*

If you would rather find something else to trade this month, *turn to page 142.*

Chrysler Bailout 1979 Stock Bullish Outcome

Oops, you just lost 25% on your investment!

Ford is really taking a beating. The stock has fallen 26% since you bought it back in September. Fear is really gripping the American auto industry as investors come to the realization that they could actually fail. Congress is going to bail out Chrysler, which is good news for now, but the American auto manufacturers are going to have to make some serious changes in their product line up if they are going to make it out of this hole. You take a substantial loss on this investment.

Ford Motor Company (F)

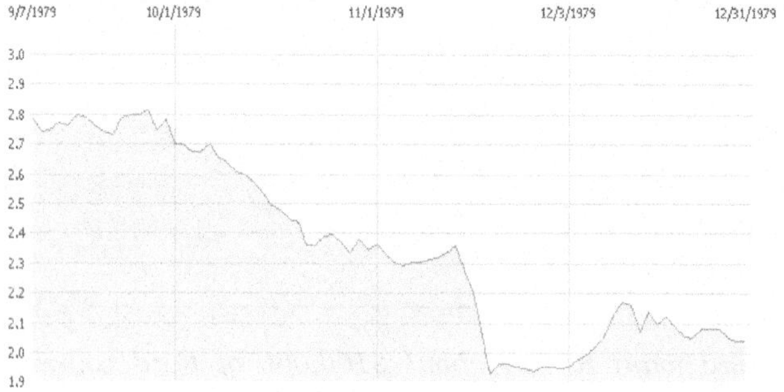

Source: MSN Money

If you would like to do more September trades, turn to page 142.

If you'd rather move onto the next month's set of trading options, turn to page 154.

Chrysler Bailout 1979 Stock Bearish Outcome

Congratulations, you just made a 25% return!

Well it looks like the bottom has been pulled out from underneath the American auto industry. With Ford down over 25% into the end of the year, you made a great move selling it when you did. Congress is going to bailout Chrysler, which is good news for now, but this could be an indication of what is happening at Ford and GM. The American auto manufacturers are going to have to make some serious changes in their product line up if they are ever going to be able to compete with the foreign auto companies.

Ford Motor Company (F)

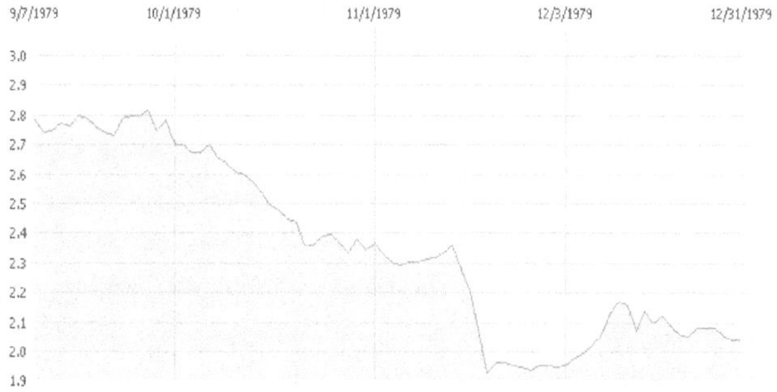

Source: MSN Money

If you would like to do more September trades, turn to page 142.

If you'd rather move onto the next month's set of trading options, turn to page 154.

Chrysler Bailout 1979 Option Bullish Outcome

Oops, you just lost 3% on your trade!

Ford stock has continued to trade lower over the last month. There is a lot of uncertainty around the auto industry right now. The bad signs at Chrysler could give traders a clue to what is going on at Ford and GM as well. However, if Congress approves this bailout, it will also set the precedent for future auto bailouts. American companies continue to lose market share to foreign companies like Toyota and Nissan. Unions continue to demand wage increases and the threat of a strike is always present. For now you will take a small loss on your call options. It certainly could have been worse.

Ford Motor Company

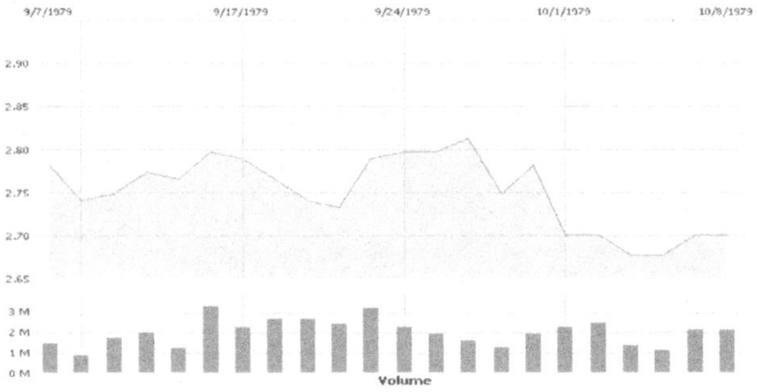

Source: MSN Money

If you would like to do more September Trades, turn to page 142.

If you would like to skip to next month's set of trading options, turn to page 154.

Chrysler Bailout 1979 Option Bearish Outcome

Congratulations, you just made a 3% return on your trade!

Over this past month it seems that the auto industry has taken a slight downturn as the threat of a lingering bankruptcy at Chrysler hangs over the horizon. Congress is now putting a bill through that will bail out Chrysler. If this passes, it could set a precedent for future auto bailouts. There is a lot of emotion wrapped around America's auto industry. They employ a large number of people and their ties with the unions have always been a source of conflict. If Chrysler were to go under, it would be a punch in the mouth to America's pride. Foreign companies like Toyota and Nissan continue to gain market share in the U.S. Your put options are up slightly and you have locked in some small gains.

Ford Motor Company

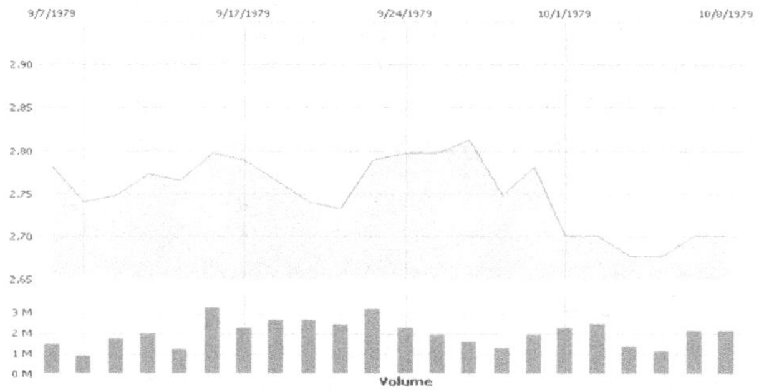

MSN Money

If you would like to do more September Trades, turn to page 142.

If you would like to skip to next month's set of trading options, turn to page 154.

RIM Playbook Setup

It's late October, 2010, and tech company Research in Motion is about to announce their very own tablet known as the Playbook. This new tablet has a seven-inch screen and is the lightest tablet for sale compared to its competitors. The tablet features 3-D graphics acceleration, a Texas Instruments dual-core processor, and a forward- and rear-facing camera.

The struggling smartphone maker has lost serious market share to Apple over the past several years and with today's release will be entering another very competitive market. The Playbook will be in direct competition with the Apple iPad, Google's Android Tablet, and the Kindle Fire, each with an established clientele. Coming in at $499, this tablet is by no means cheap and may have struggles selling.

RIMM stock has been down since the beginning of the year as the company continues to fall. The Blackberry is no longer the standard for smartphones and RIMM has failed to release an effective counter to the Apple iPhone or one of the many Android phones. This could be a great opportunity to buy RIMM if the stock were to rebound on a successful product launch (like the Playbook) or something else.

Research in Motion

Source: MSN Money

CEO Jim Balsillie says that Apple's highly-touted app marketplace really just masks iOS's sub-par web performance.

"You don't need an app for the Web," Balsillie said. Since many iOS apps are just front-end clients for web properties — stores, games, media companies, social networking sites — and RIM's app strength is in documents and productivity, it's a clear contrast.

"There's still a role for apps, but can you use your existing content?" Balsillie asked web companies. "Can you use your existing web assets? Do you need a set of proprietary tools to bring existing assets on to a device, or can you use known tools that you use for creating websites?"

As for Apple trying to take on Blackberry in the smartphone market that it has dominated for years now, when asked what he would tell Jobs if he were there, Balsillie simply said, "You finally showed up."

If you are bullish and want to buy about $100,000 of RIMM common stock and hold it for the whole year, turn to page 150.

If you are bearish and want to short about $100,000 of RIMM common stock for the whole year, turn to page 151.

If you are bullish and want to buy about $50,000 of calls in RIMM for a short-term one month trade, turn to page 152.

If you are bearish and want to buy about $50,000 of puts in RIMM for a short-term one month trade, turn to page 153.

If you would rather find something else to trade this month, turn to page 142.

RIM Playbook Stock Bullish Outcome

Ahh yeah, baby. You made 15% on this investment.

Nice pop in the stock here in the last two months of your year left to meet the 50% goal. The possibility of a significant revenue stream coming from a table lineup has inspired new faith in the company. Investors are seeing significant value in this company as it has been punished so badly in the previous year or two. The common stock is up 15% into the end of December after a significant pop the week after you bought it.

Research in Motion just might have that innovative spark that we haven't seen in a long time come out again. The Playbook won't actually sell until next year so we still have no idea on how consumers will react to the new product. Of course RIMM still faces serious competition from the likes of Apple and Google, but this could be quite the comeback story–or not.

Research in Motion

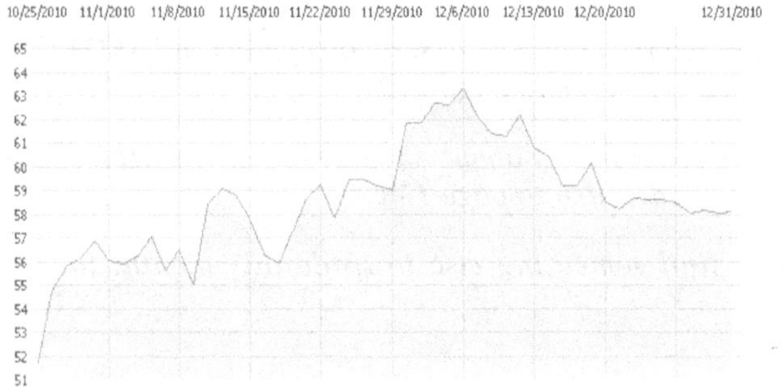

Source: MSN Money

If you would like to do more September trades, turn to page 142.

If you'd rather move onto the next month's set of trading options, turn to page 154.

RIM Playbook Stock Bearish Outcome

Ohh no, baby. You lost 15% on this trade.

You seem to be underestimating the power of innovation with this one. Investors are liking what they are hearing coming from the guys at Research in Motion. The possibility of a new stream of revenue coming from a tablet lineup seems to be music to everyone's ears.

The sentiment here may be that RIM doesn't have much more to lose. This is just a feeling you are getting as you watch the common stock rise 15% into the end of the year following the announcment. You got no satisfaction from this trade because the stock popped immediately after you bought it. We still don't know exactly how the Playbook will affect earnings because it doesn't come up for sale until next year. For now, you have to accept the fact that you were wrong on this one.

Research in Motion

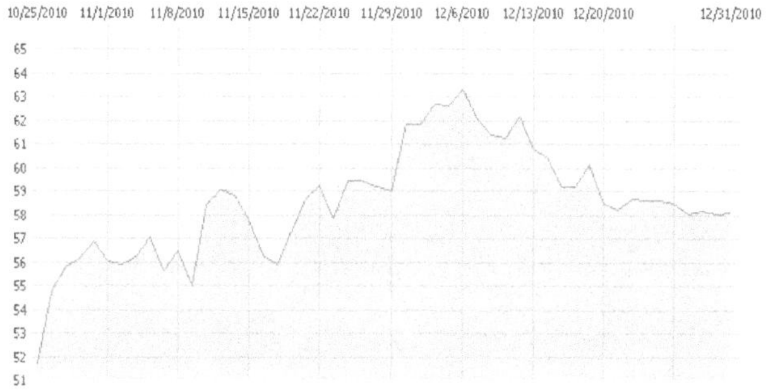

Source: MSN Money

If you would like to do more September trades, turn to page 142.

If you'd rather move onto the next month's set of trading options, turn to page 154.

RIM Playbook Option Bullish Outcome

Ahh yeah, baby. You made 15% on this trade.

Research in Motion's stock popped immediately following the announcement The stock then continued to climb into the end of the month, closing up 15% from your purchase price. It seems that the possibility of a revenue line streaming from the sale of tablets has increased investor confidence in RIM. The company has struggled for a while as it continues to lose market share to Apple and Google in the handset market.

This tablet will have to compete with the iPad and the Kindle, but the first reviews show a favorable impression of the Playbook. Some reviews are saying it is faster and that the screen has better resolution. The tablet will not actually be sold until next year so we still cannot be absolutely sure how consumers will react to the Playbook. For now you lock is some nice gains as you sell your call options.

Research in Motion

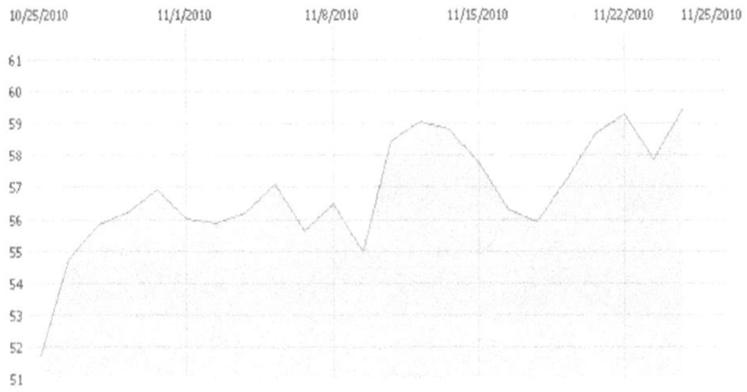

MSN Money

If you would like to do more September trades, turn to page 142.

If you'd rather move onto the next month's set of trading options, turn to page 154.

RIM Playbook Option Bearish Outcome

Ohh no, baby. You lost 15% on this trade.

Research in Motion's stock popped immediately following the announcement The stock then continued to climb into the end of the month closing up 15% from your purchase price. It seems that the possibility of a revenue line streaming from the sale of tablets has increased investor confidence in RIM. The company has struggled for a while as it continues to lose market share to Apple and Google in the handset market.

This tablet will have to compete with the iPad and the Kindle, but the first reviews show a favorable impression of the Playbook. Some reviews are saying it is faster and that the screen has better resolution. The tablet will not actually be sold until next year so we still cannot be absolutely sure how consumers will react to the Playbook. For now you take a substantial loss on your put options.

Research in Motion

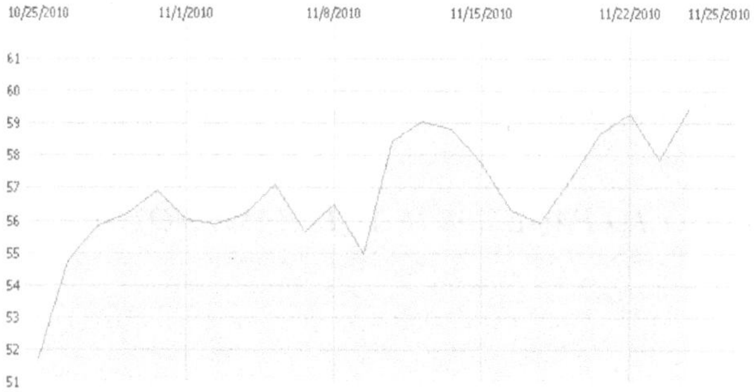

MSN Money

If you would like to do more September trades, turn to page 142.

If you'd rather move onto the next month's set of trading options, turn to page 154.

Start trading October

You pull up a chart of the DJIA, the S&P 500, and the Nasdaq. You remember on that video how your Great Uncle Buster had turned almost angry when he'd talked about how he had barely beaten the major indices last year.

And here you are supposed to be getting 50% in a single year's timeframe.

If you want to trade a footwear manufacturer just after a giant sports hero endorses them, turn to page 155.

If you want to trade an India auto manufacturer as their economy is exploding, turn to page 161.

If you want to trade a technology giant just as their new operating system is released, turn to page 167.

If you'd rather move onto the next month's set of trading options, turn to page 174.

If you've hit $1.5 million and are ready to cash in, turn to page 308.*

*(*PLEASE DO NOT GO TO PAGE 308 IF YOU HAVE NOT HIT $1.5 MILLION).*

Air Jordan Setup

It is October 18, 1985. Today Nike launched a new brand of Basketball shoes known as Air Jordans. They are riding on the brand of star basketball player Michael Jordan. Nike has not launched extensive advertising quite yet, but it is rumored that Michael Jordan will be wearing them in the game. They are pretty cool shoes and this could be a great product line for the corporation.

This stock has fallen this year as the company's net income has fallen 75% due to decreasing margins. The company's top line continues to grow but unless the issues with margins are handled, this company could continue to lose money. The stock is only trading at 3 times this year's earnings and has a serious possibility for increasing net income.

The stock also has a nice dividend that comes with it. If Nike can successfully launch this new brand, it could be a breakthrough moment for the stock.

Nike Inc. (NYSE: NKE)

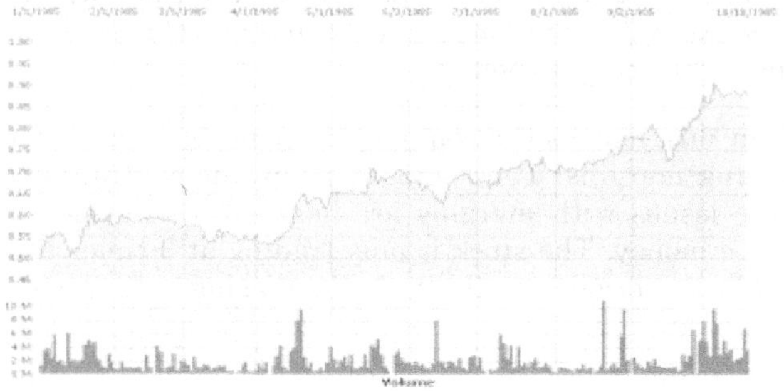

Source: MSN Money

If you are bullish and want to buy about $100,000 of common stock in NKE and hold them for the whole year, turn to page 157.

If you are bearish and want to short about $100,000 of NKE common stock for the whole year, turn to page 158.

If you are bullish and want to buy about $50,000 of calls in NKE for a short-term one month trade, turn to page 159.

If you are bearish and want to buy about $50,000 of puts in NKE for a short-term one month trade, turn to page 160.

If you would rather find something else to trade this month, turn to page 154.

Air Jordan Stock Bullish Outcome

You broke even on your investment. There is no change to your portfolio value.

This has been a little bit of a bumpy ride. However the stock closed on December 31 at your exact purchase price. The shoes have now gained major publicity–however, stock prices aren't exactly based on the number of news articles talking about it. In the future, Nike's earnings will likely reflect the massive sale of Air Jordans, but it looks like this is not going to pan out this year. Nike currently faces inventory problems along with narrowing margins that could cause problems in the future. Investors appear to be wary of the current financial problems at the company, but the stock is holding steady for now.

Nike Inc.

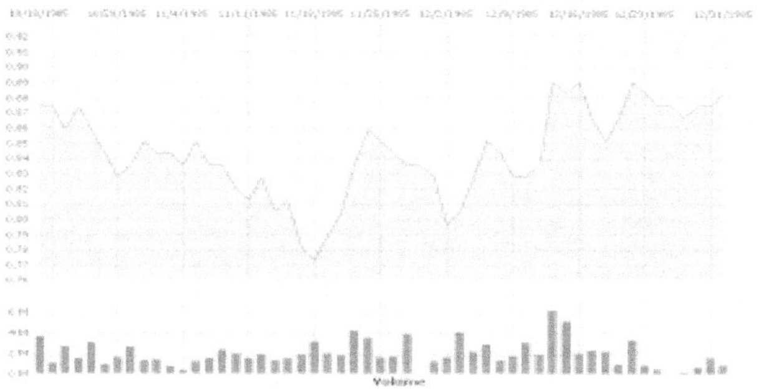

Source: MSN Money

If you would like to do more October trades, turn to page 154.

If you would like to skip to next month's set of trading options, turn to page 174.

Air Jordan Stock Bearish Outcome

You broke even on your investment. There is no change to your portfolio value.

Today you covered your sale of the stock and bought it back at the exact same price that you paid for it. Although the rapid popularity of the shoe is spreading across the nation, the stock price is holding steady as investors wait to see what kind of real earnings power that this brand can bring to the company.

The company is spending a lot of money on advertising and they are even capitalizing on the NBA ban of the shoe. The NBA officials said that every time MJ wore the shoes on the court, he would be fined $5000. In a stunning advertising event, Nike agreed to pay the fine for every game in order to keep up the popularity of the shoe. This brand may turn out to be a real money-maker for Nike, but shareholders will not be seeing those returns until some real numbers come out.

Nike, Inc.

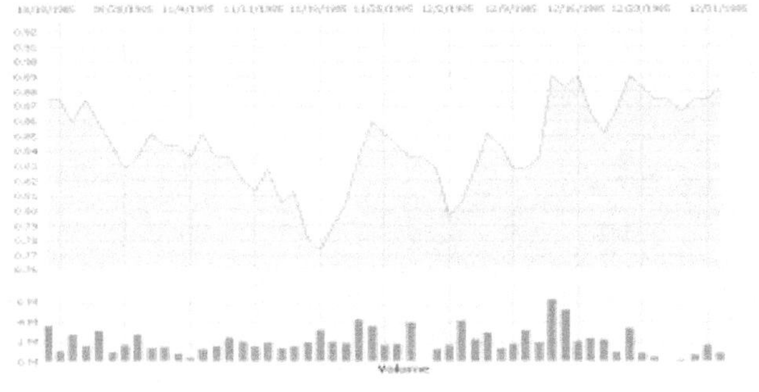

Source: MSN Money

If you would like to do more October trades, turn to page 154.

If you would like to skip to next month's set of trading options, turn to page 174.

Air Jordan Option Bullish Outcome

Oops, you just lost 11% on your trade!

Dang the luck! Nike stock has fallen drastically since you bought the call options, and it looks like you are going to have to take a loss on this trade. Nike still faces a problem with falling margins and it looks like investors are waiting to see how Nike will generate this new brand into earnings before they buy into the stock. On a positive note, a little over a month after the shoes were launched, Michael Jordan was fined for wearing them in the game. Since then the story has blown up and the shoes are finally gaining traction. Obviously it will take time before the profits start rolling in, but in the back of your mind you can know that your analysis was right–just your timeline was a little off.

Nike 1 Month

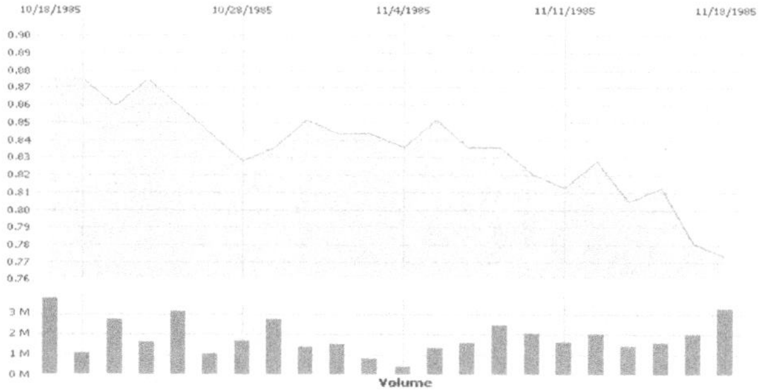

Source: MSN Money

If you would like to do more October trades, turn to page 154.

If you would like to skip to next month's set of trading options, turn to page 174.

Air Jordan Option Bearish Outcome

Congratulations, you just made a 11% return!

The stock has nearly made a straight line down the month after you bought. The introduction of the Air Jordans was not enough of a catalyst to make the stock pop. Nike is going to have to show some real earnings power coming from this brand before this stock climbs out of its hole. The problem with margins still exists and the possibility of a shrinking profit is enough to warn off any investor. Your put options are nicely in the money and this has been a very successful trade.

Nike 1 Month

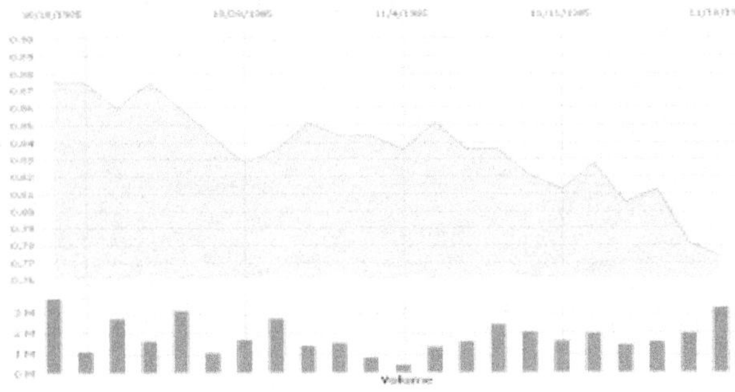

Source: MSN Money

If you would like to do more October trades, turn to page 154.

If you would like to skip to next month's set of trading options, turn to page 174.

India Auto Industry Setup

It's October of 2006, and India's economy is exploding. The liberalization of the economy has really taken hold. India nationalized Pepsi in the '50s, but now Pepsi sponsors the national cricket team and can be found everywhere. The country has a middle class of almost 300M (that all speak English) and the service economy has boomed, largely at the expense of call centers in America. With rising wealth comes the rising desire to be more American; that is, to own a car. You call up the chart of Tata Motors, a major Indian auto manufacturer, started by one of India's most prominent families. You compare how it's done since its IPO vs. the S&P 500:

Tata Motors

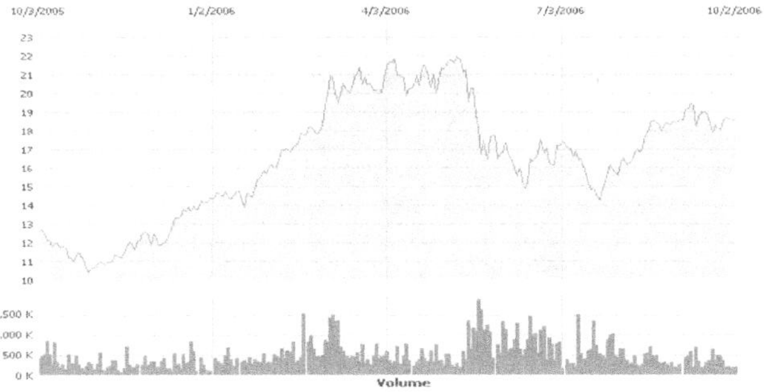

Source: MSN Money

The company has just over a billion in cash and is growing almost 50% per year. You look at the common stock and consider a one-year trade.

If you are bullish and want to buy about $100,000 of Tata Motors common stock and hold it for the whole year, turn to page 163.

If you are bearish and want to short about $100,000 of Tata Motors common stock for the whole year, turn to page 164.

If you are bullish and want to buy about $50,000 of calls in Tata Motors for a short-term one month trade, turn to page 165.

If you are bearish and want to buy about $50,000 of puts in Tata Motors for a short-term one month trade, turn to page 166.

If you would rather find something else to trade this month, turn to page 154.

India Auto Industry Stock Bullish Outcome

Congratulations, you just made a 10% return on your investment.

Tata's hot streak ended just as you got in. It's not that India slowed down, just the stock did, ending up only about 10% after a crazy volatile year. Especially nice job on buying TTM instead of just going long the S&P.

Tata Motors

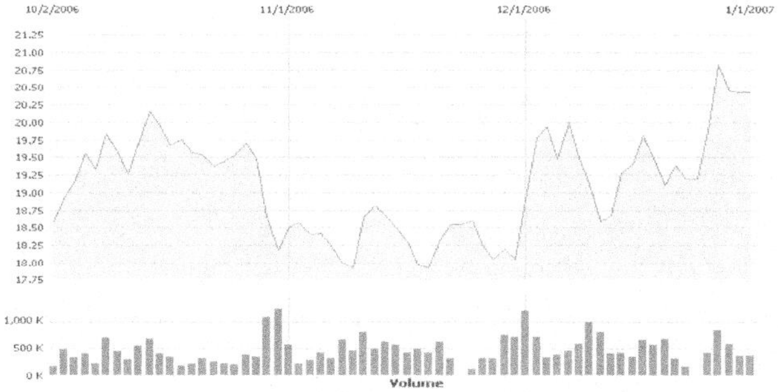

Source: MSN Money

If you would like to do more October trades, turn to page 154.

If you would rather skip to next month's set of trading options, turn to page 174.

India Auto Industry Stock Bearish Outcome

Oops, you just lost 10% on your investment.

Well it looks like Tata Motors is going to close out the year higher even after some very volatile price action. Tata Motors seems to have leveled out and is facing a lot of resistance near this current trading range. India continues to grow at a rapid pace with GDP growth at around 5% year. You shorted the leader in a rapidly growing industry and that is going to cost you.

Tata Motors

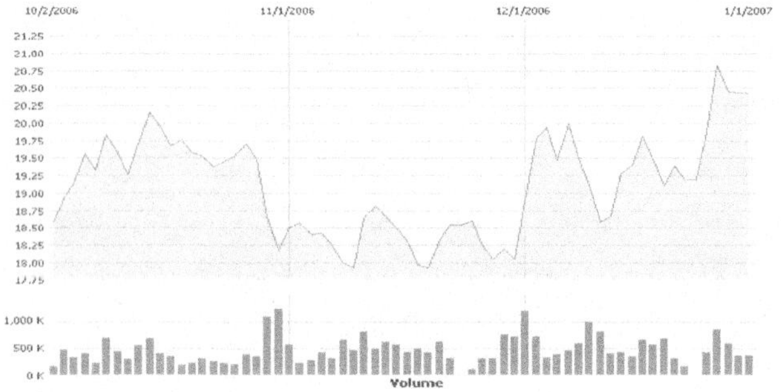

Source: MSN Money

If you would like to do more October trades, turn to page 154.

If you would rather skip to next month's set of trading options, *turn to page 174.*

India Auto Industry Option Bullish Outcome

Oops, you lost 3% on your trade.

It looks like Tata Motors stock is starting to slow down a little bit. Although India continues to grow its production at a rate of 4-5% a year, the stock seems to have gone cold. Over the course of the month, the stock was up and then fell sharply in the last few days of trading, taking your call options to a losing position. You did not have much of a catalyst to encourage a sharp increase in the price of the stock and you are going to take a small setback on this trade.

Tata Motors

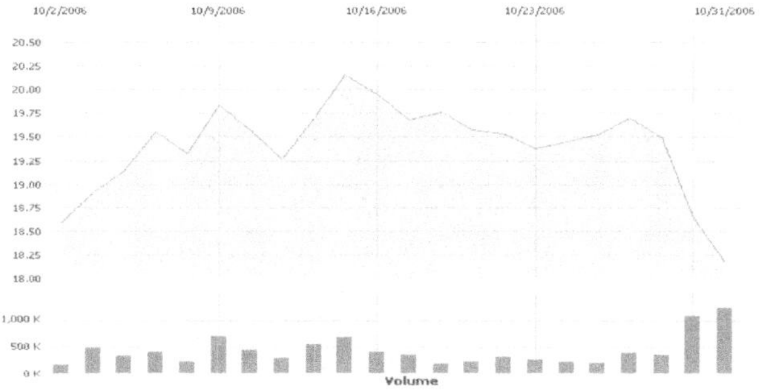

Source: MSN Money

If you would like to do more October trades, turn to page 154.

If you would rather skip to next month's set of trading options, turn to page 174.

India Auto Industry Option Bearish Outcome

Congratulations, you just made a 3% return on your trade.

This stock seems to have hit the top of its growth curve. The stock leveled out and then fell sharply in the last week of the month. India continues to grow and there has been no real shift in the fundamentals of this company. Your put options were a great play on this trade. The common stock is down only 3%, but your use of aggressive put options has increased your returns significantly. Great call (or put, technically!).

Tata Motors

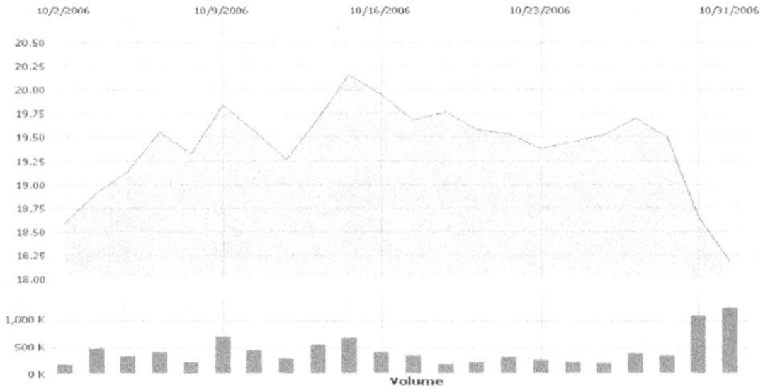

Source: MSN Money

If you would like to do more October trades, turn to page 154.

If you would rather skip to next month's set of trading options, turn to page 174.

Microsoft Windows XP Setup

Today is October 25, 2001, and Microsoft just released their latest operating system known as Windows XP.

Windows XP features both home and professional editions. While the OS upgrade is perceived largely as a consumer upgrade, Bill Gates made a special effort to highlight the Windows XP Professional features that will be useful to business users, including the real-time, audio, video and text messaging for Internet meetings, new security features and privacy controls, and support for the 802.11 wireless networking standard. Microsoft, chip maker Intel, and PC makers are expected to spend a combined total of more than $1 billion on marketing for Windows XP.

Microsoft has a lot riding on XP's success: The operating system ushers in new features tied to Microsoft's long-term strategic plans for media player software, digital photo tools and online services. Many analysts said the new operating system was the most important release of Windows since Windows 95, the forerunner to Internet Explorer and other Internet connectivity features.

"With Office XP, Windows XP will be the new standard for business," said Gates, who pointed to many product and service opportunities for Microsoft's partners.

Gates also noted that the launch of Windows XP ends one era of computing, the DOS world, and ushers the new era of Web services. Unlike the difference between Windows 2000 Pro and Windows Millennium, both the professional and home editions of Windows XP use the same code base.

"It's the end of an era," Gates said about the DOS-based code on which Windows 3.1, Windows 95, Windows 98 and Windows Millennium were built. Microsoft is already at work on the successor to Windows XP, code named Longhorn, which is aimed at exploiting Intel's McKinley chip in late 2002.

"This is a transition period and the end of too many computer crashes and the static Web era into a new dynamic Web [era]," Gates said. "XP lays the foundation for Web services."

Gates, who also serves as the company's chief software architect, noted that Windows XP supports .Net Alerts, a recently unveiled alert service that will be deployed as part of Microsoft's .Net software services platform, formerly known as HailStorm.

Gates said there are plenty of business and consumer scenarios for services such as .Net Alerts. "Built into Windows XP is this idea of supporting Web services and alerts," Gates said in earlier Q&A sessions with several other high-tech leaders. "We'll show lots of benefits of alerts to businesses and consumers."

Gartner issued a report claiming the existing Windows 2000 Professional will continue to be the leading business Windows version until 2003. But Microsoft was quick to point to businesses that have already begun deploying Windows XP, including Wells Fargo, Citigroup, BMW and Reed Elsevier.

Microsoft also noted that other enterprise customers such as Jack-In-The-Box, Digex, and Merrill Lynch, as well as Microsoft global accounts General Motors, GMAC Commercial Mortgage and Siemens, are early adopters of Windows XP.

Microsoft

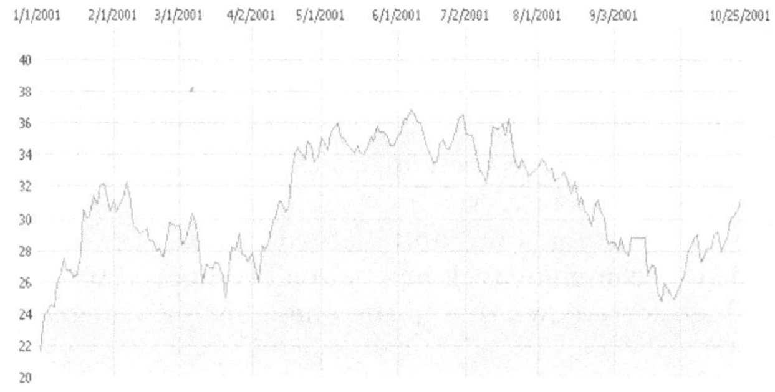

Source: MSN Money

If you are bullish and want to buy about $100,000 of MSFT common stock and hold it for the whole year, turn to page 170.

If you are bearish and want to short about $100,000 of MSFT common stock for the whole year, turn to page 171.

If you are bullish and want to buy about $50,000 of calls in MSFT for a short-term one month trade, turn to page 172.

If you are bearish and want to buy about $50,000 of puts in MSFT for a short-term one month trade, turn to page 173.

If you would rather find something else to trade this month, turn to page 154.

Microsoft Windows XP Stock Bullish Outcome

Congratulations, you just made a 6% return on your investment!

The common stock has really done well into the end of the year. It is up a little over 6% after the Windows XP launch. After almost two years of poor performance for the stock, the new operating system has restored some confidence in the company.

Microsoft has always struggled with achieving massive earnings growth even as their products have been very successful and the stock price has reflected that. Hopefully the new OS will give Softy the ability to increase its bottom line and return some of that to shareholders. Your use of common stock has paid off compared to short term call options, which were down due to the one month performance of the stock.

Microsoft Corp.

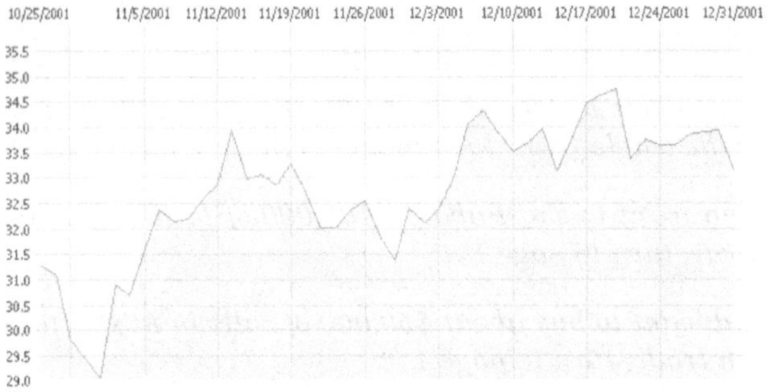

Source: MSN Money

If you would like to do more October trades, turn to page 154.

If you'd rather move onto the next month's set of trading options, turn to page 174.

Microsoft Windows XP Stock Bearish outcome

Oops, you just lost 6% on your investment!

This has been a great run up into the end of the year for Microsoft. The potential earnings derived from the sale of Windows XP has caused a run up in the stock price. With Windows huge market share, this new product will continue the tradition of Microsoft as the de facto operating system.

This has been the longest upward movement for Microsoft stock in several years. You are forced to buy back your shares at a higher price and take a loss on this trade.

Microsoft Corp.

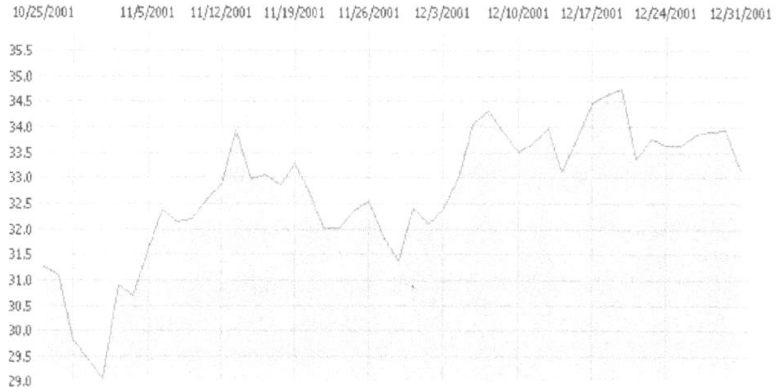

Source: MSN Money

If you would like to do more October trades, turn to page 154.

If you'd rather move onto the next month's set of trading options, turn to page 174.

Microsoft Windows XP Option Bullish Outcome

Congratulations, you just made a 4% return on your trade!

The launch of Windows XP has restored the confidence of Microsoft investors. The stock has been driven steadily lower over the past several years and this new product may help Microsoft increase earnings. They currently maintain over 90% of the operating system market share. This product will help expand that even further. Your use of call options was a great way to maximize your profits in this scenario.

Microsoft Corp.

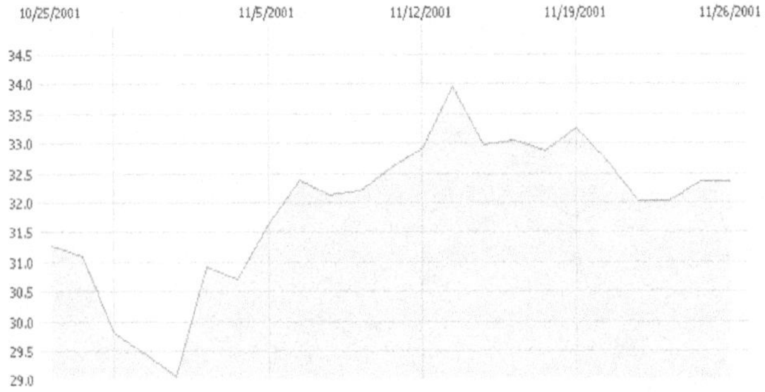

Source: MSN Money

–

If you would like to do more October trades, turn to page 154.

If you'd rather move onto the next month's set of trading options, turn to page 174.

Microsoft Windows XP Option Bearish Outcome

Oops, you just lost 4% on your trade!

The Windows XP launch has actually driven the stock slightly higher (4%). Microsoft continues to dominate which has given Windows a huge share of the market for operating systems.

Windows has struggled turning this into giant profits. While the company makes good money, the stock price has continued to fall previous to this announcement.

This new product has given investors confidence in the company again and the bears are backing off. Your put options are down slightly. Investors remain hopeful that Microsoft will turn this new product into bottom line earnings growth.

Microsoft Corp.

Source: MSN Money

If you would like to do more October trades, turn to page 154.

If you'd rather move onto the next month's set of trading options, turn to page 174.

Start trading November

You pull up a chart of the DJIA, the S&P 500, and the Nasdaq. You remember on that video how your Great Uncle Buster had turned almost angry when he'd talked about how he had barely beaten the major indices last year.

And here you are supposed to be getting 50% in a single year's timeframe.

If you want to trade a giant airline manufacturer just as a new president is elected, turn to page 175.

If you want to trade the S&P 500 just as a big financial scandal breaks out, turn to page 182.

If you'd rather move onto the next month's set of trading options, turn to page 186.

If you've hit $1.5 million and are ready to cash in, turn to page 308.*

*(*PLEASE DO NOT GO TO PAGE 308 IF YOU HAVE NOT HIT $1.5 MILLION).*

Election of Bill Clinton as 42nd President of the United States Setup

Last night was pretty dramatic. Today is November 4, 1992, and last night the news declared that Governor Bill Clinton would be the next President of the United States. Incumbent George Bush was beaten by a 10% margin with third party candidate Ross Perot picking up 29% of the vote. Some major issues linger on the horizon as Bill Clinton talks of separating the gap between the rich and the poor. The new president also has plans of balancing the budget and ending the federal deficit. Taxes are going to be raised on upper income individuals as major changes are made to the federal outlays. Defense will surely take the brunt of the budget cuts as left-wing democrat Bill Clinton ends the era of military expansion seen under the Reagan-Bush Administrations.

Companies like Boeing, Lockheed Martin, and General Dynamics have raked in the dough as the United States geared up for war with the Soviet Union. With that threat no longer present, the Clinton Administration will most likely cut defense spending to achieve the goal of a balanced budget. This could be a great opportunity to short the companies that have profited so long from huge defense spending. Boeing is down 40% from the beginning of the year and this could be the crushing blow to the stock. On the other hand, the company also has a large market for commercial airliners it makes, and it could be enough to keep the company going. Another thing to remember is that in the world of politics, nothing is set in stone and there is always the possibility of another war. The Middle East is a tinderbox waiting to be lit as tensions remains high with Israel among Islamic nations in the region. Trading at around 15 times earnings, this company could be a buy as the stock has been crushed lately.

Boeing Co.

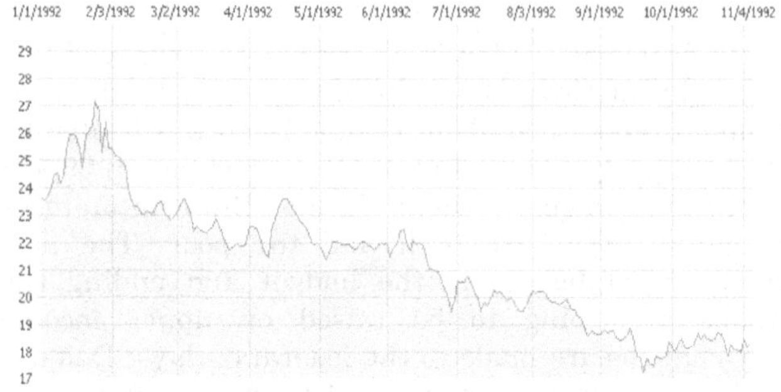

Source: MSN Money

If you are bullish and want to buy about $100,000 of BA common stock and hold it for the whole year, turn to page 177.

If you are bearish and want to short about $100,000 of BA common stock for the whole year, turn to page 179.

If you are bullish and want to buy about $50,000 of calls in BA for a short-term one month trade, turn to page 180.

If you are bearish and want to buy about $50,000 of puts in BA for a short-term one month trade, turn to page 181.

If you would rather find something else to trade this month, turn to page 174.

Election of Bill Clinton as 42nd President of the United States Stock Bullish Outcome

Congratulations, you just made a 9% return!

The stock fell hard the month after the election as uncertainty gripped the market. The stock does really not like this election. The common stock has fallen six percent and your one-month call options have lost significant value. Everyone is uncertain what this new president will bring to the table and the new direction of the federal government. Defense contractors could face serious repercussions if the budget is cut. If congress approves a budget cut, it will most likely be targeted at limiting the size of the military.

Boeing's commercial side will remain but investors are saying that it is not enough to justify the current price. It has since bounced back in the last 20 days of the year and your stock is up around 20%. Boeing will most likely continue to profit as the commercial airline industry continues to gain speed. It looks like the federal budget is going to be cut across the board and a surplus may be in sight. Taxes are also going to be raised on the upper income classes to help balance the budget. Regardless of what happens to the stock market, Clinton will surely change the way the federal government has operated over the past 12 years.

Boeing Co.

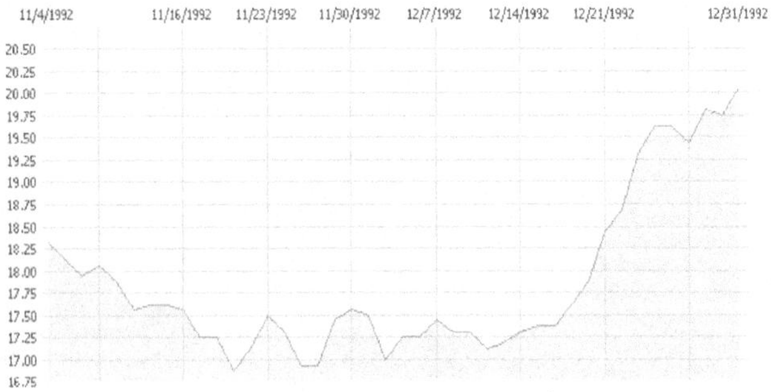

MSN Money

If you would like to do more November trades, turn to page 174.

If you would like to skip to the next month's set of trading options, turn to page 186.

Election of Bill Clinton as 42nd President of the United States Stock Bearish Outcome

Oops, you just lost 9% on your investment!

The stock fell hard the month after you bought it and you were sitting on some nice gains. In the last 20 days, however, the stock rebounded as more traders considered the future level of earnings to be worth the current price. Boeing will most likely continue to excel in the commercial airline business regardless of the military division. This is most likely going to be a new age as President Clinton leads the executive branch in a different direction than it has been led in the past 12 years.

Boeing Co.

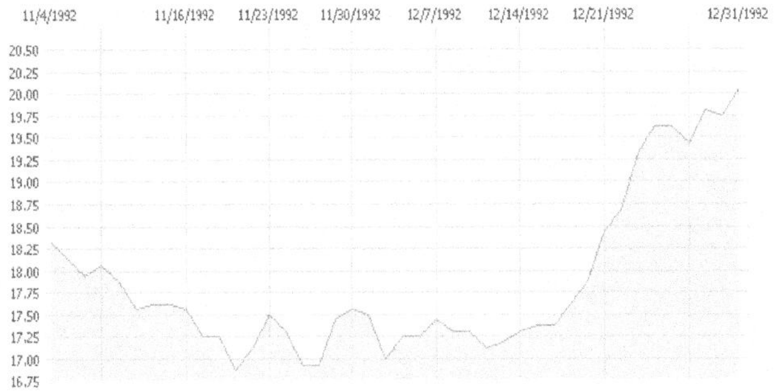

MSN Money

If you would like to do more November trades, turn to page 174.

If you'd rather move onto the next month's set of trading options, turn to page 186.

Election of Bill Clinton as 42nd President of the United States Option Bullish Outcome

Oops, you just lost 5% on your trade!

Man, you really missed this one. Uncertainty grips the defense market and prices continue to drive lower as the threat of budget cuts wards off investors. It looks like Bill Clinton is dead-set on balancing the budget and ending the federal deficit. This will likely cause major cuts in defense spending which will hurt Boeing directly. You probably shouldn't have been so aggressively long at a time like this.

Boeing Co.

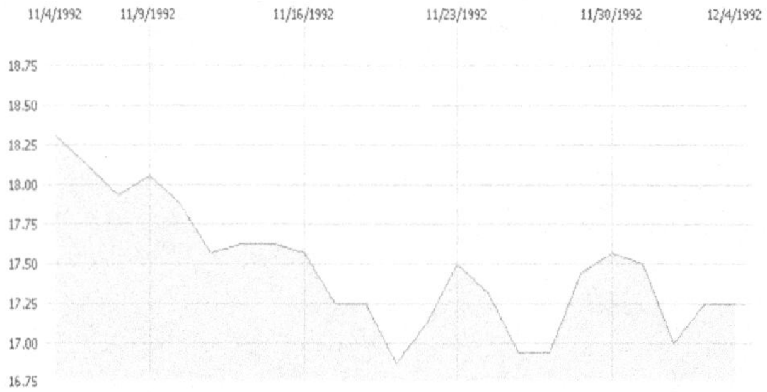

MSN Money

If you would like to do more November trades, turn to page 174.

If you would like to skip to next month's set of trading options, turn to page 186.

Election of Bill Clinton as 42nd President of the United States Option Bearish Outcome

Congratulations, you just made a 5% return on your trade!

It seems like uncertainty has gripped the markets as Bill Clinton steps into the Oval Office. The possibility of drastic cuts in defense spending is striking fear into the hearts of defense investors. The Defense-laden budget of the past 12 years is likely to be a thing of the past as Bill Clinton sets out to balance the budget and end the country's deficit. Boeing is going to have to rely on their commercial business in order to keep growing from here. Great call on the put options.

Boeing Co.

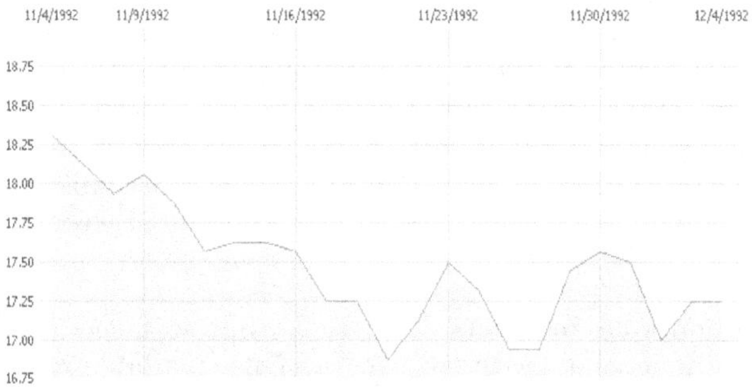

MSN Money

If you would like to do more November trades, turn to page 174.

If you would like to skip to next month's set of trading options, turn to page 186.

Enron Scandal setup

Today is November 28, 2001. This morning at 10:30 the Enron Corporation announced that its past five years of financial statements have been mostly fraud. The company has an insurmountable amount of debt and is operating at a loss. Just four months ago, the company was worth over $60 billion at a share price of $80, and as you look at the stock now on your computer, it is trading for pennies. It was listed on the S&P 500 index as well as the Dow Jones Utility Average.

Enron had over $100 billion in revenue and was a much-diversified company. Enron provided electric and natural gas utilities as well as commodities trading and many other financial products. Over the past six years, Enron was listed as Forbes #1 most innovative company. The company had been hiding their losses in "special offshore entities" which allowed them to maintain a high stock price and high credit ratings. The stock has fallen significantly over the past few months and the corporate governance was constantly reassuring shareholders that everything was alright. Meanwhile, those same officers were dumping their stock at record high prices. Enron got away with all this due to recent energy law deregulation and unregulated accounting practices.

The Enron Corporation told investors last week that it faced debt repayments over the next year vastly in excess of its available cash. Indeed, its ability to continue as a going concern is being called into question.

In the delayed quarterly filing with the Securities and Exchange Commission filed last week, the company said that it would have to repay $690 million in debt by next Tuesday if it did not come up with collateral for a loan.

Enron's independent auditors with the firm of Arthur Andersen have not been able to complete their review of Enron's financial statements for the third quarter. Andersen already faces lawsuits over its audits of Enron's books related to Enron's disclosure this month that it had overstated almost $600 million in profits in the last five years. Enron has said that it will re-release new statements that Andersen certified and that the older statements should no longer be relied upon.

This could forever change the public's view on corporations and may also have an effect on investor relations. With the current situation, we have no idea of knowing if other corporations are doing the same thing. Obviously, Enron is done and it may well drag down the rest of the S&P 500. On the other hand, this could have no effect on the broader markets and this could be a great buying opportunity. You are looking at Spider's S&P index fund (SPY) to game this action.

SPY S&P 500

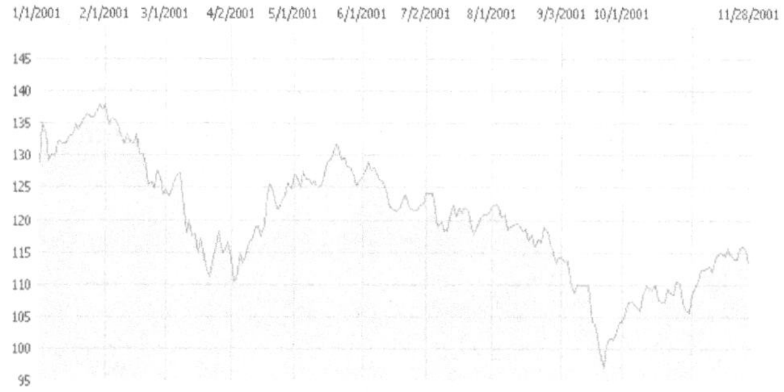

Source: MSN Money

If you are bullish and want to buy about $100,000 of the S&P 500 and hold them for the whole year, turn to page 184.

If you are bearish and want to short about $100,000 of the S&P 500 for the whole year, turn to page 185.

If you would rather find something else to trade this month, turn to page 174.

Enron Scandal Bullish Outcome

You broke even on your investment. There is no change to your portfolio value.

Turns out that the Enron Scandal has had absolutely no effect on the broader markets. Over this past month, there has been a tiny bit of movement on the S&P, but on December 31st, the SPY closed at 114.3 over your purchase price of 113.3. The 0.8% difference doesn't even cover your commission to your broker to buy and sell the shares. Although the risk still stands that other companies could be doing the same thing as Enron, the markets are holding steady as the real fundamentals have stayed constant throughout this period. We will likely see an immense amount of regulation stemming from this scandal. No movement in total returns.

SPY

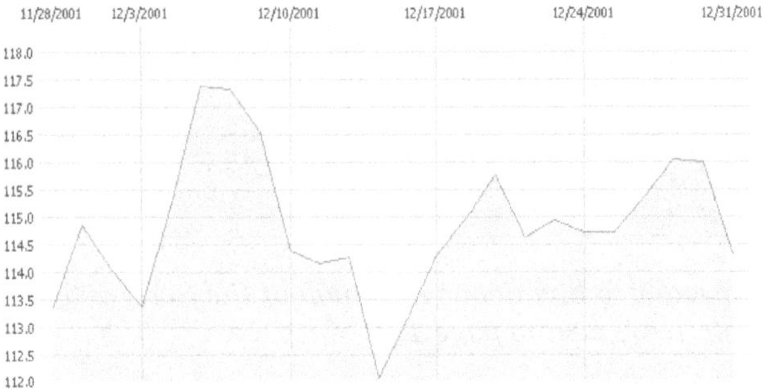

Source: MSN Money

If you would like to do more November trades, turn to page 174.

If you'd rather move onto the next month's set of trading options, turn to page 186.

Enron Scandal Bearish Outcome

You broke even on your investment. There is no change to your portfolio value.

Turns out that the Enron Scandal has had absolutely no effect on the broader markets. Over this past month, there has been a tiny bit of movement on the S&P, but on December 31st, the SPY closed at 114.3 over your selling price of 113.3. The commission cost you more than your 0.8% loss in the market. Although the risk still stands that other companies could be doing the same thing as Enron, the markets are holding steady as the real fundamentals have stayed constant throughout this period. We will likely see an immense amount of regulation stemming from this scandal.

SPY S&P 500

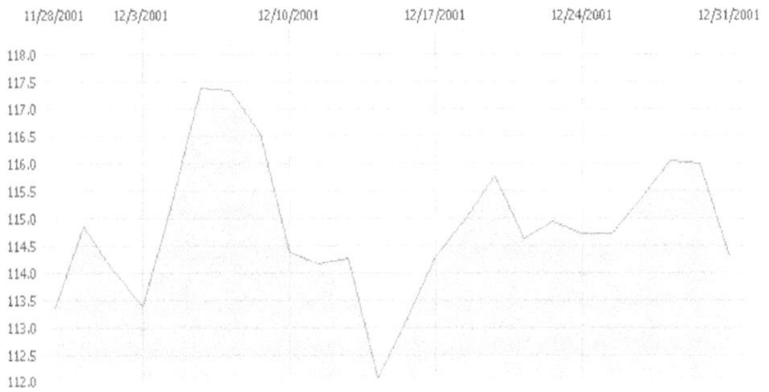

Source: MSN Money

If you would like to do more November trades, turn to page 174.

If you'd rather move onto the next month's set of trading options, turn to page 186.

Start trading December

You pull up a chart of the DJIA, the S&P 500, and the Nasdaq. You remember on that video how your Great Uncle Buster had turned almost angry when he'd talked about how he had barely beaten the major indices last year.

And here you are supposed to be getting 50% in a single year's timeframe.

If you want to trade an oil company just as a big merger is announced, turn to page 187.

If you want to trade a telecom equipment company just as a deregulation act has passed, turn to page 193.

If you've hit $1.5 million and are ready to cash in, turn to page 308.*

*(*PLEASE DO NOT GO TO PAGE 308 IF YOU HAVE NOT HIT $1.5 MILLION).*

Exxon buys Mobil Setup

It's December 1st, 1998, and the champagne corks are flying. Anti-trust legislation be damned, Exxon is buying Mobil for $75.3 billion in stock!! You see your friend's name in the Wall Street Journal as one of the deal makers. You flip through your Rolodex, call him up and inform him that the next time you two get together, the Lagavullin and steaks are on him.

As a student of financial history you know that if the FTC (and Justice Department and about twelve other regulators) allow the merger, it will mean that the Standard Oil of 1911 is practically back together.

You look through the announcement and the numbers are staggeringly huge. Texas-sized. Taken together, Exxon and Mobil pulled down $11.8 billion in profit on $203.1 billion in revenue. By merging and eliminating redundancies, the companies project to save $2.8B a year. You understand how high the stakes are when you see that the deal comes with $1.5 in *fees* and Exxon can buy 15% of Mobil–even if the whole thing falls apart.

Exxon isn't getting Mobil on the cheap though. They are paying a 24% premium and $8/barrel for the Mobil oil that's in the ground. The industry average for sourcing oil is around $5. Oil averaged $11.52 last month and prices are looking like they're heading down through the end of the year, so there isn't much room for error. Plus, the majority of analysts believe that oil prices are going to continue their nearly decade long slump. The average price of a barrel in 1990, the year of the Gulf War, was $23.19; it's declined every year save one over the last eight.

If you are bullish and want to buy about $100,000 of common stock in ExxonMobil and hold it for the whole year, turn to page 189.

If you are bearish and want to short about $100,000 of ExxonMobil common stock for the whole year, turn to page 190.

If you are bullish and want to buy about $50,000 of calls in ExxonMobil for a short-term one month trade, turn to page 191.

If you are bearish and want to buy about $50,000 of puts in ExxonMobil for a short-term one month trade, turn to page 192.

If you would rather find something else to trade this month, turn to page 186.

Exxon buys Mobil Stock Bullish Outcome

Oops, you just lost 2.5% on your investment.

Well it seems that the new stock is not doing much. Over the course of the month, there was a little price action but on the 31st the stock settled down 2.5%. This is one of the biggest companies in the world and will likely continue to generate significant profits in the future. This company will be the largest refiner of crude oil in the world, a title that was once held by parent company Standard Oil.

ExxonMobil

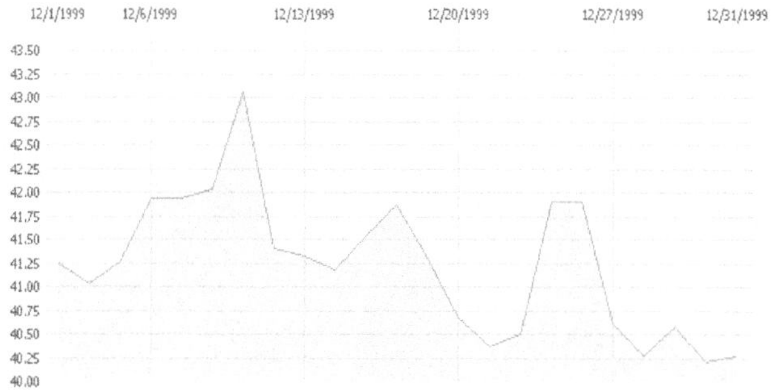

Source: MSN Money

If you would like to do more December trades, turn to page 186.

If you've hit $1.5 million and are ready to cash in, turn to page 308.

If you have exhausted your options and didn't quite make it to the $1.5 million goal, turn to page 309.

Exxon buys Mobil Stock Bearish Outcome

Congratulations, you just made 2.5% on your investment.

Well it seems that the new stock is not doing much. Over the course of the month, there was a little price action but on the 31st the stock settled down 2.5%. This is one of the biggest companies in the world and will likely continue to generate significant profits in the future. This company will be the largest refiner of crude oil in the world, a title that was once held by parent company Standard Oil.

ExxonMobil

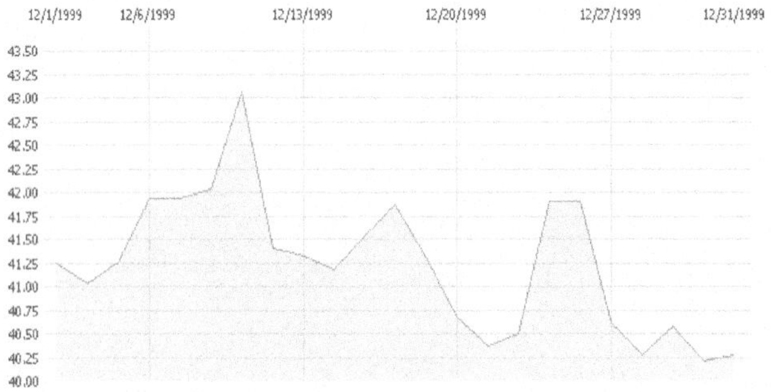

Source: MSN Money

If you would like to do more December trades, turn to page 186.

If you've hit $1.5 million and are ready to cash in, turn to page 308.

If you have exhausted your options and didn't quite make it to the $1.5 million goal, turn to page 309.

Exxon buys Mobile Option Bullish Outcome

Oops, you just lost 2.5% on your investment.

Well it seems that the new stock is not doing much. Over the course of the month, there was a little price action but on the 31st the stock settled down 2.5%. This is one of the biggest companies in the world and will likely continue to generate significant profits in the future. This company will be the largest refiner of crude oil in the world, a title that was once held by parent company Standard Oil.

ExxonMobil

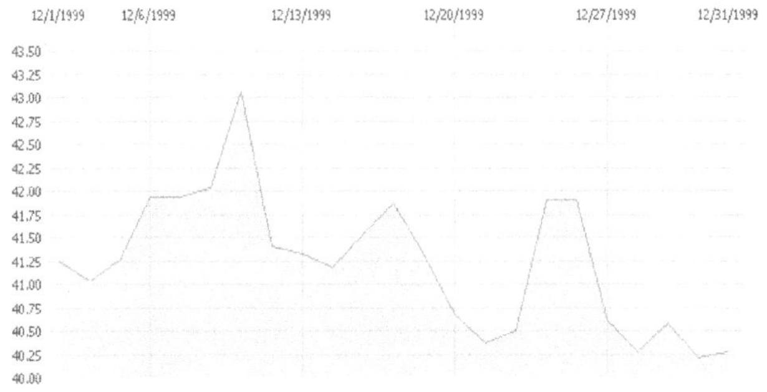

Source: MSN Money

If you would like to do more December trades, turn to page 186.

If you've hit $1.5 million and are ready to cash in, turn to page 308.

If you have exhausted your options and didn't quite make it to the $1.5 million goal, turn to page 309.

Exxon buys Mobil Option Bearish Outcome

Congratulations, you just made 2.5% on your investment.

Well it seems that the new stock is not doing much. Over the course of the month, there was a little price action but on the 31st the stock settled down 2.5%. This is one of the biggest companies in the world and will likely continue to generate significant profits in the future. This company will be the largest refiner of crude oil in the world, a title that was once held by parent company Standard Oil.

ExxonMobil

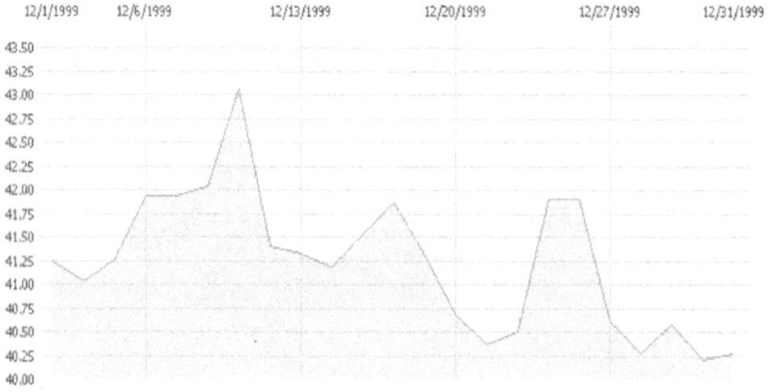

Source: MSN Money

If you would like to do more December trades, turn to page 186.

If you've hit $1.5 million and are ready to cash in, turn to page 308.

If you have exhausted your options and didn't quite make it to the $1.5 million goal, turn to page 309.

Telecommunications Deregulation Act of 1996 Setup

It's December 1st, 1995. Wow–you're almost done with your year of trading! Man, did that go fast. Recently, a bill has gone through congress known as the Telecommunications Deregulation Act. This act will be the first law to modify the Communications Act of 1934. Its purpose is to allow the expansion of entry into the telecom industry by removing regulation that hampers entry into the market. This act will most likely be made law in the next month or so and will obviously change the entire telecom environment. Today, there are only a few large telecom companies that control a majority of the market. Without the immense amount of regulation preventing market entry, this number will likely explode.

One company that stands to benefit is Cisco Systems Inc. As more and more companies are created and enter the telecom market, they will use Cisco's products to expand. Cisco has been doing great with revolutionary products and a management team that doubled revenue in the past year. The stock is already up 140% this year alone, but is only trading at 3.3x this year's earnings! This could be a screaming buy or all hype–you decide. It's the end of the year and you can use aggressive options or simply buy or sell common stock.

Cisco Systems Inc. (NASDAQ:CSCO)

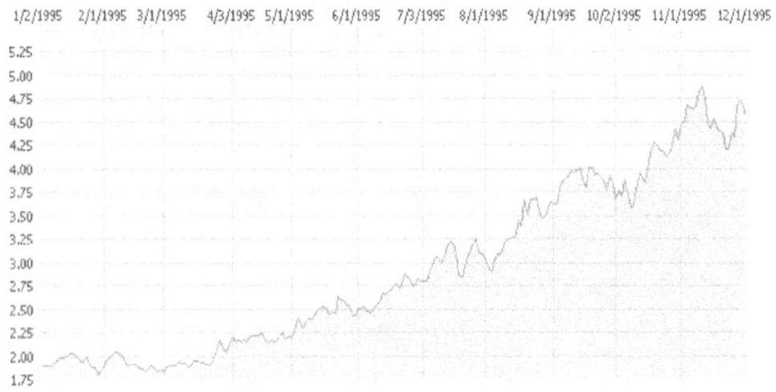

Source: MSN Money

If you are bullish and want to buy about $100,000 of CSCO common stock and hold it for the whole year, *turn to page 195.*

If you are bearish and want to short about $100,000 of CSCO common stock for the whole year, *turn to page 196.*

If you are bullish and want to buy about $50,000 of calls in CSCO for a short-term one month trade, *turn to page 197.*

If you are bearish and want to buy about $50,000 of puts in CSCO for a short-term one month trade, *turn to page 198.*

If you would rather find something else to trade this month, *turn to page 186.*

Telecommunications Deregulation Act of 1996 Stock Bullish Outcome

Can you hear me now? You just lost 9% on on your investment!

The common stock is down a modest 9%, as the broader markets are mostly flat (NASDAQ [-0.3%] and S&P [+0.8%]). This price action may be simply a sell-off as uncertainty grips the telecoms. Cisco is still set to take advantage of massive profits if/when these companies start to expand.

The company continues to grow and expand and this could certainly be a force to reckon with in the future. For now, you have to take a loss on your investment. Lucky for you, your use of common stock has limited your losses compared to if you had used options.

Cisco Systems

Source: MSN Money

If you would like to do more December trades, turn to page 186.

If you've hit $1.5 million and are ready to cash in, turn to page 308.

If you have exhausted your options and didn't quite make it to the $1.5 million goal, turn to page 309.

Telecommunications Deregulation Act of 1996 Stock Bearish Outcome

Can you hear me now? You just made 9% on on your investment!

Cisco common stock is down 9% while the broader markets have been flat in the last month of the year. The returns are mixed among telecoms in reaction to the act. Alcatel-Lucent and Verizon are both up while Sprint Nextel is down.

There appears to be a bit of uncertainty driving these telecoms. This action is strange as all telecom stocks are trading at mixed levels of volumes as well. It may be fair to say that you lucked out shorting this stock because there is about a 50% chance that this news could have sent the stock higher as it did with other telecoms.

Cisco Systems

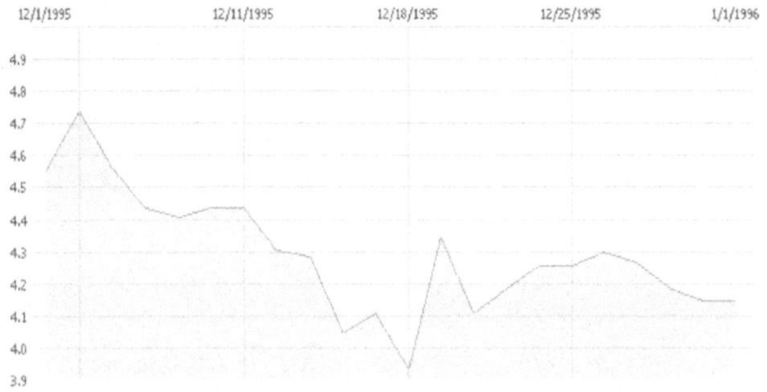

Source: MSN Money

If you would like to do more December trades, turn to page 186.

If you've hit $1.5 million and are ready to cash in, turn to page 308.

If you have exhausted your options and didn't quite make it to the $1.5 million goal, turn to page 309.

Telecommunications Deregulation Act of 1996 Option Bullish Outcome

That's not your phone ringing, that's the bell inside your head ringing from the 9% hit you just took on that trade!

The common stock is down a modest 9%, as the broader markets are mostly flat (NASDAQ [-0.3%] and S&P [+0.8%]). This price action may be simply a sell-off as uncertainty grips the telecoms. Cisco is still set to take advantage of massive profits if/when these companies start to expand.

The company continues to grow and expand and this could certainly be a force to reckon with in the future. For now, you have to take a loss on your investment. Your use of options has increased your loss rather than if you had simply used common stock.

Cisco Systems

Source: MSN Money

If you would like to do more December trades, turn to page 186.

If you've hit $1.5 million and are ready to cash in, turn to page 308.

If you have exhausted your options and didn't quite make it to the $1.5 million goal, turn to page 309.

Telecommunications Deregulation Act of 1996 Option Bearish Outcome

That's not your phone ringing, that's your head ringing from the 9% profits you just made on that trade!

Cisco common stock is down 9% while the broader markets have been flat in the last month of the year. The returns are mixed among telecoms in reaction to the act. Alcatel-Lucent and Verizon are both up while Sprint Nextel is down.

There appears to be a bit of uncertainty driving these telecoms. This action is strange as all telecom stocks are trading at mixed levels of volumes as well. It may be fair to say that you lucked out shorting this stock because there is about a 50% chance that this news could have sent the stock higher as it did with other telecoms. Your use of put options has further increased your returns on this short term trade.

Cisco Systems

Source: MSN Money

If you would like to do more December trades, turn to page 186.

If you've hit $1.5 million and are ready to cash in, turn to page 308.

If you have exhausted your options and didn't quite make it to the $1.5 million goal, turn to page 309.

Five million buckaroos

You'd rather just take the $5 million and call it quits.

Sir Topdollar asks you, "But what are you going to do with that $5 million? Are you going to invest in stock anyway? You want to put it in your mattress?

"Ha," you say to this guy you sure are starting to like an awful lot for having just met over the phone, "That'd better be a big mattress."

Sir Topdollar gets serious again, and he continues, "Your Great Uncle Buster gave you four options in his will for how to take the $5 million lump sum. You can come to my office in NYC and get a titanium briefcase filled with $100 bills totaling the $5 million. Or you can have them wire the $5 million directly to your personal account at your personal bank, Paladonia Credit Union or to your long-term stock investment account. Or you can have the prestigious firm of Goldwoman Saggs manage your money for you. They are the global leaders in investment banking, securitization and money management and I highly recommend their services."

If you want to take the $5 million home with you in a titanium briefcase, turn to page 200..

If you want to have them wire the $5 million to your bank, turn to page 208.

If you want to let this firm that Sir Topdollar is talking about, Goldwoman Saggs, manage your money for you, turn to page 209.

If you want to have them wire the $5 million to your long-term investment account, turn to page 214.

You sure you want that?

"I'll take a briefcase full of cash, please. I'll be on the next train into the city," you say into your smartphone.

"Are you sure you want to do that?" Sir Topdollar asks you, "That's an awfully big risk and I thought your Great Uncle Buster was just kidding when he included that offer in there. What would you do with $5 million in cash in a briefcase anyway? Isn't that awfully dangerous?

"Listen, the guys at Goldwoman Saggs are the best. I mean, it's very hard to even get them to consider an account as small as $5 million, but they're making an exception for you because they were such fans of your Uncle Buster."

If you want to take the $5 million home with you in a titanium briefcase, turn to page 201.

If you want to let Goldwoman Saggs manage your money for you, turn to page 209.

Picking up the cash

"Yes, I'm sure. I want the cash in a briefcase," you repeat, wondering suddenly why this guy's so insistent on you giving your newfound fortune over to this firm. I bet Sir Topdollar gets a top dollar kick back if I place that money with that firm.

"I assume you've got the briefcase ready, even if you thought this option was a joke."

"Yes, and we'll send a car service out to get you right now. I'll be here personally the rest of the day working on finalizing the other details of Buster's will." He's not calling him "Your Great Uncle Buster" anymore, is he?

The black town car of the latest year's model with all the best features driven by the overly-friendly and talkative driver drops you at the front steps of a high rise that houses Topdollar, Grant and Gold's headquarters. There's a twenty-four hour doorman at the front door who greets you with a suspicious eye. Or is there something more sinister behind that look, you think to yourself for a moment.

You say to him, "I'm here to see Sir Topdollar." After signing in, you head up to the 67th floor and are greeted by Sir Topdollar himself holding open a twelve foot mahogany door to let you into the back entrance of the floor.

In an exquisitely decorated office with an incredible view overlooking the Hudson, you make short shrift of the small talk with this guy you no longer quite trust and he gives you the briefcase full of more cash in one spot than you've ever seen in your life.

"The car service is downstairs waiting to take you back home," Sir Topdollar informs you.

And suddenly you wondering about that driver who was so darn nice to you the whole way into the city and you're also thinking back to that look you exchanged with the doorman downstairs. Do those guys know how much one you're walking out of here with? Is there some conspiracy going on to get this money? Could Sir Topdollar be a part of it?

You could catch a cab to get home. Though it might take awhile to get one while you're standing on the street on this chilly holiday weekend. Or you could just walk to the subway and catch a train back home. But what is the safest way to transport $5 million in cash?

If you want to take the car service home, turn to page 203.

If you want to try to catch a cab to take home, turn to page 210.

If you want to take the train, turn to page 212.

The ride out of the city

You have a death grip on the briefcase in your right hand as you walk briskly past the doorman's station and you're not sure whether you're relieved or freaked out when you see the car driver jump out of his car upon having seen you coming out the elevator. But you breath just a little bit easier when you realize he was simply hopping out to open the back door of his sedan for you.

You get into the car and the driver adjusts his mirror so that you're clearly in his view and he makes eye contact with you rather than with the busy avenue traffic as he strikes up another conversation.

The guy hasn't stopped talking since you got in the car, and he sure makes you nervous with these stories about his friend's Russian restaurant in the Brighton Beach area of Brooklyn that he says is the hottest place in the city. You know from experience that the Russian mafia runs most of the big Russian clubs in Brighton.

You notice the beads of sweat on your forehead turn cool when he rolls his window down to pay the toll booth operator in cash and the sweating accelerates as you wonder why he wouldn't have an E-Z pass if he drives a sedan around the city and its surrounding areas for a living. You could hop out of the car right here, right now and ask the cops who you see all around the toll booth area on foot and car patrol to take you the rest of the way home. But how would you explain such a strange request on a holiday weekend with $5 million in cash in fancy briefcase?

If you want to stay in the sedan and continue with this driver, turn to page 204.

If you want to hop out with your briefcase and try to get the police to take you the rest of the way home, turn to page 206.

Getting home and losing it all anyway

The driver presses on the gas as he presses on the button to roll his window back. Your shirt is drenched in the sweat as the dry heat from the sedan's vents and the heated leather seat beneath combine with your increasing tenseness. The driver slows as he approaches an off ramp and you sharply interrupt him when he turns on the blinker to take the off ramp, "Where the heck are you taking me?" you ask him in a terse tone.

"Oh, oh, sorry, one of my regular rides lives back there. I just was enjoying our conversation so much that I almost turned out of habit. Now what was I saying?"

He gets back to his conversation about the night club and your heart beat resumes at least a slightly more normal pace. He's talking about a woman he met from Slovenia at yet another Russian dance club in Brighton when you see two sedans of what seem to be identical year, make and model as the one you're in speed past you on both sides of the three lane highway.

The one in the far left lane makes a sudden move to its right and your driver slams on his breaks, and the briefcase flies out of your hand and flies past the driver's head and slams into the dashboard radio.

You're sure that you've just lost your entire newfound fortune to a group of Russian drivers who must also be in the Russian Mob as you see the driver reach over and grab the handle of the $5 million briefcase. You wonder if you'll get to live to see tomorrow at all. And what of that Sir Topdollar, is he in on this from the beginning? Did he set all of this up?

The driver hands the briefcase back to you and before you even realize that those other sedans are nowhere in sight — a coincidence after all — and you're turning onto the exit that takes you home. Five minutes later, you're back in your wool socks staring at an open briefcase containing five million more bucks than you had this morning. Not a bad's day work. And why didn't you have a little faith in Sir Topdollar and the driver he hired anyway?

The next night, you hear something moving in your living room. You see a shadow running out the back door and you realize you've seen that person a thousand times in your house — your housekeeper has stolen your briefcase with the $5 million in cash. There's no sign of forced entry and you know it's true.

Why hadn't you just wired it to your bank account in the first place and started your dream business?

To start a new Stock Market Events That Mattered (Or Did They?) game, turn to page 1.

Losing a lot to the system

You grab the door handle and try to open it, only to realize it's locked. So you fumble with the fancy electronic doorlock, until you hear it click and the handle gives way to your pull.

You streak by the shocked toll booth operator dealing with a car full of teenagers who are collecting enough coins to get through the gate and a cop behind him asks if you are okay. The car driver is already out of his car which remains parked and running and he walks over to you and the cop with his hands flailing in emotion.

"What's wrong, sir?" asks the cop as the car driver steps up to both of you.

"This car driver is making me feel uncomfortable and I wonder if you can give me a ride the rest of the way to my house." After much back and forth with the now obviously perplexed and seemingly innocent after all car driver who has been instructed to return to his car and be on his way, the cop tells you that he'd be happy to call you another cab.

The cop's eyes follow yours down to your briefcase and you reflexively put your other hand on it which makes the cop raise his eyebrows in suspicion and you really regret having sent that nice car driver with the club owner friends on his way. "Is there another cop who could take me?" You ask awkwardly and the cop's expression turns from still somewhat helpful to outright confrontational.

"What's in the briefcase?" the cop now demands. You get his name off his badge as he is now in your face and you realize you're in for a long trek getting this $5 million from here to your house now.

Eight months and seventeen days later, you are at your new attorney's, Sir Topdollar's, office, and he's asking you how you'd like to take possession of your $2.1 million fortune, that which is left after taxes, court and attorney fees that it took to get your $5 million in cash from your briefcase back from the system after you'd gotten arrested on drug trafficking, money laundering and a host of other charges in your paranoid episode at the E-Z Path booth on the ride home from Sir TopDollar's offices eight months and seventeen days ago.

Sir Topdollar gets that same serious look on his face that he had last time, and he says, "Would you like the $2.1 million wired directly to your personal account at your personal bank, Paladonia Credit Union? Or would you, as I've suggested to you from the beginning, would you rather have prestigious firm of Goldwoman Saggs manage your money for you. They are the global leaders in investment banking, securitization and money management and I highly recommend their services."

If you want to have them wire the $2.1 million to your bank, turn to page 208.

If you want to let this firm that Sir Topdollar keeps talking about, Goldwoman Saggs, manage your money for you, turn to page 209.

Your dream business

"Okay, well, no problem then. You should see the money hit your bank account before noon on Monday," Sir Topdollar sighs into the phone with obvious disappointment. You again wonder just how much kickback he was going to get from Goldwoman Saggs.

And sure enough, when you check your bank account balance online Monday during lunch, you feel a rush inside your gut as it has seven full digits behind in it. In your personal bank account.

Six weeks later, your new business is in full out launch mode and you've barely used 1/10 of that inheritance. Six months later, you've turned down multiple seven digit offers for your business even as you've had to use almost a 1/3 of that nut you started with. Sales are doubling month over month though, and you're willing to risk your inheritance from dear Great Uncle Buster's to pursue your dream.

Six years later, you top $100 million in sales and you're looking at several offers of almost a billion dollars for your dream business. But you love what you're doing and you're making more money than you ever dreamed possible. So why would you quit?

To start a new Stock Market Events That Mattered (Or Did They?) game, turn to page 1.

Screwed by GS

"I think letting the fine folks at Goldwoman Saggs manage your money for you is a great idea. I'll make a few calls today and open you an actively managed account at their shop and take care of all the details for you. I'll be back in a few days and there will be a few papers to sign, but don't worry. The normally have a $10 million account minimum, but since they took more than one of your Great Uncle Buster's tech companies public over the years, they're making an exception for you. We'll take care of everything for you from here on out."

You shake hands feeling relieved that somebody else will take care of all your money, and what a miracle to have this kind of small fortune left to you by a Great Uncle Buster you never even knew that you had.

Three years later, you're out $300,000 in attorney fees as you've sued Sir TopDollar, his entire firm, your so-called money managers at Goldwoman Saggs as well as that entire firm, but in the final arbitration hearing that at the kangaroo arbitration court that you were forced to use via an agreement on every one of those contracts you ever signed with these folks, you lose any chance of retribution as the verdict comes against. In fact, you end up in bankruptcy just two years later as you had overleveraged yourself with a variety of failed angel, real estate and stock market investments thinking that you had that multi-million dollar cushion over at Goldwoman Saggs. Little did you know that Sir TopDollar got a 25% kickback on the 3/30% payout agreement you'd had with GS. And while your brokers took out their quarterly payouts from your account every quarter that it ever went up at all, they eventually had all your money in CDOs, RMBS, and other toxic real estate securities and their derivatives in a spider web mess of conflicts of interest. You took suit against GS when they had the gall to send you a final amount due on some latent money management fees from your account. What a mess.

You should have took the money and started your dream business instead.

To start a new Stock Market Events That Mattered (Or Did They?) game, turn to page 1.

Hailing a taxi can be hell

You decide not to raise suspicion in Sir TopDollar by telling him your plan, so you simply say, "Okay, sounds good," and you take the briefcase from him and head to the elevator.

You get in the elevator and push the button for the 2nd floor, figuring that you'll get out on the 2nd floor and find some stairs and go out the backside so the driver waiting for you won't see you. Just in case it really is a conspiracy, you don't want the driver or the doorman to see you on your way out.

At the second floor, you get out and you're surprised to see that there's an open door at the long end of the hallway of this giant midtown highrise that runs for an entire block. You exit out the door past another set of doormen who don't raise their eyes from the Knicks game in front of them and you're onto the avenue a full two blocks drive away from the car and the driver who might have Russian Mob friends and the suspicious doorman waiting for you to leave.

The bad news is that you can't find a taxi with his light on top in service anywhere. So you start walking north and the bitter cold wind starts biting into your bare hand holding the briefcase. Twenty minutes later you're still looking for a cab when you see the sedan that brought you into the city turning onto the block that you're walking up. You wonder if he's looking for you now.

Your hands are numb so you step into a coffee shop to warm up, get off the street, and essentially hide from that driver in case he is looking for you and that money in the briefcase grasped tightly by your freezing fingers. You set the briefcase down to get your wallet out and pay.

You pick the briefcase back up, hardly thinking of just how valuable that money inside really is and sit down at a single empty seat at a small table. You're blowing on your cupped hands in front of you and are happy that you've got some feeling coming back into them and that you're about to be holding a warm cup of java when the barista calls your name. You go to pick up your order and stop to grab a napkin. The lid on your cup isn't on quite right and you stop to use the counter as leverage to get it back on.

By the time you get back to your table, it's happened. Somebody stole your whole briefcase with the $5 million in cash.

Why hadn't you just wired it to your bank account in the first place and started your dream business?

To start a new Stock Market Events That Mattered (Or Did They?) game, turn to page 1.

Subway blues

You decide not to raise suspicion in Sir TopDollar by telling him your plan, so you simply say, "Okay, sounds good," and you take the briefcase from him and head to the elevator.

You get in the elevator and push the button for the 2nd floor, figuring that you'll get out on the 2nd floor and find some stairs and go out the backside so the driver waiting for you won't see you. Just in case it really is a conspiracy, you don't want the driver or the doorman to see you on your way out.

At the second floor, you get out and you're surprised to see that there's an open door at the long end of the hallway of this giant midtown highrise that runs for an entire block. You exit out the door past another set of doormen who don't raise their eyes from the Knicks game in front of them and you're onto the avenue a full two blocks drive away from the car and the driver who might have Russian Mob friends and the suspicious doorman waiting for you to leave.

The bad news is that the subway station here is closed because the train is being re-routed this weekend while they do service on the track line. Typical New York City, closing down a subway system on a crazy busy weekend like this and you know its either a terrorist prevention measure or incompetence by city planners or a litle bit of both. Whatever the case, you're now stuck with a $5 million briefcase in the freezing wind in the middle of NYC without a train to get you home on the down low.

So you start walking north looking for a cab or an open subway station while the bitter cold wind starts biting into your bare hand holding the briefcase. Twenty minutes later you're still looking for a cab when you see the sedan that brought you

into the city turning onto the block that you're walking up. You wonder if he's looking for you now.

Your hands are numb so you step into a coffee shop to warm up, get off the street, and essentially hide from that driver in case he is looking for you and that money in the briefcase grasped tightly by your freezing fingers. You set the briefcase down to get your wallet out and pay.

You pick the briefcase back up, hardly thinking of just how valuable that money inside really is and sit down at a single empty seat at a small table. You're blowing on your cupped hands in front of you and are happy that you've got some feeling coming back into them and that you're about to be holding a warm cup of java when the barista calls your name. You go to pick up your order and stop to grab a napkin. The lid on your cup isn't on quite right and you stop to use the counter as leverage to get it back on.

By the time you get back to your table, it's happened. Somebody stole your whole briefcase with the $5 million in cash.

Why hadn't you just wired it to your bank account in the first place and started your dream business?

To start a new Stock Market Events That Mattered (Or Did They?) game, turn to page 1.

Your Buy-And-Hold-Forever Investment Approach

You have the opportunity to go back in time to some of the most famous stock market events in history and decide if you'd like to invest a small amount of your $5 million in each opportunity. You are a long-term, true buy-and-hold-forever investor and you're about to work your way through 30 investment opportunities.

But be careful, you might think you know how easy it is to go back in time and buy the best stocks at the right time, but there are plenty of pitfalls and losses in these investment opportunities and you don't want to lose your money by buying a stock that drops 90%.

To check out the first long-term investment opportunity, turn to page 215.

Chrysler Bailout 1979 Long-Term Investment Setup

Today is September 7, 1979. Today the CEO of Chrysler ,Lee Iacocca, asked congress for $1.5 billion in loan guarantees to keep the company from filing bankruptcy. The company is struggling with foreign competition and there is little demand for it's current lineup of vehicles.

This is a bold request by a private company however it is not the first time the government has bailed out a corporation. In 1970, the government did it's first corporate bailout in history when it gave Penn Central Railroad $676 million in loan guarantees. Again in 1971 and 1974 the federal government bailed out Lockheed and Franklin National Bank with loan guarantees of $1.4 billion and $1.75 billion respectively.

Regardless, this is a sign that the Auto Industry may be struggling. Ford Motor Company is the second of the three major auto makers based in the United States. Could this possibly mean that Ford is in the same shape as Chrysler. On the other hand, this could be a great opportunity for Ford. They could in fact be beating Chrysler in the Auto Market and this could be a sign of Ford's strength. The decision is up to you. How will this affect Ford?

Ford Motor Company (F)

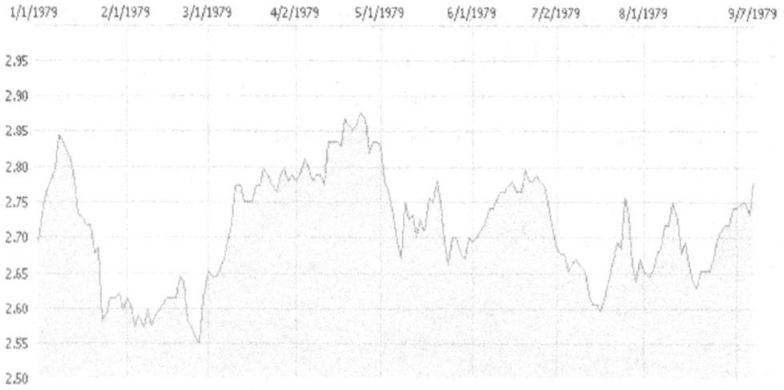

Source: MSN Money

If you want to invest about $500,000 in Ford forever, turn to page 217.

If you'd like to move onto the next invest opportunity, turn to page 218.

If you'd like to retire, turn to page 309.

Chrysler Bailout 1979 Long-Term Investment Outcome

Congratulations, you just made a 230% return on your long term investment!

Through the years, Ford has proven to be a good investment. They continue to produce cars that consumers want.

Today Ford is the fifth largest automaker in the world with revenues of $130 billion. Ford never received any form of bailout during the 1970's but in 2008, the entire auto industry received a $25 billion bailout to stimulate sales. The government has always kept the auto industry under it's wing and Ford has done well since you bought it.

Ford since Chrysler Bailout

Source: MSN Money

If you are ready to go on to the next investing opportunity, turn to page 218.

If you would rather skip to retire now, turn to page 309.

New Coke Long-Term Investment Setup

Today is April 19, 1985 and the Coca-Cola Corporation (KO) has announced that the classic coke formula will be replaced by a new, sweeter formula.

This announcement comes as a response to the loss of market share experienced by Coca-Cola to Pepsi. Many drinkers prefer Pepsi due to the fact that it has a sweeter taste. Coca-Cola has been working on the project for several months and they have a big marketing and sales plan ready to go. Coke has lost major ground in the area of supermarket sales and today only has 24% of the total market share for carbonated drinks. Coke is still the leader at fast-food restaurants as well as in vending machine sells.

Coca-Cola stock is up nicely over the past year and appears to be on a steady climb. Pepsi has long been the leader in soft drinks and this new formula could possibly give Coke the chance to challenge that. Although there is the possibility that traditional Coke drinkers will stop buying the product if they do not like the new formula.

This could be a great long-term investment. The economy is in a steady rate of growth and everything seems to be going well after the recession of 1980. Coke will likely be around for plenty of years to come and this could be a great entry point for the stock.

Coca-Cola (KO)

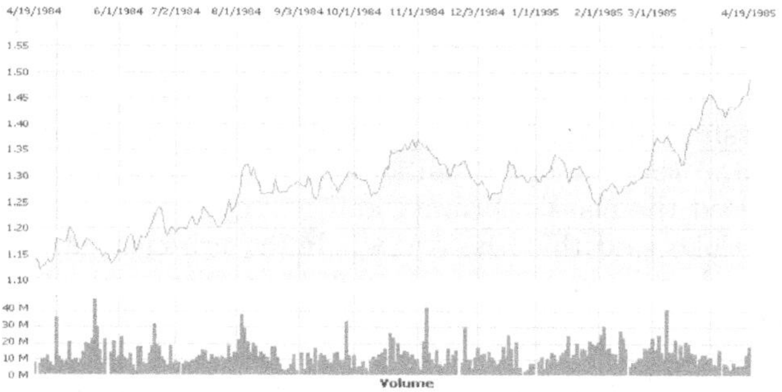

Source: MSN Money

If you want to invest about $500,000 in KO forever, turn to page 220.

If you'd like to move onto the next invest opportunity, turn to page 221.

If you'd like to retire, turn to page 309.

New Coke Long-Term Investment Outcome

Congratulations, you just made a 2,600% return!

Today, Coca-Cola is the number one selling soft drink in the world. The company has consistently grown revenue and profit and continues to see good growth moving forward. The company currently sells over 50 brands of drinks around the world including Coke, Minute Maid, Fanta, Dasani, and Dr. Pepper (Europe).

It is the most successful beverage company in the world with a market cap of $173 billion and revenue of $80 billion a year. In July of 1988, Coco-Cola reintroduced the classic formula and it has remained ever since. The guys at Coke said that the overwhelming criticism of the new formula caused them to remove the brand. Since then, coke has been very successful.

They have exhibited one of the most successful and popular advertising campaigns in corporate history and today the Coca-Cola brand is known world wide. This has been a great investment and has paid off big time with the common stock up 2600% since you bought it.

Coca-Cola since New Coke launch

Source: MSN Money

If you are ready to go on to the next investing opportunity, turn to page 221.

If you would rather skip to retire now, turn to page 309.

Air Jordan Long-Term Investment Setup

Today is October 18, 1985. Today Nike launched a new brand of Basketball shoes known as Air Jordan's. They are riding on the brand of Star Basketball player Michael Jordan. Nike has not launched extensive advertising quite yet buy it is rumored that Michael Jordan will be wearing them in the game. They are pretty cool shoes and this could be a great product line for the corporation.

This stock has fallen this year as the company's net income has fallen 75% due to decreasing margins. The company's top line continues to grow but unless the issues with margins are handled, this company could continue to lose money. The stock is only trading at 3 times this year's earnings and has a serious possibility for increasing net income. The stock also has a nice dividend that comes with it. If Nike can successfully launch this new brand, it could be a breakthrough moment for the stock.

Nike Inc. (NYSE: NKE)

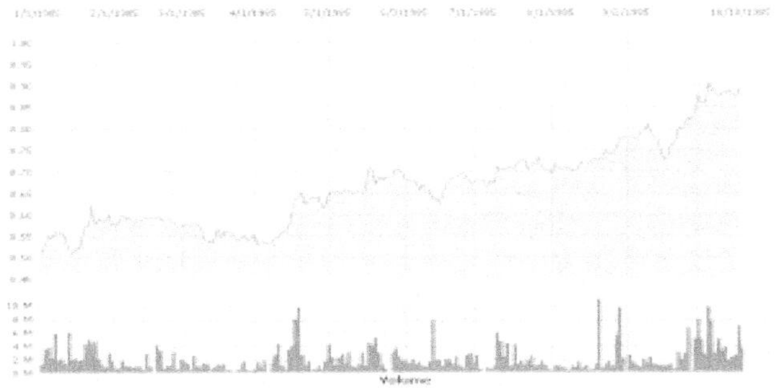

Source: MSN Money

If you want to invest about $500,000 in NKE forever, turn to page 222.

If you'd like to move onto the next invest opportunity, turn to page 223.

If you'd like to retire, turn to page 309.

Air Jordan Long-Term Investment Outcome

Congratulations, you just made a 9,400% return on your investment!

Nike has turned into the most successful and widely known sports apparel manufacture since you invested in the company back in 1995. Although it took some time, the Air Jordan brand is perhaps the companies most successful venture. Today, Air Jordan's along with other Nike shoes can be found in almost every shoe store you visit.

The Nike brand is extremely valuable and the company has crushed competitors like Adidas. Since the rollout of the Air Jordans, Nike has continued to grow, introducing more extremely successful brands like Converse and Hurley. Nike along with it's brands currently maintain over 50% of the shoe market share with Adidas coming in at around 20%. This has been a great investment and you are proud to say that you own such a successful and popular company.

Nike, Inc. since Air Jordan rollout

Source: MSN Money

If you are ready to go on to the next investing opportunity, turn to page 223.

If you would rather skip to retire now, turn to page 309.

Election of Bill Clinton as 42nd President of the United States Long-Term Investment Setup

Last night was pretty dramatic. Today is November 4, 1992 and last night the news declared that Governor Bill Clinton would be the next president of the United States. Incumbent George Bush was beaten by a 10% margin with third party candidate Ross Perot picking up 29% of the vote. Some major issues linger on the horizon as Bill Clinton talks of separating the gap between the rich and the poor. The new president also has plans of balancing the budget and ending the federal deficit. Taxes are going to be raised on upper income individuals as major changes are made to the federal outlays. Defense will surely take the brunt of the budget cuts as left-wing democrat Bill Clinton ends the era of military expansion seen under the Reagan-Bush Administrations.

Companies like Boeing, Lockheed Martin, and General Dynamics have raked in the dough as the United States geared up for war with the Soviet Union. With that threat no longer present, the Clinton Administration will most likely cut defense spending to achieve the goal of a balanced budget. This could be a great opportunity to short the companies that have profited so long from our huge defense spending. Boeing is down 40% from the beginning of the year and this could be the crushing blow to the stock.

On the other hand, the company also has a large market for commercial airliners it makes and it could be enough to keep the company going. Another thing to remember is that in the world of politics, nothing is set in stone and there is always the possibility of another war. The Middle East is a tinderbox waiting to be lit as tension remains high with Israel among Islamic nations in the region. Trading at around 15 times earnings, this company could be a buy as the stock has been crushed lately.

Boeing Co.

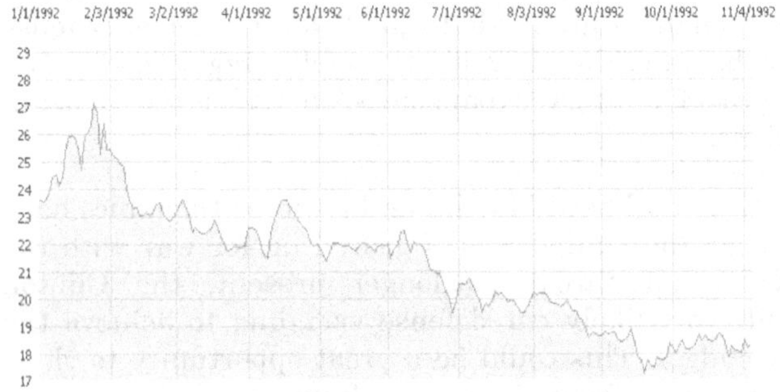

Source: MSN Money

If you want to invest about $500,000 in BA forever, turn to page 225.

If you'd like to move onto the next invest opportunity, turn to page 226.

If you'd like to retire, turn to page 309.

Election of Bill Clinton as 42nd President of the United States Long-Term Investment Outcome

Congratulations, you just made a 250% return on your long term investment!

The stock fell hard the month after the election as uncertainty gripped the market. This stock did not like this election. Everyone was uncertain what this new president would bring to the table and the new direction of the federal government and defense spending. As it turns out, Boeing was a great investment through the years and Clinton's election was an exceptional buying opportunity. You've made a 250% return on your investment.

Boeing Co. Today

Source: MSN Money

To continue onto the next investment opportunity, turn to page 226.

If you would like to skip to retire now, turn to page 309.

Netscape IPO Long-Term Investment Setup

It's August 9,1995. A lot of new technology is starting to change the way that we live our lives. Mobile Phones allow us to instantly contact each other and along with the internet and email, communication has increased to a new level. One of the companies that is helping to expand on the capabilities of the internet is Netscape. Ninety percent of web users are using the Netscape internet browsers and now the company is coming public.

The stock came public today and their was so much demand for the stock that the NYSE had to stop trading by request of one of the underwriters (Morgan Stanley). When trading began, the stock skyrocketed to $75, more than 2.5x the IPO price of $28. It's later in the day now and the stock has sold off to $50. Is this a great buying opportunity? This company is changing the way we use computers. Maybe common stock is the way to go. The stock is now trading at 126 times it's earnings. Maybe it is all hype. Microsoft will soon be releasing their own browser called "Internet Explorer" and it could pose a serious threat to Netscape's Navigator Browser.

This company is made of innovators and may be a leader in the technology sector for years to come. This could be a solid investment and no one knows just how high these internet stocks might be going.

If you want to invest about $500,000 in Netscape forever, turn to page 227.

If you'd like to move onto the next invest opportunity, turn to page 229.

If you'd like to retire, turn to page 309.

Netscape IPO Long-Term Investment Outcome

Congratulations, you just made a 450% return on your investment!

Today is March 17, 1999 and a deal between Netscape and AOL closed today for an acquisition of $10 billion. You bought the company when it was worth $2.2 billion. The acquisition was a stock for stock transfer and you were given AOL stock which you immediately sold.

Since you bought Netscape, the internet and everything having to do with it has really taken off. Stock in Companies with no revenue, much less profit, are touching the skies.

Netscape has made the internet more accessible through it's browsers and continues to innovate in new ways. As a part of AOL, the company will continue to make browsers and expand on the AOL platform. You have made out like a bandit on this trade.

Netscape Communications

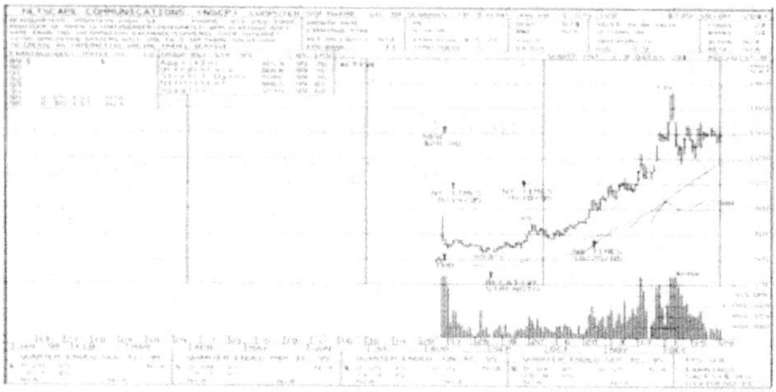

Source: Bloomberg

Nasdaq 1995-1999

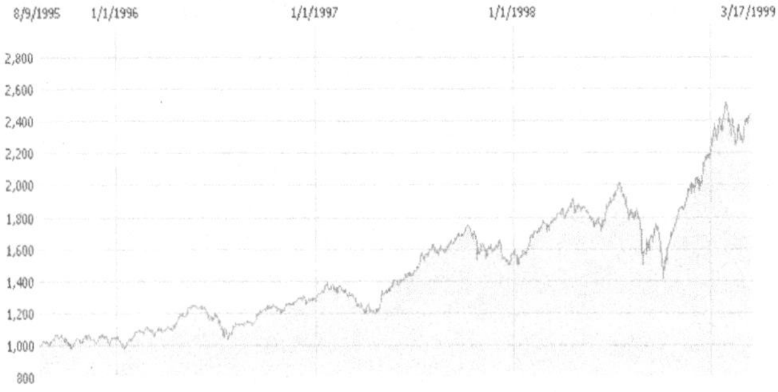

Source: MSN Money

To continue on to the next investing opportunity, turn to page 229.

If you would like to skip to retire now, turn to page 309.

Telecommunications Deregulation Act of 1996 Long-Term Investment Setup

It's late 1996, and a bill is going through congress known as the Telecommunications Deregulation Act. This act will be the first law to modify the Communications Act of 1934. Its purpose is to allow the expansion of entry into the Telecom Industry by removing regulation that hampers entry into the market. This Act will most likely be made law in the next month or so and will obviously change the entire telecom environment. Today, there are only a few large telecom companies that control majority of the market. Without the immense amount of regulation preventing market entry, this number will likely explode.

One company that stands to benefit is Cisco Systems Inc. As more and more companies are created and enter the Telecom market, they will use Cisco's products to expand. Cisco has been doing great with revolutionary products and a management team that doubled revenue in the past year. The stock is already up 140% this year alone but is only trading at 3.3x this year's earnings! This could be a screaming buy or all hype, you decide. Cisco seems to have great revolutionary management and will probably continue to be a leader in the internet sector for many years to come.

Today could be a good entry point into this company as it seems that the internet sector is really taking off.

Cisco Systems Inc. (NASDAQ:CSCO)

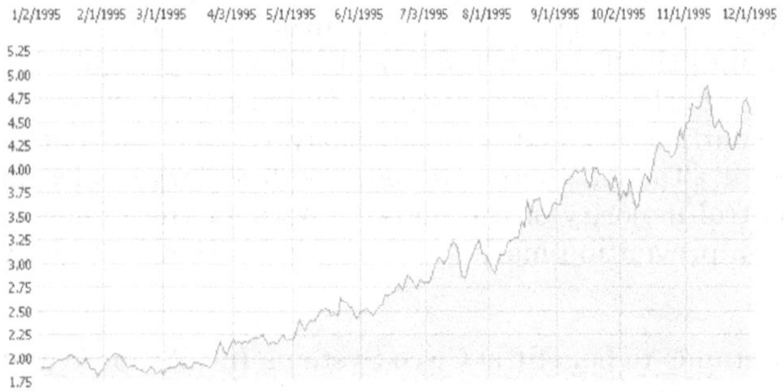

Source: MSN Money

If you want to invest about $500,000 in CSCO forever, turn to page 231.

If you'd like to move onto the next invest opportunity, turn to page 232.

If you'd like to retire, turn to page 309.

Telecommunications Deregulation Act of 1996 Long-Term Investment Outcome

Ring that bell, baby, you made 344% on this investment.

Today Cisco Systems remains the leader in networking. As the internet took hold of our world, Cisco was their all along the way to help make it happen. Cisco's routers, switches, servers, and other networking products helped transform the world. Today if your 8 year old son asked, "Who makes the internet", your answer could simply be, Cisco. During the internet bubble of 1999-2000, Cisco stock skyrocketed. Cisco stock reached an all time high of $82 on March 27, 2000.

At that point your stock with a split adjusted purchase price of $4.50 was up a remarkable 1722%. These remarkable gains were soon wiped away by the bursting of the internet bubble. Today the stock trades close to $20 and you still have gains of around 344%.

Cisco faces competition from companies like Juniper Networks and Alcatel-Lucent. The internet continues to grow and Cisco has remained a profitable company for many years. This has been a good investment and you have really beaten the markets on the this one.

Cisco Systems since Telecommunications Deregulation Act of 1996

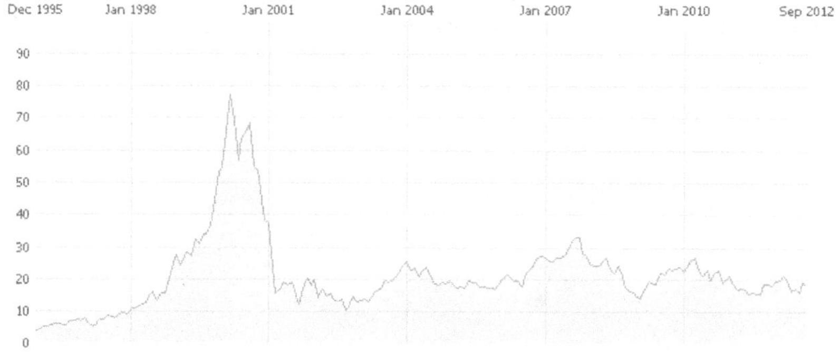

Source: MSN Money

To continue on to the next investment opportunity, turn to page 232.

If you want to skip to retire now, turn to page 309.

Return of Steve Jobs Long-Term Investment Setup

It's July 9, 1997. Apple Computers announced today that founder and former CEO Steve Jobs is going to replace current CEO Gil Amelio. The struggling company has lost some of its momentum and this visionary may just be what the company needs. Since he left Apple, Jobs has been very successful with his ventures at Pixar and NeXT Computers.

The tech industry is booming. Personal Computers are now cheaper and more powerful than ever. The internet is really starting to take off and it seems that any stock having to do anything with the internet is going sky high. If Steve Jobs can capitalize on this, then maybe this could be the comeback story of the century. Then again, Apple is not even in the top five computer makers by market share. Apple faces serious competition from other computer makers like Compaq, IBM, and Hewlett-Packard. Also, Steve Jobs is known to be a sporadic and harsh manager.

Apple has been crushed badly lately. The company struggles in the computer business as it continues to lose what little market share it had to begin with. The computer companies that are making all of the money right now are all business centered. Apple has continued to fall even as this internet bubble continues to take off. In many people's mind, Apple's future is doomed. The company will truly have to come out with some revolutionary software or product in order to get back up on top.

You must also not forget that it has been 13 years since Steve Jobs left Apple. The reason that Apple is struggling could be simply due to the fact that Steve Jobs hasn't been running it. With Jobs back on board, Apple might be reignited.

Apple Inc.

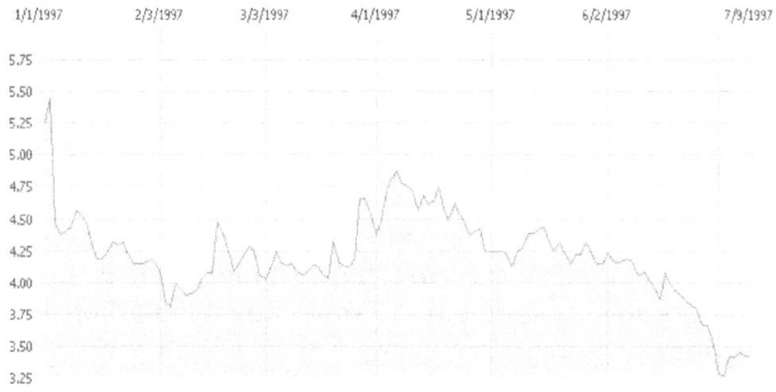

Source: MSN Money

If you want to invest about $500,000 in AAPL forever, turn to page 234.

If you'd like to move onto the next invest opportunity, turn to page 236.

If you'd like to retire, turn to page 309.

Return of Steve Jobs Long-Term Investment Outcome

Congratulations, you just made a 15,000% return on your investment!

Wow what a phenomenal trade. As you look back over the last 27 years, Apple is probably the best investment that you could have made. As you look at the price of Apple during the internet bubble, it pales in comparison in what Apple trades at today. Most tech companies set all time highs in 2000 that they have never even got close to again since then. Today, Apple is the most valuable company on the face of the earth with a market cap of over $600 billion.

The craziest part of this whole trade is that Apple is still relatively cheap trading at 12 times next year's earnings. Apple stock is up a remarkable 15,000%. Talk about some gains. Apple has done all of this by building it's ecosystem.

With the release of 6 versions of the iPhone (which is possibly the most revolutionary phone to ever hit the market), two iPads, a revolutionary lineup of Macs, and the expansion of iTunes and the Apple platform, Apple has created the perfect scenario for itself to be in. People get sucked into the Apple brand and in turn they use more and more products and services provided by Apple.

Steve Jobs has led this charge. He is the visionary that saw just how revolutionary Apple could be. He envisioned these products and created one of the most profitable companies on the planet.

Apple Inc. since the Return of Steve Jobs

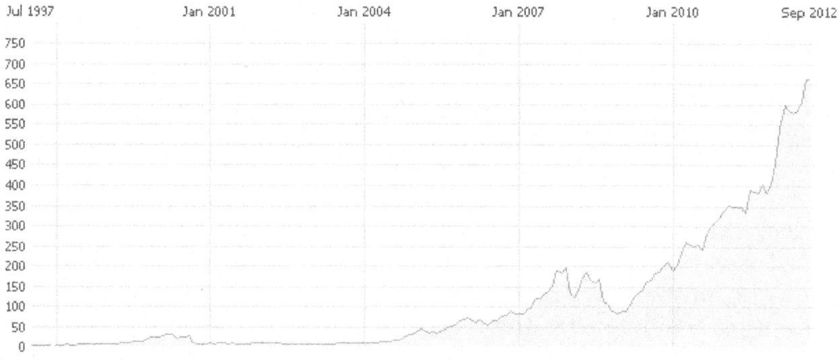

Source: MSN Money

To continue to the next investment opportunity, turn to page 236.

If you want to skip to retire now, turn to page 309.

Exxon buys Mobil Long Term Investment Setup

It's December 1st 1998 and the champagne corks are flying. Anti-trust legislation be damned, Exxon is buying Mobil for $75.3 billion in stock!! You see your friend's name in the Wall Street Journal as one of the dealmakers. You flip through your Rolodex, call him up and inform him that the next time you two get together, the Lagavullin and steaks are on him.

As a student of financial history you know that if the FTC (and Justice Department and about twelve other regulators) allow the merger, it will mean that the Standard Oil of 1911 is practically back together.

You look through the announcement and the numbers are staggeringly huge. Texas-sized. Taken together Exxon and Mobil pulled down $11.8 billion in profit on $203.1 billion in revenue. By merging and eliminating redundancies the companies project to save $2.8B a year. You understand how high the stakes are when you see that the deal comes with $1.5 in *fees* and Exxon can buy 15% of Mobil even if the whole thing falls apart.

Exxon isn't getting Mobil on the cheap though. They are paying a 24% premium and $8/barrel for the Mobil oil that's in the ground. The industry average for sourcing oil is around $5. Oil averaged $11.52 last month and prices are looking like they're heading down through the end of the year, so there isn't much oroom for error. Plus the majority of analysts believe that oil prices are going to continue their nearly decade long slump. The average price of a barrel in 1990, the year of the Gulf War, was $23.19; it's declined every year save one over the last eight.

This could be a great opportunity to get in on one of the biggest companies in the world for a long term investment. The new ExxonMobil is going to be one of the most powerful and profitable companies in the world. If you would like to take part in the growth of this company and want to invest, now is the time.

If you want to invest about $500,000 in ExxonMobil forever, turn to page 237.

If you want to skip to the next investing opportunity, turn to page 238.

If you want to retire now, turn to page 309.

Exxon buys Mobil Long Term Investment Outcome

Congratulations, you just made a 125% return on your investment.

You invested in one of the most successful oil producers in the world. Since you invested in the stock the common stock is up, 125%. The merger of the two companies increased the companies power and profitability throughout the world.

One of the reason's for ExxonMobil's success is the dramatic increase in the price of oil since you bought into the company. Oil was around $12 when you bought into the company and today a barrel of crude oil sells for close to $90.

ExxonMobil is today's biggest refiner of oil, a title was held by parent company Standard Oil. This was a great investment and you have also had some nice dividends along the way.

ExxonMobil since Merger

Source: MSN Money

To go to the next investment opportunity, turn to page 238.

If you want to skip to retire now, turn to page 309.

Hollister Co. Long-Term Investment Setup

It is May 2000 and next month Abercrombie & Fitch is going to launch a new brand of stores known as Hollister Co. These stores are based on the So-Cal theme off trendy/colorful clothes and targets 14-18 year olds. The lineup will include graphic tees, polo shirts, long and short sleeve collared shirts, jeans, cologne/perfume, and bath products among other things. The clothes are likely to be very trendy coming from higher end clothing retailer Abercrombie & Fitch. Abercrombie & Fitch states that their main target age is college level 18-22 year olds. This new brand will give them exposure to a demographic that they have yet to reach. This new brand will face significant competition from existing teen retail outlets like American Eagle, Aéropostale, and Old Navy.

Management at A&F has continued to do well even in a struggling retail environment. The company has reported record revenue each year over the past five years and continues to increase their bottom line. The stock is off 75% over the last year and the stock only trades at 5.6x this year's earnings. The highly competitive and cyclical retail stores are always a risk and the teen clothing market may well be saturated. Hollister clothes will most likely be expensive if they follow suit with A&F.

"Abercrombie's been the most profitable in the industry, but I don't see where it has room to grow," said Deutsche Banc Alex. Brown retail analyst Marcia Aaron said recently in an interview.

Although the company reported profits rose 27% in the last quarter, mark-downs cut into the hip retailer's sales growth, which has consistently been slowing the past two years.

Marino-Nachison with Lonnie Fogel, Investor Relations and Communications Director for Abercrombie said on the most recent earnings report:

"It's a very simple profitability model. The general idea is to open new stores at the approximate rate of 20% per year to achieve comparable-store sales in the range of 5% to 6% and with leverage on your fixed expense base you can achieve 30% EPS growth. Now, clearly the kids' business now is above and beyond the 20% profitability model so there's some upside to that, but in terms of a long-term profitability model that's our focus.

"Now, we have nearly 200 Abercrombie & Fitch stores at this point in time. Conservatively, our thinking is that 400 domestically is pretty much where we max out, although some people on Wall Street are arguing that there's more room. For us, we're feeling conservative. So we figure at some point you become close to at least theoretical saturation domestically. We haven't even really begun to seriously consider anything international."

The projections are still that the company will be growing at an earnings per share rate of 30%, and comp-store sales are targeted for a range of perhaps 3-6%.

Abercrombie & Fitch Co. (NYSE: ANF)

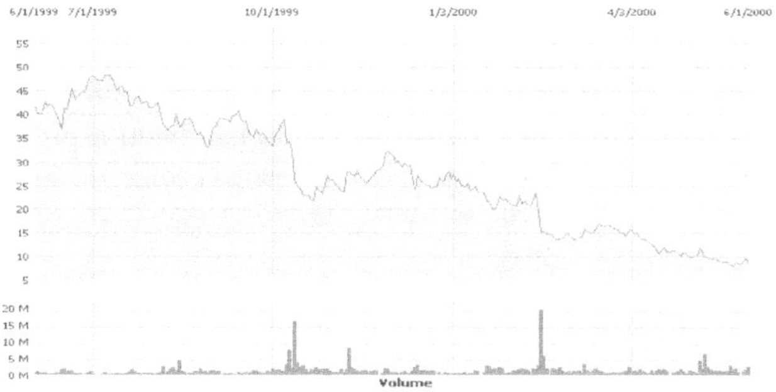

Source: MSN Money

If you want to invest about $500,000 in ANF forever, turn to page 240.

If you'd like to move onto the next invest opportunity, turn to page 241.

If you'd like to retire, turn to page 309.

Hollister Co. Long-Term Investment Outcome

Congratulations, you have a 250% return on your investment.

People are really excited about this new line up of clothes. The first store which opened in Columbus, Ohio was followed by four more stores in the next two weeks. CEO of A&F said that the performance of the five Hollister stores continues to exceed expectations. All of this has happened without marketing or advertising support and he sees the brand as a key driver for growth in the future.

These stores are all going to be located within malls and the theme is very much like a west coast beach house. The stores present a feel that is very different from any other existing retail outlets. With the great success of the brand, we can expect that A&F will expand these outlets more and more. The common stock popped as soon as you bought it and it went on to more than double in price into the end of the year. ANF has experienced a general upward trend . This has been a great investment in a long term trend. The new prosperity of the 21st century is allowing people to purchase more stylish, more expensive clothes than ever before.

ANF since Hollister Co. was launched

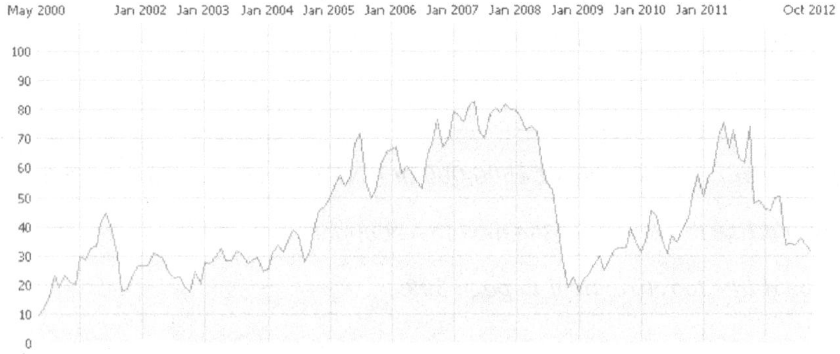

Source: MSN Money

To go to the next investing opportunity, turn to page 241.

If you want to skip to retire now, turn to page 309.

Internet Sector Long-Term Investment Setup

It's January 2000...There's a hot new tech sector called the "Internet" that enables people and companies to connect and do business easier than ever before through their computers. Most of the recent IPOs there are flying high, although you can also find some of the stocks in this sector have missed their earnings estimates and have been pummeled. The NASDAQ, the exchange where all these high-flyers have been listing, was up 88% in 1999, almost 60% in the last 6 months alone. Last October a startup called Akamai that does something with the speed of the internet came public at $26 and closed that first day at $145.19 at a market capitalization of $15 billion. Your friends who have never traded before in their life are opening accounts are all making money buying and flipping internet stocks, doubling their Etrade accounts in a matter of months. When you turn on TV the analysts are saying that the right way to value companies without revenues and earnings is with "eyeball" and "click" multiples, not earnings. Absolutely everyone will be on the internet in the next five, this is the most profound technology shift in 100 years.

Nasdaq Composite Index-1999

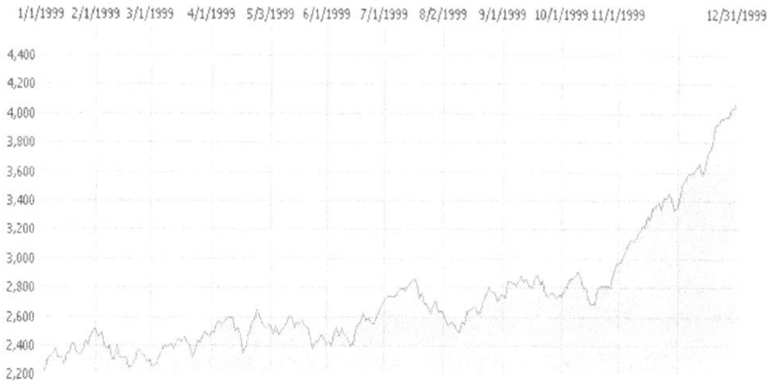

Source: MSN Money

If you want to invest about $500,000 in the Nasdaq forever, turn to page 242.

If you'd like to move onto the next invest opportunity, turn to page 243.

If you'd like to retire, turn to page 309.

Internet Sector Long-Term Investment Outcome

Oops, you lost 25% on your investment.

Sorry, you just literally top-ticked the Internet tech bubble. I mean, your timing couldn't be any worse. You bought Amazon at a split-adjusted $76 in January 2000 and by November of next year it was under $7 bucks. And that isn't even your worst trade. Lycos, HotBot, a host of other internet portals are in Chapter 11 or have been sold for the office furniture. Globe.com was up 600% on it's first day of trading in 1998; it was delisted in April 2001. The Nasdaq fell to a new low in 2002 and since has steadily recovered. Of all those stocks you bought in 2000, about half of them are around today. Even those stocks that are still trading are in the red and it will take a few more years of increased earnings before these stocks get back to your purchase price.

Nasdaq Composite Index since Jan-2000

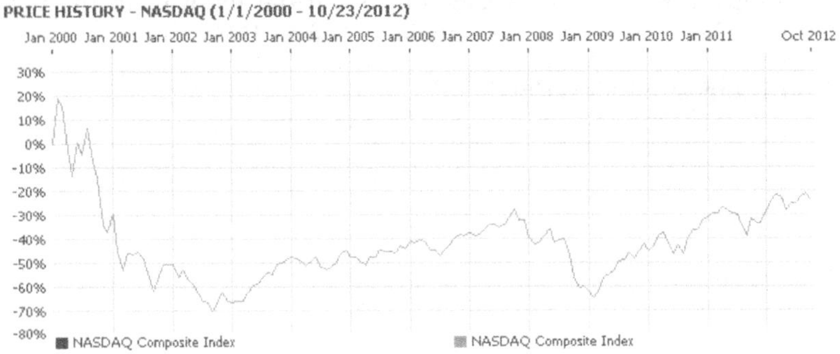

Source: MSN Money

To go to the next investing opportunity, turn to page 243.

If you want to skip to retire now, turn to page 309.

Enron Scandal Long-Term Investment Setup

Today is November 28, 2001. This morning at 10:30 the Enron Corporation announced that its past five years of financial statements have been mostly fraud. The company has an insurmountable amount of debt and the company is operating at a loss. Just four months ago, the company was worth over $60 billion at a share price of $80 and as you look at the stock now on your computer, it is trading for pennies. It was listed on the S&P 500 index as well as the Dow Jones Utility Average.

Enron had over $100 billion in revenue and was a much diversified company. Enron provided electric and natural gas utilities as well as commodities trading and many other financial products. Over the past six years, Enron was listed as Forbes #1 most innovative company. The company had been hiding their losses in "special offshore entities" which allowed them to maintain a high stock price and high credit ratings. The stock has fallen significantly over the past few months and the corporate governances was constantly reassuring shareholders that everything was alright. Meanwhile, those same officers were dumping their stock at record high prices. Enron got away with all this due to recent energy law deregulation and unregulated accounting practices.

The Enron Corporation told investors last week that it faced debt repayments over the next year vastly in excess of its cash available. Inded its ability to continue as a going concern is being called into question.

In the delayed quarterly filing with the Securities and Exchange Commission filed last week, the company said that it would have to repay $690 million in debt by next Tuesday if it did not come up with collateral for a loan.

Enron's independent auditors with the firm of Arthur Andersen have not been able to complete their review of Enron's financial statements for the third quarter. Andersen already faces lawsuits over its audits of Enron's books related to Enron's disclosure this month that it had overstated almost $600 million in profits in the last five years. Enron has said that it will restate statements that Andersen certified and that those statements should no longer be relied upon.

This could forever change the public's view on corporations and may also have an effect on investor relations. With the current situation, we have no idea of knowing if other corporations are doing the same thing. Obviously Enron is done and it may well drag down the rest of the S&P 500. On the other hand, this could have no effect on the broader markets and this could be a great buying opportunity. You are looking at Spider's S&P index fund (SPY) to game this action.

SPY S&P 500

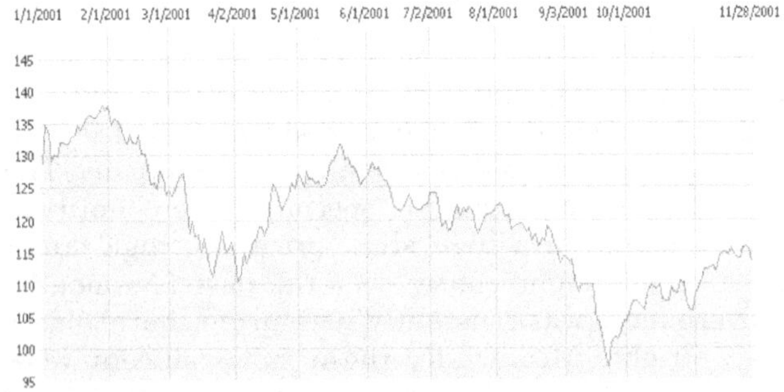

Source: MSN Money

If you want to invest about $500,000 in the S&P 500 forever, turn to page 245.

If you'd like to move onto the next invest opportunity, turn to page 246.

If you'd like to retire, turn to page 309.

Enron Scandal Long-Term Investment Outcome

Congratulations, you just made a 26% return on your long term investment!

Turns out that the Enron Scandal did not have much of an effect on the broader markets. We've had some volatile times since the Enron Scandal, including the financial crisis of 2008 – 2009, but overall investing in the S&P 500 during the Enron Scandal proved to be a good investment.

SPY Today

Source: MSN Money

To go to the next investment opportunity, turn to page 246.

If you want to skip to retire now, turn to page 309.

Microsoft Windows XP Long-Term Investment Setup

Today is October 25, 2001 and Microsoft just released their latest operating system known as Windows XP.

Windows XP features both home and professional editions. While the OS upgrade is perceived largely as a consumer upgrade, Gates made a special effort to highlight the Windows XP Professional features that will be useful to business users, including the realtime, audio, video and text messaging for Internet meetings, new security features and privacy controls, and support for the 802.11 wireless networking standard. Microsoft, chipmaker Intel and PC makers are expected to spend a combined total of more than $1 billion on marketing for Windows XP.

Microsoft has a lot riding on XP's success: The operating system ushers in new features tied to Microsoft's long-term strategic plans for media player software, digital photo tools and online services. Many analysts said the new operating system was the most important release of Windows since Windows 95, the forerunner to Internet Explorer and other Internet connectivity features.

"With Office XP, Windows XP will be the new standard for business," said Gates, who pointed to many product and service opportunities for Microsoft's partners.

Gates also noted that the launch of Windows XP ends one era of computing, the DOS world, and ushers the new era of Web services. Unlike the difference between Windows 2000 Pro and Windows Millennium, both the professional and home editions of Windows XP use the same code base.

"It's the end of an era," Gates said about the DOS-based code on which Windows 3.1, Windows 95, Windows 98 and Windows Millennium were built. Microsoft is already at work on the successor to Windows XP, code-named Longhorn, which is aimed at exploiting Intel's McKinley chip in late 2002.

"This is a transition period and the end of too many computer crashes and the static Web era into a new dynamic Web [era]," Gates said. "XP lays the foundation for Web services."

Gates, who also serves as the company's chief software architect, noted that Windows XP supports .Net Alerts, a recently unveiled alert service that will be deployed as part of Microsoft's .Net software services platform, formerly known as HailStorm.

Gates said there are plenty of business and consumer scenarios for services such as .Net Alerts. "Built into Windows XP is this idea of supporting Web services and alerts," Gates said in an earlier Q&A sessions with several other high-tech leaders. "We'll show lots of benefits of alerts to businesses and consumers."

Gartner issued a report claiming the existing Windows 2000 Professional will continue to be the leading business Windows version until 2003. But Microsoft was quick to point to businesses that have already begun deploying Windows XP, including Wells Fargo, Citigroup, BMW and Reed Elsevier.

Microsoft also noted that other enterprise customers such as Jack-In-The-Box, Digex, Merrill Lynch as well as Microsoft global accounts General Motors, GMAC Commercial Mortgage and Siemens are early adopters of Windows XP.

Microsoft will most likely maintain it's dominance in the PC market for years to come and this could be a great investment opportunity. Technology is changing at such a rapid pace that no one knows what is around the turn and how fast these companies could grow. With that said, a new technology could arise that would wipe Microsoft off the map. The threat of competition is very high all across the technology sector.

Microsoft Corp.

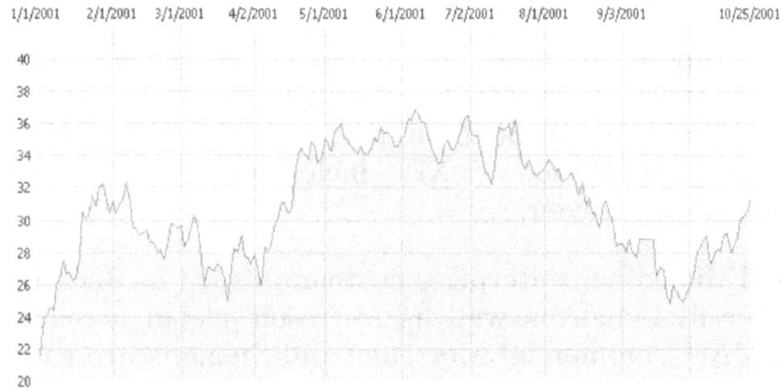

Souce: MSN Money

If you want to invest about $500,000 in MSFT forever, turn to page 249.

If you'd like to move onto the next invest opportunity, turn to page 250.

If you'd like to retire, turn to page 309.

Microsoft Windows XP Long-Term Investment Outcome

You broke even on your investment. There is no change to your portfolio value.

After the launch of Windows XP, Microsoft successfully launched two more operating systems, Windows Vista and Windows 7. Today these three operating systems make up 92% of the operating system market share. Microsoft has been an extremely successful company.

The stock has moved a lot over the years but to date is up only single digits. Meanwhile the Nasdaq was up almost 80%. You have made decent money on this investment if you count all of the dividends that you have been paid but besides that, this investment has not done much.

MSFT Corp. since Windows XP launch

Source: MSN Money

To go to the next investment opportunity, turn to page 250.

If you want to skip to retire now, turn to page 309.

American Idol Long-Term Investment Setup

It's May 2002, and next month, News Corp's FOX Television stations will be airing a brand new series called *American Idol: The Search for a Superstar*. Simon Fuller will to bring the show to the US from his native UK in a deal in which he is believed to be paid around $50m (£34.9m).

Fox will air 15 episodes of the show, which will be called American Idol, this summer with the hope that it will emulate the success of the show in the UK, where as many as 8.7m voted in the final show.

Fuller, who was the former manager of the Spice Girls, will, in addition to selling the News Corporation-owned station the format, also benefit from lucrative sponsorship and telephone revenue-sharing deals.

In its most recent quarter, Rupert Murdoch's News Corporation has posted a quarterly loss of more than $3 billion after writing down the value of its stake in Gemstar-TV Guide International.

Shares in Gemstar, which provides on-screen TV programme guides, have lost more than two thirds of their value since last year, leading to the massive write-down. The company is 38% owned by News Corp.

However, News Corp's revenues for the first three months of 2002 rose 18% to more than $3.5 billion as its 20th Century Fox movies Moulin Rouge and Ice Age boomed at the box office. Without the effect of the $4.23bn write-off in Gemstar and other one-time effects, profits nearly doubled to $236m from $127m a year ago.

News Corp also owns the Fox TV network, StarTV in Asia and the News International newspapers in the UK, which include the Sun and the Times.

Operating income at the UK newspapers was in line with expectations but higher circulation revenues and savings on newsprint prices could not offset a drop in advertising revenue, which was 16% down on the first three months of last year.

In its third quarter statement News Corp said the advertising slump was affecting all categories.

"The advertising weakness was principally the result of lower volumes and yields across all major advertising categories," it said.

News Corp owns 36% of BSkyB and last week's draft communications bill lifted the barrier preventing it from buying Channel 5 or a commercial radio station.

News Corp (NWS)

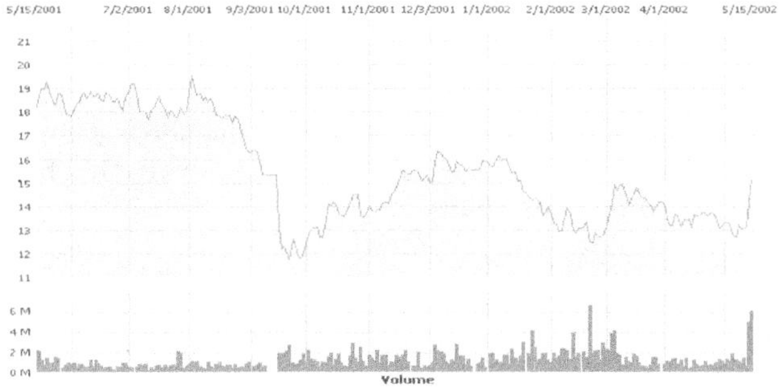

Source: MSN Money

If you want to invest about $500,000 in NWS forever, turn to page 252.

If you'd like to move onto the next invest opportunity, turn to page 253.

If you'd like to retire, turn to page 309.

American Idol Long-Term Investment Outcome

Congratulations, you just made a 53% return!

This stock has been on a wild ride through the years. At one point, your investment was down almost 50% but its now bounced back significantly. The first episode of American Idol aired on June 11 with around 9.85 million viewers. After watching the show, you decide that you really like it and this could definitely be a growth driver in the future.

One neat part about the show is that it locks the viewer into it thus providing a steady audience throughout the course of the show. People have their favorites and they want to see how they do. Overall, this has been a good investment through the years.

News Corp

Source: MSN Money

To go to the next investment opportunity, turn to page 253.

If you want to skip to retire now, turn to page 309.

Apple iTunes Rollout Long-Term Investment Setup

It's March 29th 2003 and you're walking to the office. It's a particularly dreary morning and the indexes have been whipping around all year and are basically flat. To top it all off, the U.S. has just invaded Iraq to go and root out what the adminstration and the press call "Weapons of Mass Destruction" aka anthrax and nuclear material. Fun stuff.

As you get off the subway you notice that everyone is doing the same thing you are: bobbing their head with little white earbuds stuck into the side of their head. You look down at your own iPod:

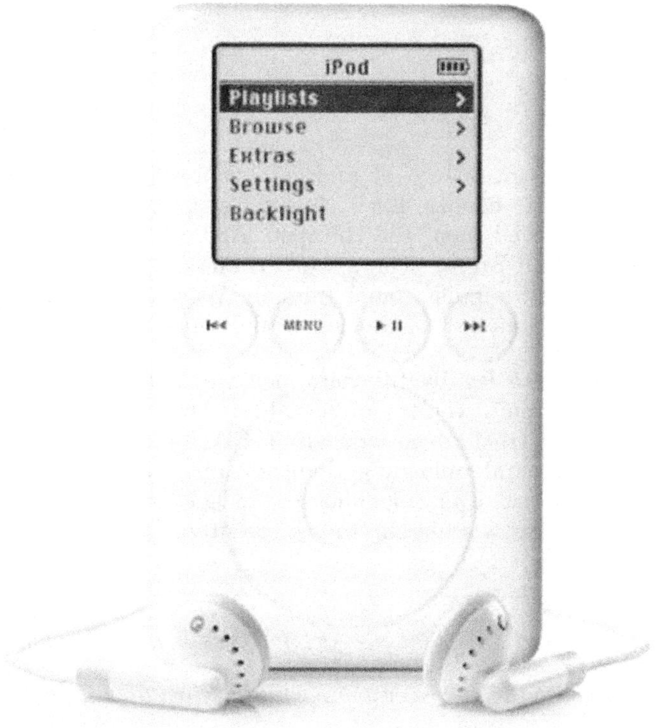

When you get to the office you call up what Apple's stock has done since they introduced the ipod and basically killed off the competition:

APPL

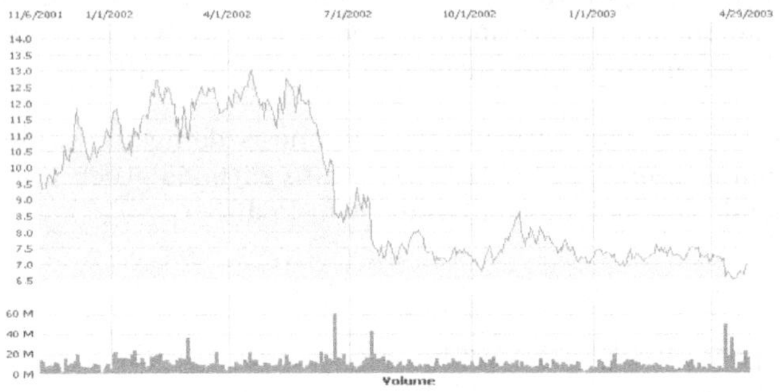

MSN Money

Not so hot. You look up the financials and you see a stock trading at about $7 per share with $8 in cash. Even after two successful consumer launches, the candy-colored imac and the ipod, Apple is stuck in the muck and hated on Wall Street. There were rumors last week that Apple was about to buy a music label (namely Warner Music) but instead they launched an mp3 through their itunes software.

Songs are 99 cents, so to legally fill your ipod would cost a couple hundred dollars. At this point you've purchased Bob Dylan's 'Blonde on Blonde" as a vinyl, an 8-track, a cassette and a CD. You can also just keep ripping your CDs and uploading them as mp3's to your ipod, which takes hours. Most everyone chooses to go another route, downloading the music free via torrent and warez sites.

If you want to invest about $500,000 in AAPL forever, turn to page 255.

If you'd like to move onto the next invest opportunity, turn to page 256.

If you'd like to retire, turn to page 309.

Apple iTunes Rollout Long-Term Investment Outcome

Congratulations, you just made a 9,600% return on your investment!

Wow, what an investment. The stock immediately popped after you bought it and never looked back. The common stock is up almost 9,600% since you bought it. Their was really a lot of basis for this investment that you caught on to.

First from a value perspective, Apple at $7 wasn't dirt cheap, it made dirt look good. In other words, if Apple were to liquidate, you would get more cash for each share than what you even paid for the shares. That's not counting earnings and the other millions of dollars of assets that Apple owns.

Next, Apple was a great growth play. You saw the platform that Apple was starting to build and you jumped on it. The iPod was the number one selling mp3 player in the world and iTunes just expounded on an already great product. Apple has continued to expand this platform. You really did good on this one!

Apple since iTunes rollout

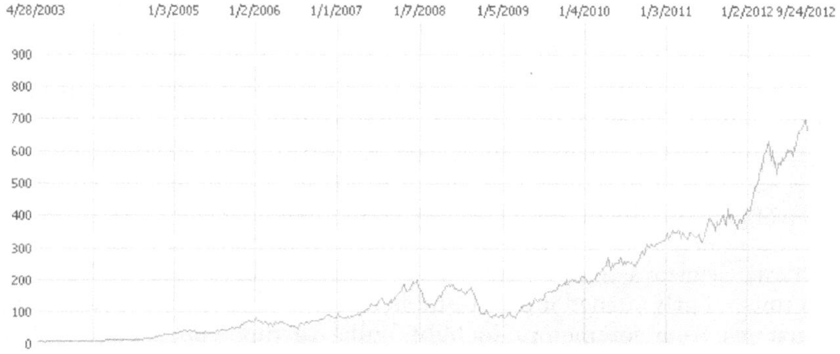

Source: MSN Money

To go to the next investment opportunity, turn to page 256.

If you want to skip to retire now, turn to page 309.

Operation Iraqi Freedom Long-Term Investment Setup

Today is March 12 2003. The world is a mess. Europe's economies are in total disarray with Germany leading the collapse and all the major indices hitting new 300 year lows every day. Japan remains mired in its mess and the Nikkei looks to be headed for triple digits. Venezuela is a pit. Argentina is left for dead. The dollar can't stop falling. Treasuries are through the roof. We've got a housing bubble to contend with still. Serbia's PM is assassinated today. The UN is falling apart and the US is burning all bridges. Consumers are overleveraged and can't sustain the economy any longer.

President Bush will soon announced that a coalition of Allied troops will be invading Iraq. The reason for the invasion is to remove the current tyrannical Saddam Hussein Regime. The relations between the United States and Iraq have been deteriorating for months now. Back in October of last year, President Bush announced that the US would use armed forces to counter Iraq. Reportedly, Iraq has amassed weapons of mass destruction and has repeatedly threatened to attack US ally Israel. This move by the United States will definitely increase tension with many other Middle Eastern nations such as Iran and Turkey. Iraq has the fifth largest military in the world and a highly trained unit known as the Republic Guard. This is most likely going to be a much extended war and occupation of the country could run into next year.

General Electric (GE) is an American conglomerate that is typically very cyclical. How do you think this announcement will affect a company like GE? How will GE behave in this type of an Economy? Obviously the US is going to spend a lot of money on this war and some of GE's products could possibly be in demand.

General Electric is one of the oldest companies listed on the DJIA. It has consistently turned a profit and is exposed to hundreds of different industries from jet motors to light bulbs to financial services.. The stock may be a great buy right now since it has been crushed so bad lately. GE's large size also means that it is going to be less volatile as it's many revenue streams balance each other out. Also, GE has the ability to aggressively acquire new companies that could possibly be competitors and use them for their own good.

General Electric

Source: MSN Money

If you want to invest about $500,000 in GE forever, turn to page 258.

If you'd like to move onto the next invest opportunity, turn to page 259.

If you'd like to retire, turn to page 309.

Operation Iraqi Freedom Long-Term Investment Outcome

Oops, you just lost 10% on your investment!

Well General Electric turned out to not be so hot of an investment. The financial crash of 2008 seemed to derail GE. Since then the stock has recovered but is till 10% below your 2003 purchase price. The reason that the financial crash had such a toll on GE was because a third of it's revenue was coming from GE Capital which was exposed to some of the same risky investment's that the banks were exposed to.

When you bought the stock, the company was making $15 billion a year and last year they only made $12 billion. Over this same time period, most companies have increased their earnings and the S&P 500 is up almost 80%.

General Electric

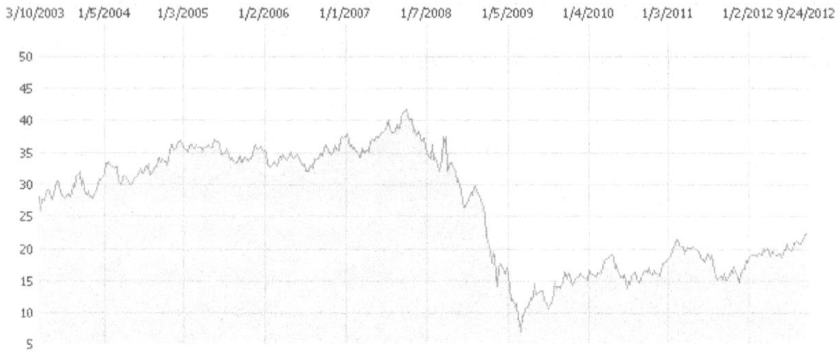

Source: MSN Money

To go to the next investment opportunity, turn to page 259.

If you want to skip to retire now, turn to page 309.

Google IPO Long-Term Investment Setup

It's August 19, 2004 and the SEC requires that companies make their information public "20 days after the close of the year in which the company reaches $10 million in assets and/or 500 shareholders, including people with stock options". At that point most companies figure they might as well raise capital, and Google is not an exception. Nerds that they are Google is seeking to raise up to $2,718,281,828, or the mathematical constant "e" to the 10th-digit.

Google has replaced every other search engine for you and it's now your homepage. And on April Fool's Day earlier this year, Google released Gmail as beta, a free web email service with a whole gigabyte of free storage; you immediately switch over from Microsoft's Hotmail when you're friend gets you in as a beta-tester. Google gives you five Gmail invites which are a hot commodity and are trading for $150 on Ebay.

You call around to other investors and bankers and you hear something you can't even believe: Google is going to cut Wall Street out of the IPO process all together and use a 'Dutch Auction" to go publicly directly. Time to dig into the S-1.

Even though it was just founded in 1988 Google already has $961.9 billion in revenue for 2003 and a profit of $106.5 million. So if the IPO prices at about 20x earnings that would make Google worth about $20 billion on the first day. You scratch your head and look at previous tech IPOs from the tech bubble that are now trading at market caps about 95% lower. Google is a great business but there are some things that worry you in the S1. You take out your highlighter and mark the following:

If opportunities arise that might cause us to sacrifice short term results but are in the best long term interest of our shareholders, we will take those opportunities. We will have the fortitude to do this. We would request that our shareholders take the long term view. ***(Umm, how long is this "long-term"? Founder's can convince themselves of a lot, and while you want to buy into a long-term business, the IPO is at a pretty large market cap so the short-term does matter.)***

We aspire to make Google an institution that makes the world a better place. With our products, Google connects people and information all around the world for free.

(So your capital will be used to make things that are given away?)

We provide advertising, web search and other services to members of our Google Network. The net revenues generated from the fees advertisers pay us when users click on ads that we have delivered to our Google Network members' web sites represented approximately 15% of our net revenues in 2003, and approximately 21% of our net revenues for the three months ended March 31, 2004, and we expect this percentage to increase in the future. We consider this network to be critical to the future growth of our net revenues. However, some of the participants in this network may compete with us in one or more areas. Therefore, they may decide in the future to terminate their agreements with us. If our Google Network members decide to use a competitor's or their own web search or advertising services, our net revenues would decline.

(A fifth of revenues are from direct competitors?)

Advertising revenues made up 77%, 92%, 95% and 96% of our net revenues in 2001, 2002, 2003 and in the three months ended March 31, 2004.

(So this **is an advertising company? You consider the stocks of ad companies and the total pie of ad spending.)**

iShares S&P Global Technology (IXN)

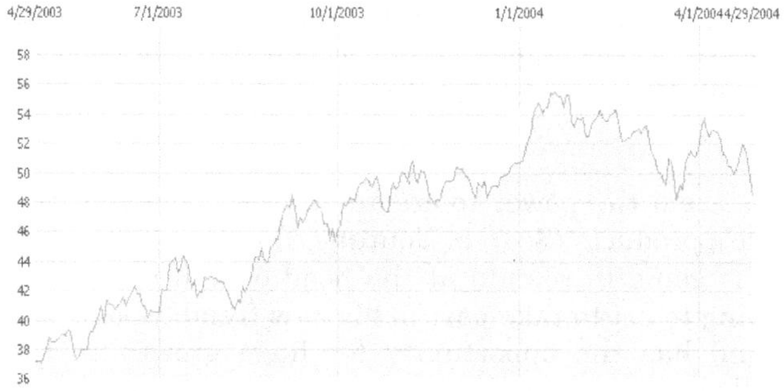

Source: MSN Money

If you want to invest about $500,000 in GOOG forever, turn to page 262.

If you'd like to move onto the next invest opportunity, turn to page 263.

If you'd like to retire, turn to page 309.

Google IPO Long-Term Investment Outcome

Congratulations, you have a 782% return on your investment.

Since it's IPO, Google has gone up 123% into the end of the year. From there, it has continued and today is up 782% from your $85 purchase price. Google has a great search engine and from that they are creating a magnificent platform. Google is by far the most widely used search engine on the web.

This user base gives them the power to create an ecosystem that ties together all of Google's products (Search, Youtube, Docs, etc) and profit off of them. Google is going to remain at the head of web innovation and investors are going to get to take part in big new trend. Google is a great investment and has the opportunity for huge growth in the future. This has really been a fun trade.

Google since IPO

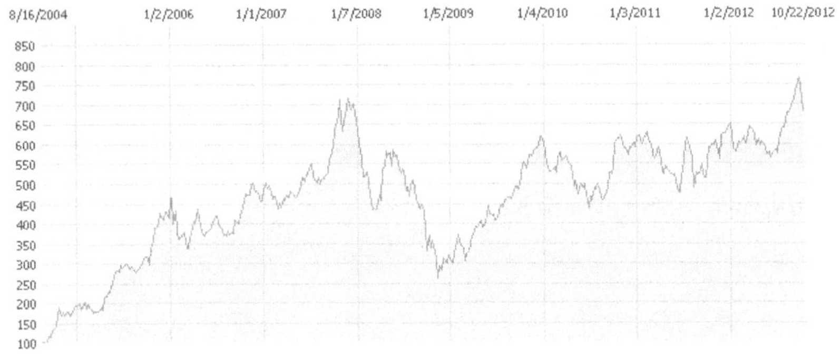

Source: MSN Money

To go to the next investment opportunity, turn to page 263.

If you want to skip to retire now, turn to page 309.

Ethanol Mandate Long-Term Investment Setup

It's August and President George W. Bush has just signed the Energy Policy Act of 2005 in Albuquere, NM. You go to the website of Rep. Joe Barton (R) from the Texas 6th, sponsor of the Bill. The table of contents is eleven pages long. You're gonna need some energy of your own, so you down that second can of sugar-free Red Bull.

You start by reading all the subsection in the TOC. The very first one makes you laugh out loud:

Sec. 101. Energy and water saving measures in congressional buildings.

Nice to see that Congress is learning about personal conservation, odd to see it in federal legislation. A kindergarten refresher or a Home Depot visit couldn't do. You wonder if Senators are being told "If it's yellow, let it mellow…". No matter, you move on.

The bill is chock-full of seemingly every energy idea ever think tank has ever had. There's a re-consideration of daylight savings and a study about elevator efficiency. But the real pattern you pay attention to is all the ink given over to energy technologies.

Sure there's stuff for nuclear, wind, coal, hydroelectric, fuel cells, natural gas and methane (how come no one ever just says cow farts?) but the big daddy king kahuna in the bill is ethanol.

Some company named Pacific Ethanol went public earlier this year and you remembering your pestering you about it. You've seen at least ten pitch decks in the past year from ethanol companies looking for VC mezzanine funding. You start searching around your room and you find one with Sequoia as the lead investor under an unholy pile of papers and notebooks. The company is based in Iowa and you realize why Congress is lavishing so much attention on ethanol; you need corn to make this stuff and Iowa is the first presidential primary, so any money for ethanol is money for Iowa. What politician wouldn't want to make that trade?

Now you get excited and start digging into the scale of the mandates. 7.5 *billion* barrels of ethanol and bio-diesel to be used by 2012. Wait, what? You start checking the math. Last year (2004) saw 1.26 billion bushels of domestic corn production go towards ethanol production. These mandates would mean that eventually 40% of the corn crop would go towards ethanol.

You lean back in your chair. Then you lean forward and re-check the math. Yeah, looks like a huge chunk of the corn crop is about to be diverted to making fuel. Now what you really want to know is how this will impact corn prices. International demand for American corn has been ticking up. You know that most corn is fed to livestock and processed into sugar, neither of which seem to be slowing down but aren't really going up either. Americans ate 27.8 billion pounds of beef last year and that's probably going to stay the same this year. So if other sources of demand for corn will likely be flat over the next half decade as ethanol ramps up what does that mean for prices? And if corn prices go up because of ethanol won't that make Americans eat chicken instead of beef, which will put downward pressure on corn? You remember your mentor's saying about commodities: "The cure for high prices is high prices".

You go back to your original premise, that corn is all about Iowa, and you consider the supply side of corn prices. 2004 was a pretty good year for corn, prices were the best in a couple years and the crop yielded about 142 bushels per acre. What didn't go up that much was new acres for planting, only about 800K came on line. Farmers are predicting $2.90/bushel for this year, a big spike from today, unless almost another 50% or 1.2M acres comes online. With land prices going up as fields are plowed over for housing, you doubt that will happen. Ethanol already accounts for one out of every ten acres of corn. The weather has been pretty good and advances in crop technologies have meant better yields so maybe farmers will do more with less.

You're not about to start trading the futures in any scenario (you've learned from the last time) so you start looking for derivative plays on ethanol and corn. You consider Archer Daniels Midland but think that the company just has too many moving parts. Then you start thinking about what it takes to make corn...water, a little sun, luck, fertilizer,more luck, seed and...farming equipment!

There's only one farming equipment name to consider and that's John Deere, which you discover goes by the corporate name Deere & Co. You think about the riding mower your parents had and regret that you can't drink a beer and mow Central Park for a couple hours. You punch up a one year chart and see that it's up about 14% since last August; YTD mighty Deere is down slightly. You dig into the financials and see that Deere earned $1.4 billion in 2004, almost double 2003. Revenues were up 29% to almost $20 billion (seriously almost, just $14 million short). You see that the manufacturing side takes huge capital investment, with Deere managing 29.4 million square feet of factory space! Deere has upped the dividend every year since 1982. All this adds up to a market cap around $17 billion trading about 12x earnings.

So what do you do?

Deere & Co.

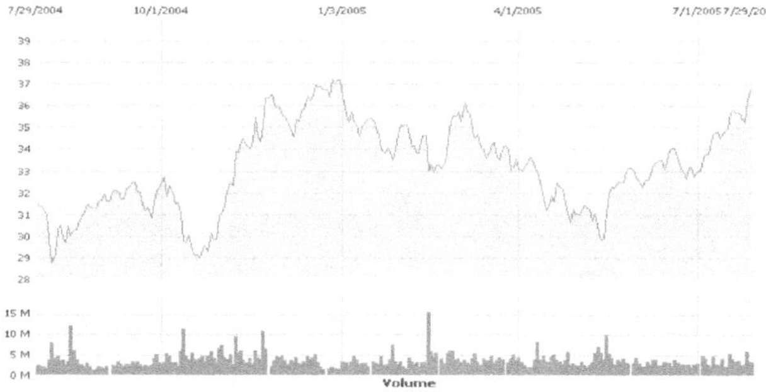

Source: MSN Money

If you want to invest about $500,000 in DE forever, turn to page 266.

If you'd like to move onto the next invest opportunity, turn to page 267.

If you'd like to retire, turn to page 309.

Ethanol Mandate Long-Term Investment Outcome

Congratulations, you have made 114% on your investment.

You made a great call buying Deere at those levels. Since then the stock has rallied significantly as revenue and earnings have increased dramatically since 2005. The ethanol mandate did end up having an effect on the stock price. The strong demand for corn and has increased food prices across the board.

The farmers of America are expanding their farms and buying up equipment in order to take advantage of these changing markets. This has been a great investment for you.

Deere & Co since Ethanol Mandate

Source: MSN Money

To go to the next investment opportunity, turn to page 267.

If you want to skip to retire now, turn to page 309.

Housing Sector Long-Term Investment Setup

It's January 2005 and housing stocks have been on a multi-year run. Okay that's an understatement. Hovanian Enterprises is up almost 1400% in the last five years. Lennar is up 500% and KBH is up 300%. Every time you're up late (instead of sleeping and resting up for the trading day) you see a new infomercial about buying and flipping houses.

Your junk mail is full of mortgage offers. Some company called Ditech has been able to offer loans on the phones with increasingly weird terms; 10% down, nothing down, adjustable rates and now something called a 1+3+6+20 year loan. And they promise you can refinance later.

Something smells funny to you. You look at Department of Labor and Federal Reserve data. Your alarm bells go off.

The line of housing prices is starting to veer away from everything that could justify those prices (income, rents). Median housing prices have increased faster than median incomes! You don't see how people can keep buying houses on just credit.

Lennar Corp.

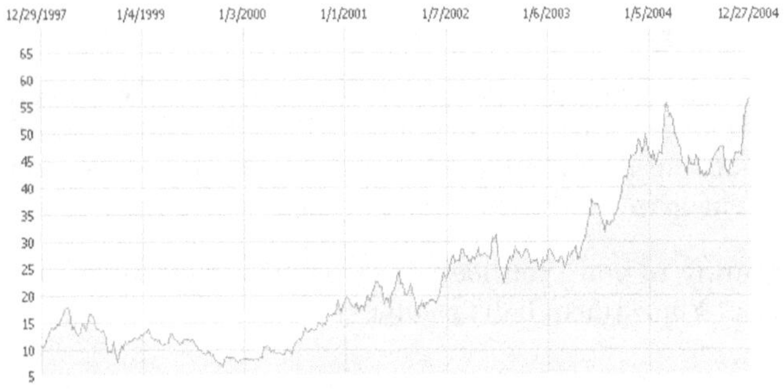

Source: MSN Money

If you want to invest about $500,000 in Lennar forever, turn to page 269.

If you'd like to move onto the next invest opportunity, turn to page 270.

If you'd like to retire, turn to page 309.

Housing Sector Long-Term Investment Outcome

Oops, you just lost 36% on your investment.

The housing sector remained steady to higher in the first couple of years after you bought it. In 2007, the truth about the mortgage crisis as well as the banking fraud caused the housing sector to collapse. By the beginning of 2008, Lennar was down 70% from where it was a year earlier. Foreclosures are happening everywhere and brand new subdivisions look like ghost towns. Nobody can afford to keep their home much less build a new one. The homebuilder stocks are taking it hard and only in the past year or so have they finally recovered partially.

Lennar Corp. since 2004

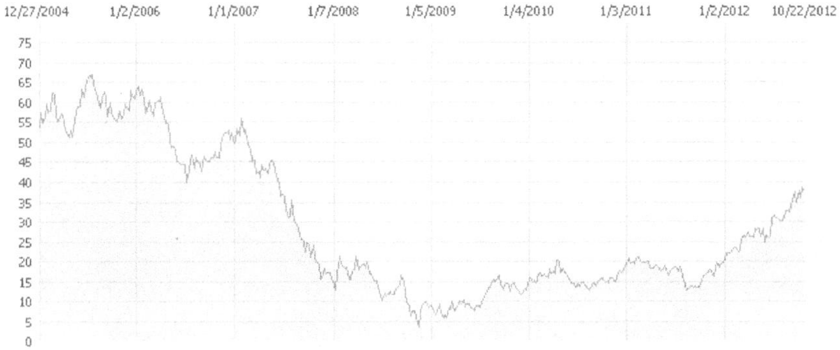

Source: MSN Money

To go to the next investment opportunity, turn to page 270.

If you want to skip to retire now, turn to page 309.

China Exposure Long-Term Investment Setup

It's January of 2006 and you want some China exposure. Since liberalization of the economy in the 1990s everything has been going gangbusters. The Hong Kong index, where foreign investors can buy in, has been pretty volatile over the last couple years but has absolutely destroyed the S&P 500:

Stock Market Events That Mattered (Or Did They?)

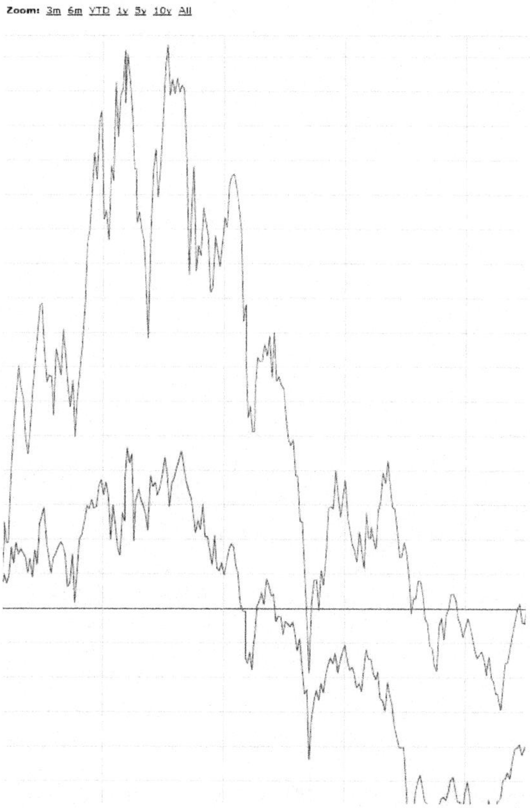

You start looking through the universe of Chinese ADRs and you land on Focus Media, a company that places ads in elevators and the 55,000 displays that it owns. It has 1,200 foreign clients that are seeking its services to advertise on the mainland. It just purchased rival Framedia for about $40 million. Focusmedia IPOd just last year, so you call up a 2005 chart:

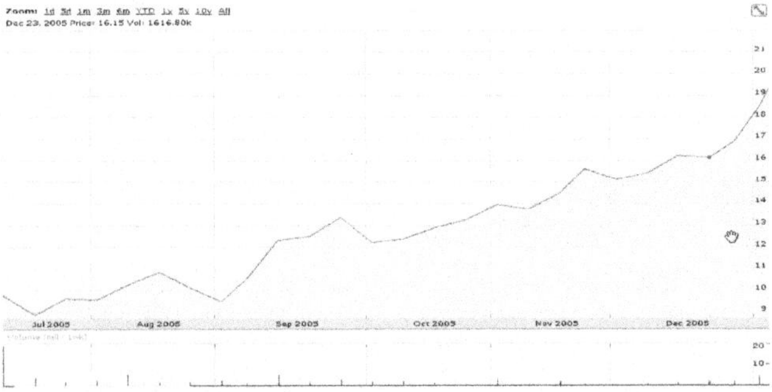

Source: MSN Money

FMCN has had the market to itself for years but that's changing rapidly. Viacom has just bought a local interest and Clear Channel is poking around. 2005 Third quarter revenues were up 146% y-o-y, with a $7.1 million profit vs a $1 million loss in 2004. Piper Jaffrey just raised their target to $40. Focus Media has had to cut ad rates in Tier II cities and their operating margin has dropped from 44.7% in Q3 2004 to 33.2% in Q3 2005. But every single other metric is up and has been going up in a straight line. What do you do?

If you want to invest about $500,000 in FMCN forever, turn to page 273.

If you'd like to move onto the next invest opportunity, turn to page 274.

If you'd like to retire, turn to page 309.

China Exposure Long-Term Investment Outcome

You broke even on your investment. There is no change to your portfolio value.

There has essentially been no change to Focus Media's stock over the years.

FMCN

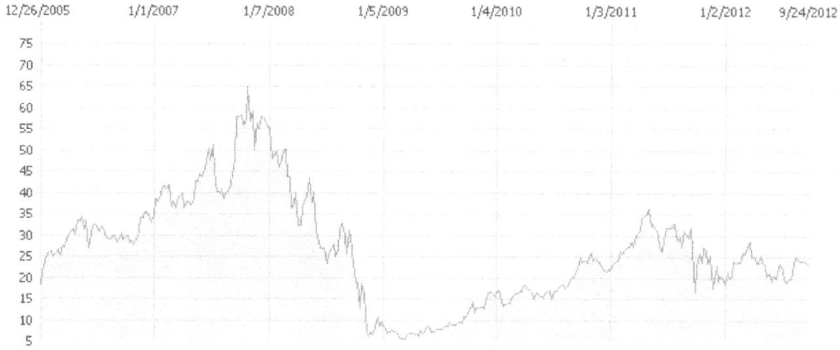

Source: MSN Money

To go to the next investment opportunity, turn to page 274.

If you want to skip to retire now, turn to page 309.

India Auto Industry Long-Term Investment Setup

It's October of 2006 and India's economy is exploding. The liberalizations of the economy has really taken hold. India nationalized Pepsi in the 50s but now Pepsi sponsors the national cricket team and can be found everywhere. The country has a middle class of almost 300M (that all speak English) and the service economy has boomed, largely at the expense of call-centers in America.

With rising wealth comes the rising desire to be more American; that is, to own a car. You call up the chart of Tata Motors, a major Indian auto manufacturer, started by one of India's most prominent families. You compare how it's done since it's IPO vs the S&P 500:

Tata Motors

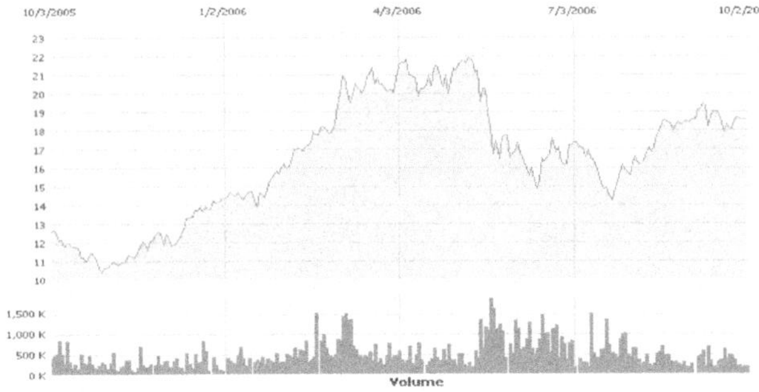

Source: MSN Money

The company has just over a billion in cash and is growing almost 50% per year. You look at the common stock and consider a one year-trade.

If you want to invest about $500,000 in Tata Motors forever, turn to page 275.

If you'd like to move onto the next invest opportunity, turn to page 276.

If you'd like to retire, turn to page 309.

India Auto Industry Long-Term Investment Outcome

Congratulations, you made a 40% return on your investment.

India continues to experience rapid growth. Real GDP outgrows American GDP by 4-6 times. The industrialization of the nations of India and China are key drivers in today's global economy. Unfortunately, Tata Motors stock has stopped going up and has essentially gone flat. The stock acts very cyclical and no longer outperforms the markets. Over six years, the common stock is up 40% only barely outperforming the S&P 500. Not necessarily a bad trade and you have even made money. A goal on a trade like this over the same time period should actually be to double or triple.

Tata Motors since 2006

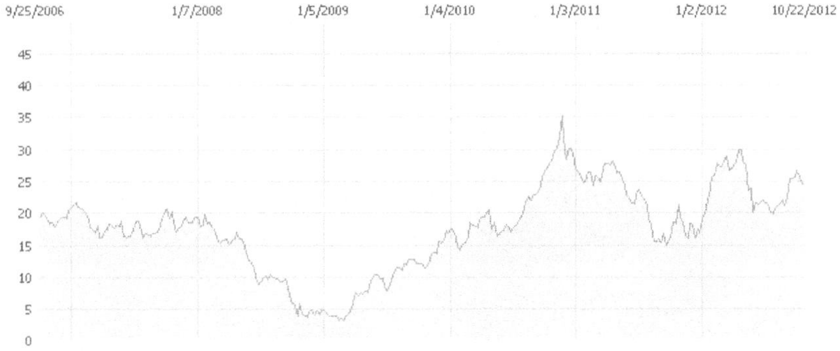

Source: MSN Money

To go to the next investment opportunity, turn to page 276.

If you want to skip to retire now, turn to page 309.

First iPhone Setup Long-Term Investment Setup

It's January 2007...Apple's about to release their first ever cell phone, rumored to be called the iPhone. There have been so many Apple whispers over the last couple years that it's hard to keep track. Remember when everyone said Apple would buy a music label?

What isn't hard to keep track of is how Apple's stock has done since Steve Jobs returned in August of '97: it's up more than 1600%. The market has bid up Apple almost 50% in the last six months and with good reason. The ipod is a monster hit and has obliterated every other mp3 player from the market.

But Apple isn't without missteps. You bought a Rokr in 2005, Apple's phone collaboration with Motorola, when renewing your Cingular contract. Blackberry and Nokia are already established giants in mobile devices, with enterprise and global consumer bases. Apple has always been a niche player in computers and smartphones are a totally new market for them and everyone else.

Apple Inc.

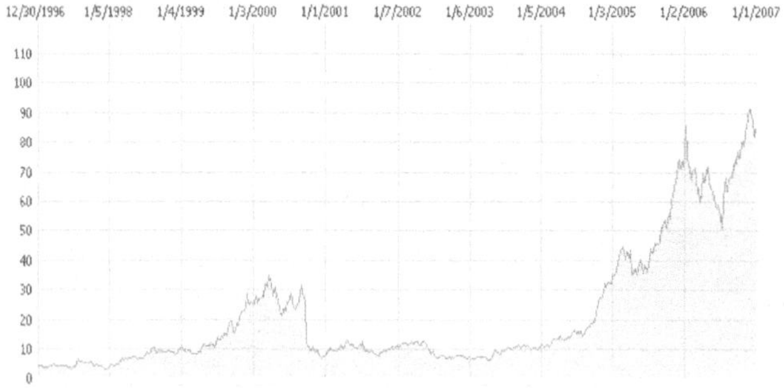

Source: MSN Money

If you want to invest about $500,000 in AAPL forever, turn to page 277.

If you'd like to move onto the next invest opportunity, turn to page 278.

If you'd like to retire, turn to page 309.

First iPhone Long-Term Investment Outcome

Congratulations, you have a 775% gain on your investment.

Wow this stock is on fire and on the rise. The iPhone was met with huge demand and service providers struggled to provide all of the data that the phones are using. Apple sold 1.65 million units in the first 6 months after the launch at a price of $599 a piece. The iPhone has even been called the Jesus phone.

Since then, Apple has released five more versions of the iPhone. Today, Apple is the most valuable company in the world with a market cap of over $600 billion. Apple products are top of the line and each new release is eaten up by consumers.

The iPhone has further expounded on the already successful Apple ecosystem. The company continues to lock users into it's platform via devices, operating systems, software, and music. As Apple continues to innovate, they will continue to profit and grow. Apple is still a growth company at $650. You really did well on this trade.

Apple Corp. since first iPhone rollout

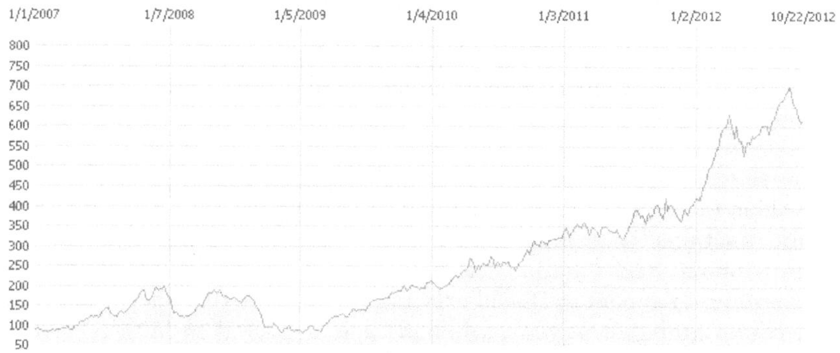

Source: MSN Money

To go to the next investment opportunity, turn to page 278.

If you want to skip to retire now, turn to page 309.

RIM 8800 Long-Term Investment Setup

Today is February 12, 2007. The famous smartphone company Research in Motion just released their all new lineup of Blackberry's known as the RIM 8800 series. These new phones are everything good about the previous Blackberry's with new features and a sleek new look. These series of smartphones now come standard with the trackball and will now feature a Wi-Fi capability. Research in Motion is one of the most innovative companies on the planet and continues to rock the world with their great lineup of unique smartphones.

RIM has doubled in price over the last year and is facing resistance around the $47 level. It has had some big displacement in the last few months and looks primed for a breakout or a crash. This new product launch is likely to be spectacular as this phone faces high demand from businesses as well as consumers. People love their PDA's and businesses have a lot of utility for them. RIM has been making phones for several years and new competition is starting to come out. Apple just released their first version of a Phone called the iPhone in January. Samsung and Motorola also have similar smartphones.

Unstrung describes the new RIM 8800 phones as "for the cognoscenti, almost as hotly anticipated as was the iPhone".

The Blackberry 8800 will be a wider version of the Blackberry 8100 Pearl, with a full ASCII keyboard. There will be two versions – with and without a camera.

Like the Pearl, the 8800 series will play heavily on multimedia functions (a camera and a music player) alongside the existing strong email functions. By comparison, the iPhone is taking multimedia, and adding phone and email – though without a Qwerty keyboard, it's never going to appeal to Blackberry users. Another Blackberry upgrade will come later in the year, when RIM is expected to launch a 9000 series, which will operate on 3G (and one might hope, Wi-Fi), and will "feature a completely redesigned Blackberry GUI". It is also expected to feature a full system back-up and restore to a micro-SD card.

Research in Motion may be reaching the top of their exponential growth curve. The company is facing serious competition from new smartphone makers and this could cut into RIM's earnings. Basic economics states that if a company does not innovate, it will soon fall of the growth curve. This could be the case for RIM and this may not be the investment you want.

On the other hand, RIM is the leader in smartphones. They have an extraordinary team who makes and designs these phones and this ability to innovate could keep the company rising. Even if this stock falls short-term due to competition from Apple, RIM could still innovate and return to the top of the smartphone market. This is a wildly popular and nobody is saying that the repercussions from the iPhone are going to be significant enough to hurt the stock in any way.

Research in Motion

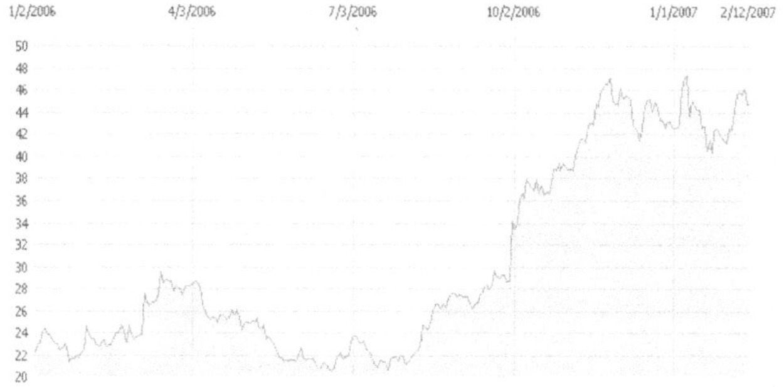

Source: MSN Money

If you want to invest about $500,000 in RIMM forever, turn to page 280.

If you'd like to move onto the next invest opportunity, turn to page 282.

If you'd like to retire, turn to page 309.

RIM 8800 Long-Term Investment Outcome

Oops, you just lost 86% on your investment!

Research in Motion has fallen 86% since you bought it 5 years ago. As Apple took the mobile world by storm with the release of 6 version of the iPhone and 2 iPads, RIM was left on the sidelines. Blackberry's continue to lose market share and RIM's attempt at a tablet (Playbook) has been a disaster. Today the Blackberry represents a 1% market share while the Playbook holds 1.78% of the market. Compare that to the Blackberry's 20% market share in 2009 and you can see how much ground this company has lost.

While Research in Motion is still releasing new products to compete with Android and Apple, the products face very little demand. Apple and Android are now in a war with each other and in the process have wiped out much of the competition. iPhones are one of today's most sought after phones and Androids are the number one selling operating system in the world.

The story of RIM is a sad one in that such a profound and revolutionary company can be passed by the wayside in such a short matter of time. Although the stock could possibly rise again if RIM develops some new product that people like, the stock would have to gain 750% before you could even break even on the trade.

Research in Motion since RIM 8800 launch

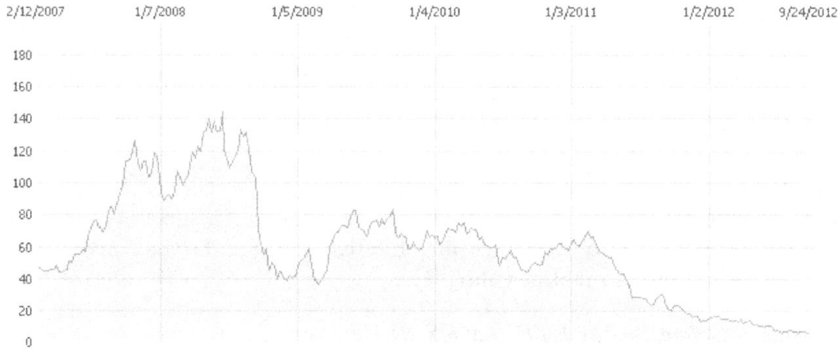

Source: MSN Money

To go to the next investment opportunity, turn to page 282.

If you want to skip to retire now, turn to page 309.

Financials in Collapse Long-Term Investment Setup

It's January 2008 and financials have been taking it on the chin. The XLF is down 25% in the last six months. The housing bubble is in full scale collapse and the fallout is starting to hit Wall Street.

Last July Bear Stearns had to close two multi-billion mortgage hedge funds when their holdings cratered in a matter of days. Even vaunted Goldman Sachs is down 15% since just October.

But the Fed and the Treasury insist that there is no issue with the financial system with Treasury Secretary Paulson saying that the fallout from subprime is "largely contained".

The Dow was just at an all-time high and money center banks are trading below their long-term earnings multiples. Citigroup, Bank of America and Lehman Brothers pay healthy dividends that provide a buffer against stock market volatility.

Financial Select Sector ETF (AMEX:XLF)

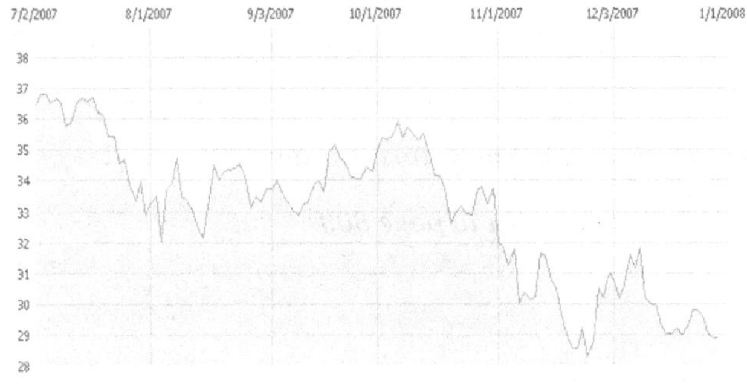

Source: MSN Money

If you want to invest about $500,000 in XLF forever, turn to page 283.

If you'd like to move onto the next invest opportunity, turn to page 285.

If you'd like to retire, turn to page 309.

Financials in Collapse Long-Term Investment Outcome

Oops, you just lost 50% of your investment.

It was only a matter of time. The entire banking system was fragile and literally every single giant bank was insolvent despite what the balance sheets they were filing with the SEC and despite what every CEO denial that the system was collapsing. Over the course of the year, there was a total run on the banking system and it took trillions of dollars of covert and overt bailouts and welfare distributions to the banks to keep them afloat.

And you blew it.

But the amount of pain from this disastrous trade depends upon the time frame you had for it. The short term returns on the options weren't nearly as painful as the returns for those who bet on the sector stocks going to all-time new highs and held on for the whole year. The system truly collapsed and the stocks did too, but it wasn't overnight. It took months.

Financial Select Sector ETF (XLF) Today

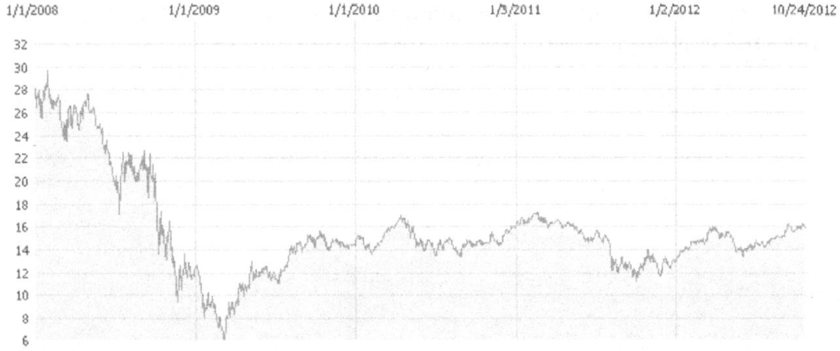

Source: MSN Money

On November 11, 2008, it was announced that the XLF would be moved from AMEX to the NYSE Arca.

To go to the next investment opportunity, turn to page 285.

If you want to skip to retire now, turn to page 309.

Quantitative Easing-Round 1 Long-Term Investment Setup

It is November 25, 2008 and the Federal Reserve just announced that they will begin implementing a new monetary policy known as Quantitative easing (QE). The economy has just fallen into a deep recession. Real GDP is at -0.5%. Unemployment has been rising rapidly and is now at 7.5%. It seems like the bottom has been pulled out from underneath the Stock Market.

President-elect Barack Obama brought hope to many Americans during his campaign and it seems like that hope has been stripped away by a bad economy. People's 401K's have lost a third of their value and the bottom doesn't seem to be in sight. The Fed has agreed to expand its balance sheet by purchasing up to $600 billion in Mortgage-Backed Securities. By the Fed assuming the debt of America's financial institutions, hopefully businesses will be able to acquire more capital, thus increasing the productivity of the nation.

Caterpillar (CAT) is a very cyclical equipment manufacturer and is off more than 50% from it's summer high's. This new stimulus could possibly be what it needs to get the great American company back on it's feet. Is this what our economy needs right now? On the other hand, this could simply be a scheme on the taxpayer by the Big Banks. In reality, the financial institutions are the only ones receiving direct help. If the banks choose not to lend, then the stimulus helps no one. Is CAT a tremendous by right now? Or are the greater macroeconomic forces going to shove this stock lower.

CAT has typically been the leader in construction equipment and a big player in farm equipment for a long time. They are a solid American company with good financials to back it up. The company sees revenue growth in emerging markets as well and has good exposure to China, a place that typically spends a lot on infrastructure build up.

Dow Jones Industrial Average

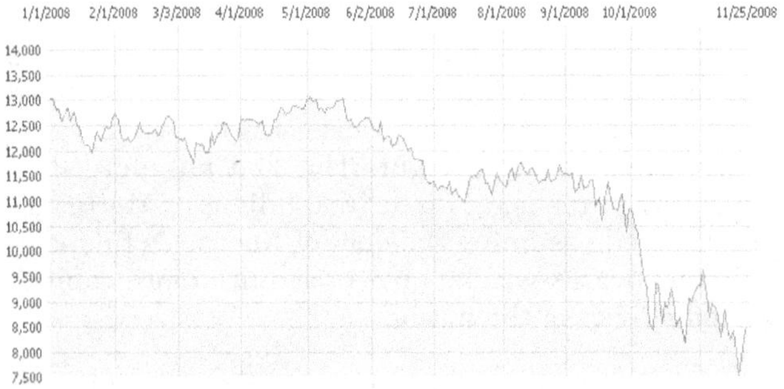

Source: MSN Money

Caterpillar Inc.

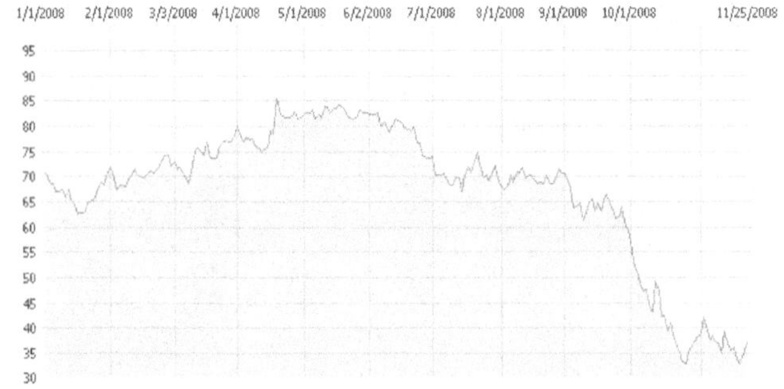

Source: MSN Money

If you want to invest about $500,000 in CAT forever, turn to page 287.

If you'd like to move onto the next invest opportunity, turn to page 288.

If you'd like to retire, turn to page 309.

Quantitative Easing-Round 1 Long-Term Investment Outcome

Congratulations, you just made a 125% return on your investment!

Congratulations, CAT has been a great investment. With America's Financial entities now free and willing to lend, more businesses can get the capital they need to buy CAT equipment. The government has also passed several rounds of stimulus that involve a large buildup of infrastructure within the United States. With more capital available and more work to be done, construction companies have bought more CAT equipment.

Since 2009, CAT has increased its net income by five times racking in a record $5 billion profit in 2011. The companies stock has reflected this as well; up 125% since you bought it at the end of 2008. CAT maintains its dominance in the construction and mining equipment industry and will likely continue to grow for some time into the foreseeable future.

Caterpillar since QE1

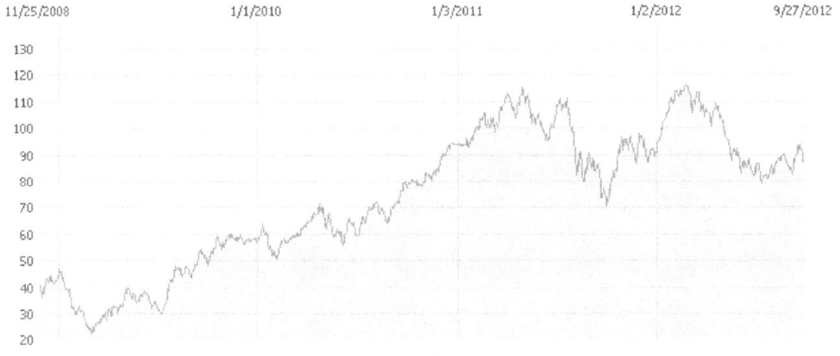

Source: MSN Money

To go to the next investment opportunity, turn to page 288.

If you want to skip to retire now, turn to page 309.

WTI Crude Oil Long-Term Investment Setup

It's late June, 2008. West Texas Intermediate Crude Oil August contracts just hit a record high of $142 as the supply of Oil seems to be dwindling. Everybody on TV is talking about how strong the economy is. It seems like every investor, hedge fund manager, and investment banker you know is leveraging everything they have to get as much exposure to oil, gold and silver as they can. Even your neighbor, a premium car salesman, is so proud of his commodity investments that you can't get him to stop talking about all the money he's been making on them.

The President of OPEC has quoted all over saying that oil could easily reach $170 a barrel in the next few months and Libya threatened to cut output. You are looking at the July contracts that expire in a month or looking at December Contracts and you can choose to buy them, or sell them short today hoping the price will fall.

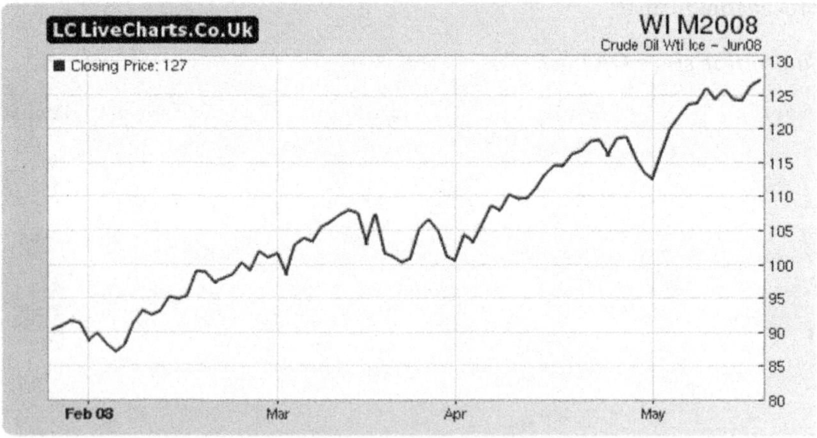

If you want to invest about $500,000 in Crude Oil forever, turn to page 289.

If you'd like to move onto the next invest opportunity, turn to page 290.

If you'd like to retire, turn to page 309.

WTI Crude Oil Long Term Investment Outcome

Oops you just lost 43% on your investment.

Not long after you bought oil did it crash. Oil went from $140 to $33 in a matter of weeks. Everyone and their dog was highly leveraged going into the crash and when the prices started falling and the margin calls went out, investors had to liquidate to raise capital. In turn, the prices of commodities, equities, homes, derivatives, and just about everything else crashed along with oil. The housing crisis is a mess and the banks are insolvent. The economy is in a recession and 2008 was the worst market downturn since the great depression.

Since then the markets have recovered and oil prices have risen back to around $80. You are still in the red on this trade and it is going to be a long while before, if ever, you see green numbers on this oil trade.

WTI Crude Oil since 2008

To go to the next investment opportunity, turn to page 290.

If you want to skip to retire now, turn to page 309.

Gilead Long-Term Investment Setup

It's April of 2009 and you're looking for shelter from the storm. The stock market has been nothing but a heartache for the last two years. So you figure that lots of other people must be feeling ill and they'll need drugs too. You start looking at companies that sell blood pressure medication.

You land on Gilead, a biotech giant with a promising new hypertension drug, Darusentan. You see a press release with an image of the molecule:

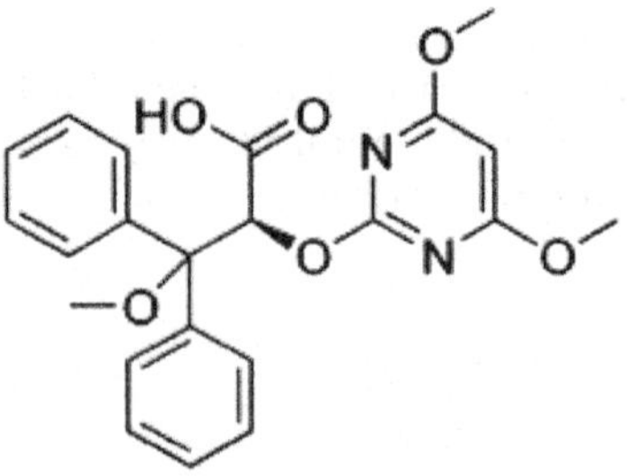

You think back to Organic Chemistry, shudder, and need to take a break.

After a 30-minute pause to play Halo you're feeling well enough to start researching. Gilead is best known for making Tamiflu, the only thing that stopped the bird-flu panic two years agao. Gilead is primarily in the business of treating HIV/AIDS–and what a lucrative business it is. The average HIV-positive patient can expect to live twenty years and will spend $600K over that time. And as the drugs get better, life-expectancy will go up and so will that revenue stream. In 2008 Gilead's revenues were up 26% to $5.34 billion, with the profits in Q4 alone hitting $568.2 million.

Gilead's management wants to leverage their cash and know-how to crack into the lucrative blood pressure. About 68 million people in the U.S. have high blood pressure and Gilead wants to sell them something. In 2006 Gilead bought Myogen Inc, the maker of ambrisentan (Letairsis in the U.S.) an endothelin receptor antagonist that works for pulmonary hypertension. While Letairsis will bring in about $184 million this year, that's not going to pay for the $2.6B acquisition cost without new drugs. That's where Darusentan comes in.

Myogen licensed Darusentan from Abott Labs (which was working on it for cancer treatments). Since then Darusentan has done very well in trials. In 2006 put the drug on its Phase III Fast Track. In 2005 Credit Suisse pegged the total Darusentan opportunity at $500M; the consensus now is that the drug would easily do $1B. One of the Phase III trials just completed and those results look great. The results will be presented next month at the American Society of Hypertension but the medical community is already buzzing. In a double-blind, placebo-controlled trial 379 patients were given the drug. 14-weeks later, both systolic blood pressure (trough sitting SBP) and ambulatory blood pressure were down much more significantly in the patients taking Darusentan. Best of all the most common side effects, peripheral edema and fluid retention, are very manageable. The results of the other, larger, Phase III trial will be announced in December. If that is also as successful, FDA approval for a full release isn't far behind.

Gilead is down 6% on the year and is down about 5% over the 52-weeks but that's nothing when compared to the broader market. The S&P is down 3.47% YTD and about 34% since April of 2008. Gilead just last month picked up CV Therapeutics for $1.4 billion. Gilead trades for about 22x earnings; for comparison traditional drug maker Pfizer is selling for 11x earnings.

Gilead

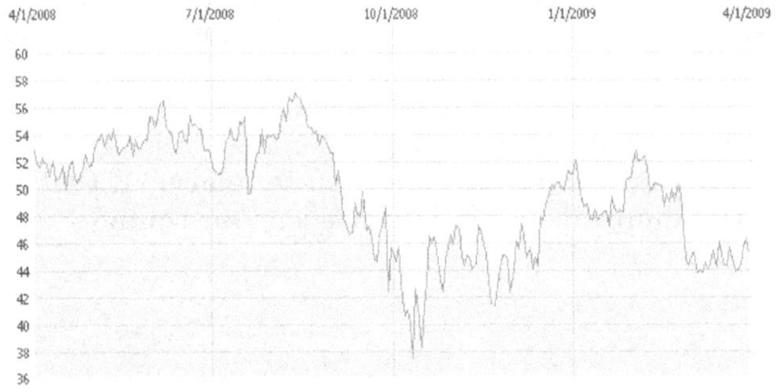

Source: MSN Money

If you want to invest about $500,000 in Gilead forever, turn to page 293.

If you'd like to move onto the next invest opportunity, turn to page 294.

If you'd like to retire, turn to page 309.

Gilead Long-Term Investment Outcome

Congratulations, you have a 55% return on your investment.

While results from early clinical studies suggested that darusentan might emerge as new treatment option in patients with resistant hypertension, results from recent studies suggests that darusentan appears unlikely to find its way in the armamentarium for treatment of resistant hypertension.

But it turns out that Gilead has developed and/or bought plenty of other drugs that are selling and the stock is one of many healthcare stocks that have rallied after Obamacare was passed as government spending on such drugs looks set to climb indefinitely.

Gilead Sciences Inc. since 2009

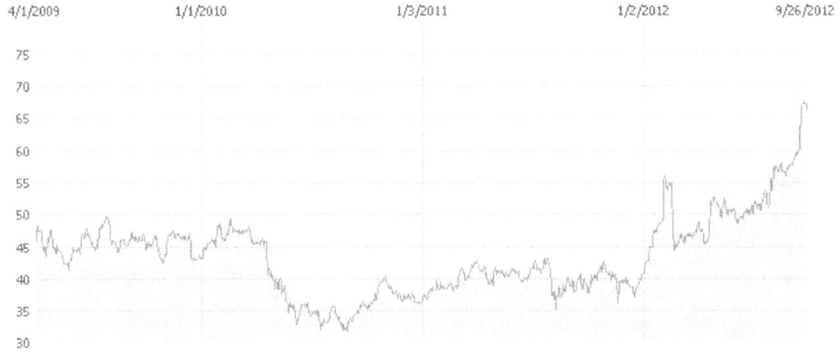

Source: MSN Money

To go to the next investment opportunity, turn to page 294.

If you want to skip to retire now, turn to page 309.

Obamacare Long-Term Investment Setup

Today is February 24, 2009. Today in a joint session of Congress, newly elected President Barack Obama said "So let there be no doubt: Health care reform cannot wait, it must not wait, and it will not wait another year." This is a very powerful statement.

Throughout his campaign, Barack Obama pledged that he would make healthcare affordable for all Americans. He has some big plans to change America's current health insurance industry. Most likely health insurers will have to provide insurance regardless of preexisting conditions. They will also not be allowed to cap the amount of insurance you can receive. For example if you get cancer and have millions of dollars worth of treatment, there is a good chance that your insurance has a cap around 1 million dollars. These could spell doom for the current insurance providers in America.

UnitedHealth Group (UNH) is America's largest Insurance provider. This bill could seriously cut into their profits. On the other hand, this company is known for spending big bucks on lobbyists. They may be able to sway politicians to make the bill where it could actually increase their profits. If they can get subsidized for providing this insurance, they will likely double or triple their revenue as people who were never allowed to get insurance before (preexisting condition, low income) are now being paid for by the government. One thing to consider is that 65% of healthcare providers had a disapproval rating on United Healthcare, the lowest of all insurance providers.

UnitedHealth Group Inc.

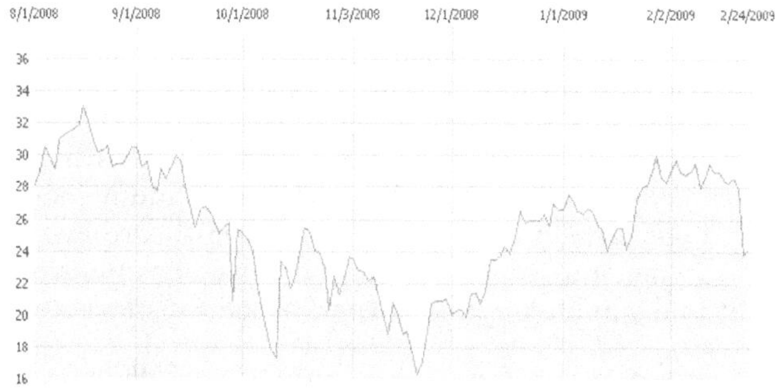

Source: MSN Money

If you want to invest about $500,000 in UNH forever, turn to page 296.

If you'd like to move onto the next invest opportunity, turn to page 297.

If you'd like to retire, turn to page 309.

Obamacare Long-Term Investment Outcome

Congratulations, you just made a 250% return on your investment!

Great Call. You caught the bottom of this healthcare stock. You have gotten to enjoy a nearly straight up ride as UNH is now up some 250% from your purchase price. Since you bought the stock, the Affordable Healthcare act went through committee and passed the Senate on December 24.

Investors have continued faith in management's ability to navigate through the government and still generate returns. Not long after you bought them did the common stock jump 33%. Healthcare in the United States is now going to be a different animal as this 2,074 page bill is picked through and administered by the Bureaucracy.

UnitedHealth has increased their revenue 22% since 2009 with net income up 37%. The company continues to do outstanding and it seems that they have figured out how to navigate the new healthcare law in order to stay in the game and stay on top. This has been a very successful investment and you have really outperformed the markets.

UnitedHealth Group Inc. since Obamacare

Source: MSN Money

To go to the next investment opportunity, turn to page 297.

If you want to skip to retire now, turn to page 309.

Tiffany's vs. Wal-Mart Long-Term Investment Setup

It's May of 2009 and you are just plain tired. The last two years have been brutal; all-time high's in the market just before the crash, a financial crisis that nearly wiped out the banking system and a never ending stream of foreclosures. You pull up a chart of the market, YTD.

Source: MSN Money

Flat (or slightly down) is the new up as far as everyone is concerned.

And the epidemic is nationwide. The total number of foreclosures is the third highest on record, up 18% year-over-year. 40, 870 foreclosures notices were sent out this month to Californians alone. When lenders do decide to sell a foreclosed home in California they're only getting about 60% of the *loan amount*. You start working out the hypothetical numbers and see just how bad the problem is. A house purchased for $500K (with a 20% down payment) is now selling for $240K. And all those loans are bundled and collateralized and spread in banks all over the world.

Unemployment is at 9.4%. The government just keeps handing out bailout cash, even to foreign corporations. Fiat is close to buying Chrysler. The bailout for Main Street isn't quite on the same scale but it's not nothing. A tax-credit along with a payroll tax-cut is already juicing consumer spending, which was up 2.2% in the first quarter.

If this is the new normal, a perma-poorer consumer that doesn't have a house, you want to know about both ends of the spectrum. You pull up a YTD chart of Wal-Mart vs Tiffany's:

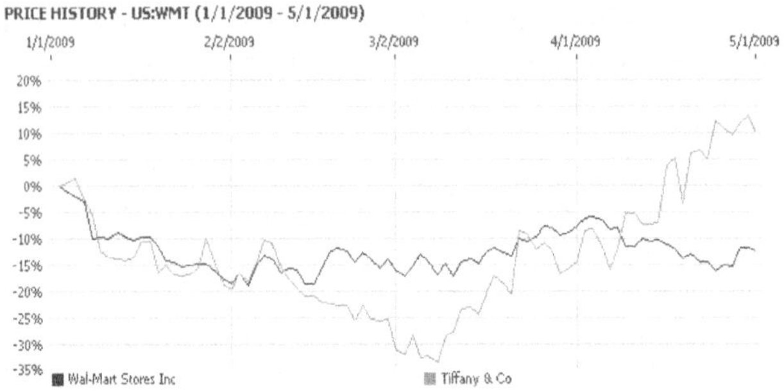

Source: MSN Money

Whoa, Tiffany's is totally beating the Wrangler-pants off Wal-Mart. You look back over a year and the situation looks much different:

Source: MSN Money

Do you bet on the trade down of the average consumer or the resillency of the rich? Is Wal-Mart the bargain or is Tiffany's the one on rollback special?

If you want to invest about $500,000 in TIF forever, turn to page 300.

If you want to invest about $500,000 in WMT forever, turn to page 301.

If you'd like to move onto the next invest opportunity, turn to page 302.

If you'd like to retire, turn to page 309.

Tiffany's vs. Wal-Mart TIF Long-Term Investment Outcome

Woohoo, you have made a 100% return on your investment!

Tiffany's stock is up a whopping 100% since you bought the stock in May. This has definitely been an outperformer and has blown everyone's mind. This stock continues to climb and lead the way out of recession. Fighting all of the bad news coming from the leading financial broadcasters paid off.

You are the kind of value investor that Warren Buffet would be proud of. Trading at only 11 times earnings, TIF was a great buy. Remarkably, TIF has even outperformed Wal-Mart, the low-end retailer that would typically benefit off of lower incomes. Even as Tiffany's earnings fell 25% year over year, the stock continues to climb. Over the same time period, Walmart was up only 50%.

Tiffany since May 2009

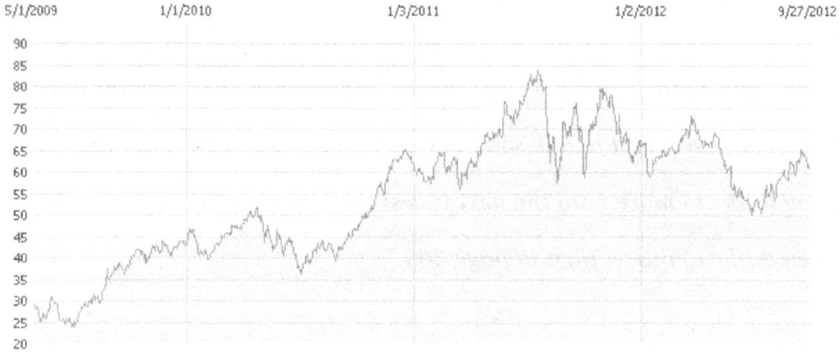

Source: MSN Money

To go to the next investment opportunity, turn to page 302.

If you want to skip to retire now, turn to page 309.

Tiffany's vs. Wal-Mart WMT Long-Term Investment Outcome

Woohoo, you have made a 50% return on your investment!

Wal-Mart is today the biggest retailer in the world. It is bigger than the next four American retailers (Kroger, Target, Walgreens, and Costco) combined in terms of revenue. Running $446 Billion dollars across their books in 2012 shows the kind of sales that this company is seeing. Wal-Mart is the largest employer in America (next to the federal government) with a workforce of 1.5 million people. The company has floor space, that if combined, would equal the size of Manhattan Island. Operating at a respectable 4% profit margin, Wal-Mart made $16.3 billion this last year.

This investment has been extremely successful. Most American families–along with yourself–frequently use Wal-Mart to buy common household items and food, among other things. Wal-Mart has successfully ventured abroad and currently makes over 30% of its revenue overseas. Today Wal-Mart goes on the list as one of the great American companies and continues to see growth for the future.

Wal-Mart since May 2009

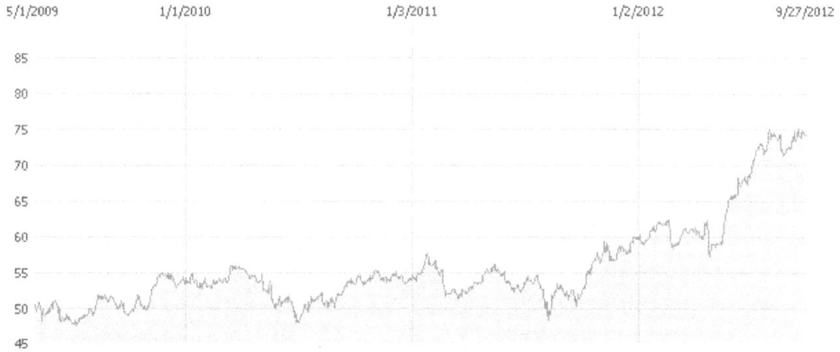

Source: MSN Money

To go to the next investment opportunity, turn to page 302.

If you want to skip to retire now, turn to page 309.

RIM Playbook Long-Term Investment Setup

It's late October, 2010 and tech company Research in Motion is about to announce their very own tablet known as the Playbook. This new tablet has a 7 inch screen and is the lightest tablet for sale compared to its competitors. The tablet features 3D graphics acceleration, a Texas Instruments dual-core processor, and a forward and rear facing camera.

The struggling smartphone maker has lost serious market share to Apple over the past several years and with today's release will be entering another very competitive market. The playbook will be in direct competition with the Apple iPad, Google's Android Tablet, and the Kindle fire, each with an established clientele. Coming in at $499, this tablet is by no means cheap and may have struggles selling.

RIMM stock has been down since the beginning of the year as company's growth continues to fall. The blackberry is no longer the standard for smartphones and RIM has failed to release an effective counter to the Apple iPhone or one of the many Android phones. This could be a great opportunity to buy RIMM if the stock were to rebound on a successful product launch (like the playbook) or something else. RIM has long been a leader in handset technology and this could be a great opportunity to get on the revolutionary company.

Research in Motion

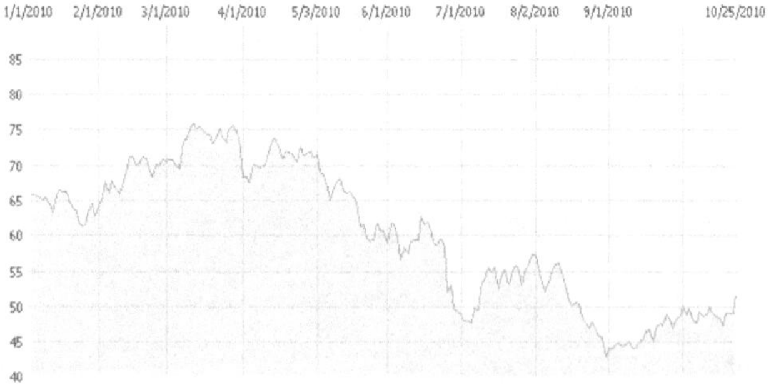

Source: MSN Money

CEO Jim Balsillie says that Apple's highly-touted app marketplace really just masks iOS's subpar web performance.

"You don't need an app for the Web," Balsillie said. Since many iOS apps are just frontend clients for web properties — stores, games, media companies, social networking sites — and RIM's app strength is in documents and productivity, it's a clear contrast.

"There's still a role for apps, but can you use your existing content?" Balsillie asked web companies. "Can you use your existing web assets? Do you need a set of proprietary tools to bring existing assets on to a device, or can you use known tools that you use for creating websites?"

As for Apple trying to take on Blackberry in the smartphone market that it has dominated for years now, when asked what he would tell Jobs if he were there, Balsillie simply said, "You finally showed up."

If you want to invest about $500,000 in RIMM forever, turn to page 304.

If you'd like to move onto the next invest opportunity, turn to page 305.

If you'd like to retire, turn to page 309.

RIM Playbook Long-Term Investment Outcome

Oh no, baby. You lost 90% on this investment.

Since the launch of the Playbook, RIM has been on a downhill slope. The stock actually did well the year after the launch but as the products met little demand in the marketplace, the stock sunk. Net income fell 67% from 2011 to 2012. The company continues to struggle with the intense amount of competition presented by Apple and Google.The former leader in cell phones has become a sort of relic. RIM has fallen some 80% while Apple and Google were up 120% and 20% respectively Apple has released a new iPad, a new iPhone, and continues to build the Apple ecosystem.

The story of RIM is a basic lesson on economics and the business cycles. RIM experienced exponential growth after they created a revolutionary new product. Competition soon entered the market and RIM did not innovate enough to keep their products as the market leaders. RIM was an $80 stock when you bought it and today it trades close to $8.

Research in Motion since Playbook Launch

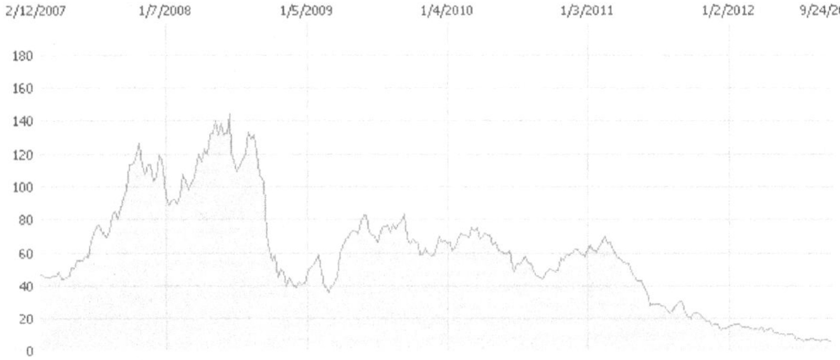

Source: MSN Money

To go to the next investment opportunity, turn to page 305.

If you want to skip to retire now, turn to page 309.

Sino-Forest Long-Term Investment Setup

Today is June 2, 2011 and Muddy Waters research just released a report that Canadian Forestry company Sino-Forest has expanded and lied about their assets and income. Sino-Forest claims to own major stakes in Chinese forests and this report claims that it was all one big lie.

The company has become a favourite of investors, both because it offers exposure to China and because it is one of the only successful forestry companies of the last decade. Unlike its rivals, it has reported consistent revenue and earnings growth and constantly expanded its operations. For 2010, Sino-Forest reported net income of US$170.9-million, up 52% from 2009.

The company had a market value of almost $5 billion, but the stock has fallen 60% today after Muddy Waters Research last night released an extensive report by a short-seller that called the operation an "established institutional fraud."

The Muddy Waters report claims that Sino Forest was a "multibillion-dollar Ponzi scheme" that was "accompanied by substantial theft".

Sino-Forest is fighting back against the report though: "It is important that our independent committee thoroughly address Muddy Waters' allegations, and they will have my full support and those of the management team in doing so," chairman and chief executive Allen Chan said in a statement.

"However, let me say clearly that the allegations contained in this report are inaccurate and unfounded."

Sino-Forest noted that Muddy Waters held a short position in the company. A short position allows an investor to profit when a share falls in price.

"Muddy Waters' shock-jock approach is transparently self-interested and we look forward to providing our investors and other stakeholders with additional information to rebut these allegations," Chan said.

If what management said is true, then this could be a great entry point for the stock. If Sino-Forest is telling the truth, this will be a great buying opportunity.

Sino-Forest Corp.

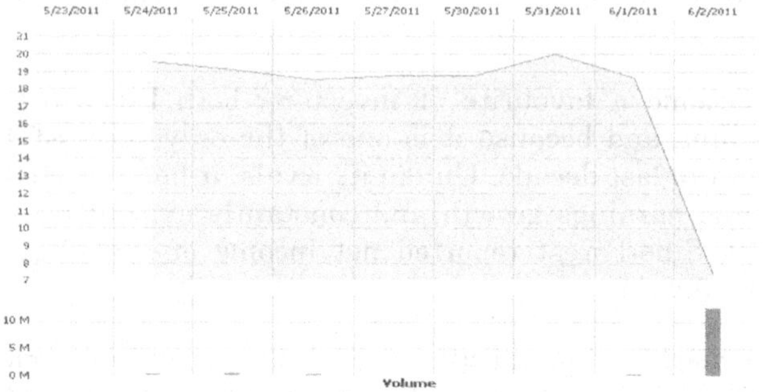

Source: MSN Money

If you want to invest about $500,000 in Sino forever, turn to page 307.

If you'd like to retire, turn to page 309.

Sino-Forest Long-Term Investment Outcome

Brutal. You lost all of your capital on this investment. 100% of it.

This trade is going down as one of the worst you've ever done as a trader. Turns out that the report hit the nail on the head. Sino-Forest lied about their assets, income, and debt in a disgusting statement of fraud. The company was essentially a giant Ponzi-Scheme and you took the bait. Sino-Forest stock was suspended from trading on August 26, 2011 by the Ontario Securities Commission.

Canadian authorities are currently investigating the company to find out what exactly is going on. Until the stock is allowed to trade again, you are out 100%. That's right, you lost everything you put in this stock (10% of your portfolio). Someday the stock will trade again after the authorities release it and you might get lucky and sell the stock for a few pennies a piece. This was a horrible trade and it looks like the report by the Muddy Waters research agency was true.

Sino-Forest Corp

Your trading career is over, time to retire, turn to page 309.

That's a big chunk of change

Congratulations! You've won the whole $150 million, plus the amount that you ended up with in the trading account that you used. Look at the the Top 10 Traders list on the right to see how you've made it–or how much better you need to be next time to make it.

It's been quite a life

Well your trading career has finally come to an end. Throughout the course of your life, you have gotten to invest in some of the most interesting and profound events in history.

END OF BOOK:

ABOUT THE AUTHORS

Cody Willard is an American investor, television anchor and formerly the manager of a successful hedge fund. He is the founder of CL Willard Capital. Willard also serves as an adjunct professor at Seton Hall University where he teaches a class called "Revolutionomics" focused on technology and businessand serves on Finance Committee of the University of New Mexico Alumni Board. He is the author of a subscription-based investment newsletterTradingWithCody.com and the author of The Cody Word on the Wall Street Journal's Digital Network.

He wrote a monthly investment column for The Financial Times and a trading diary for TheStreet.com and was the long-time featured tech investor and expert economist on CNBC's Kudlow & Company.

Cody's approach to the markets and his insights on trading and investing have been featured on The Tonight Show with Jay Leno, ABC's 20/20 and Good Morning America, CBS Evening News, CNBC's SquawkBox, Jon Stewart's The Daily Show, as well as in the Financial Times, Wall Street Journal, New York Times, and many other outlets.

He was an anchor on the Fox Business Network, where he was the co-host of the long-time #1-rated show on the network, Fox Business Happy Hour.

He is a musician who has played backup guitar for Bob Weir, Neil Sedaka, Lorrie Morgan and others, and is a songwriter and producer with the indie rock band The Muddy Souls.

Contributor, **William Fox**, is the Chief Technology Officer for Willard Media Ventures. Previously, Bill was the Information Technology Manager at a financial services company in San Diego where he developed a proprietary software system for the company. He has worked as a technology manager in the financial industry for over 15 years and has over 25 years experience in information technology. Bill holds a B.S. degree in Computer Science from California State University, Chico.

Contributor, **Bryce Smith**, is a student at New Mexico State University, a competitive rodeoer and runs a small fund for his family office.

Published by Willard Media Ventures, LLC, New York, NY.

For general information on our other products and services or for technical support, please contact our Customer Care Department within the United States at (646) 397-7244.

Willard Media Ventures also publishes its books in a variety of electronic formats. For more information about Willard Media Ventures' publications, including Cody Willard's TradingWithCody.com products, visit our web site at www.TradingWithCody.com.

You should not treat any opinion expressed by Cody Willard as a specific inducement to make a particular investment or follow a particular strategy, but only as an expression of his opinion. Willard's opinions are based upon information he considers reliable, but neither Willard Media Ventures nor Cody Willard warrants its completeness or accuracy, and it should not be relied upon as such. Willard Media Ventures and Cody Willard are not under any obligation to update or correct any information provided on in this book. Willard's statements and opinions are subject to change without notice.

Past performance is not indicative of future results. Neither Willard Media Ventures, LLC nor Cody Willard guarantees any specific outcome or profit. You should be aware of the real risk of loss in following any strategy or investment discussed on this website or on the show. Strategies or investments discussed may fluctuate in price or value. Investors may get back less than invested. Investments or strategies mentioned in this book may not be suitable for you. This material does not take into account your particular investment objectives, financial situation or needs and is not intended as recommendations appropriate for you. You must make an independent decision regarding investments or strategies mentioned in this book. Before acting on information in this book, you should consider whether it is suitable for your particular circumstances and strongly consider seeking advice from your own financial or investment adviser.

Made in the USA
Monee, IL
04 November 2026

67378025R00177